Writing in the Margin

From Annotation to Critical Essay

Ronald Primeau

Central Michigan University

DAVID McKAY COMPANY, INC.
New York

McKAY ENGLISH AND HUMANITIES SERIES

ADVISORY EDITOR: Lee A. Jacobus
University of Connecticut, Storrs

WRITING IN THE MARGIN

COPYRIGHT © 1976 BY David McKay Company, Inc.

Developmental Editor: Gordon T. R. Anderson
Editorial and Design Supervisor: Nicole Benevento
Cover and Interior Design: Angela Foote
Production and Manufacturing Supervisor: Donald W. Strauss
Composition: Typographic Services, Inc.
Printing and Binding: Hamilton Printing Company

Library of Congress Cataloging in Publication Data

Primeau, Ronald.
  Writing in the margin.

  1. Criticism. 2. Rhetoric. I. Title.
PN81.P67   801'.95   75-21561
ISBN 0–679–30296–4

MANUFACTURED IN THE UNITED STATES OF AMERICA

Introduction

Inventiveness in writing is universally admired. That it is sadly lacking in so many of our most "educated" writers is a scandal overshadowing even outcries about "the good old days" in education. We derive our term "invention" from the Latin verb *invenire* meaning "to come upon" or "to find out." Other associated terms are "venture" (with its suggestions of creativity and risk) and "adventure" from the Latin *adventura* meaning "about to happen" and the French *aventure*, "a chance" or "an occurrence." Although "inventiveness" appears often to be an innate talent, the word itself suggests an ongoing process of discovery through search, the taking of risks, and the ability to make things happen. To be inventive on paper means first, then, to discover something to say that is worth hearing. And it obviously means as well the ability to get that discovery into words and *onto paper* as soon as possible.

People have always argued about whether inventiveness is a result of genius or identifiable and repeatable habits of hard work. When the arguments have run their course, some hybrid of inspiration and disciplined technique usually wins out. Geniuses thrive in spite of educational systems. But for the rest of us, some procedures for generating thought and then preserving it and developing it in writing are desirable and—when they work—welcome.

This short book is an extended exercise in invention. It presents a method for putting into written form ideas that would otherwise go unexpressed. Its basic assumption is that most successful writers are not geniuses who compose effortlessly but people who have developed talents systematically and know how to use those talents to advantage. The techniques described in these pages are hinged on the twofold process of active reading and creative revision. A writer discovers what he or she has to say in the process of saying it. A reader becomes a writer only when his or her thoughts have been put in words and on paper. Marginal comments get this process started, and revision keeps it going. Inventiveness is not prewriting; revision is not correction. The two are never mutually exclusive. Each reinforces the other in one continuous process of written communication.

The organization of this book is intended to reinforce the continuity between the earliest marginal comments and the most highly developed revisions. The first five chapters offer suggestions for recording thoughts on paper and *in the process developing* one's thinking on a topic. Specific examples of marginal comments, outlines, and finished drafts illustrate the method. Chapters 6 through 10 review the decisions writers must make when they want an audience for their ideas. The relationship between marginal comments and revision is stressed in chapter 9. Two final chapters explain techniques for drafting through the use of marginal comments when the method might at first seem unworkable.

The principal goal of "thinking in the margin" is to get started sooner and keep going longer in the processes of inventing and communicating ideas. Many of the activities described as distinct in these pages occur almost simultaneously as people think and write. But there are benefits to looking at the process in stages. One advantage of consciously systematic inquiry is that breakdowns in expectations are more easily located. Short-circuits in the process of written composition can be found and communication restored if specific problems are discovered where and when they occur. Too often instructors and students alike decide that writing problems are due to lack of innate talent. Such conclusions (generally foregone and vaguely stated) fuel excuses for dogging it and produce writing classes with an endless repetition of exercises that do little more than pass time.

A recent television commercial depicts a superrich eccentric spending a good deal of time and effort securing a guarantee on what is surely for him a meager purchase. When asked why he bothers with the drudgery of seeming trivialities, he answers aptly for the student of writing: "My boy, how do you think a man like me got to be a man like me?"

Contents

1/Marginal Comments: Reader as Participant

How well an audience responds to any performer often affects how well he or she performs. Similarly, actively engaged readers help create what they read as they read it. When readers involve themselves with a printed page, in a sense they contribute to what we ordinarily think of as "communication." Media specialists refer to this process as the decoding of a message that had been sent by an encoder. Although few people today would argue with this view of audience or reader as participant, we nonetheless continue to think of "meaning" as something that is embedded into lines on a page. We continue to talk, that is, of the seemingly one-way action in which the reader is a passive receiver who either does or does not "get" what is being transmitted.

This view of perceiver as a more or less talented "sponge" has been destructive in our schools and has robbed readers on the whole of the fun they, as audience, are entitled to have. Reading ability has often been measured as one would count holes in a sponge to test its absorbency. The creative activity of response to language has been passed over and replaced with tests that cover "material." Not least among problems caused by neglect of audience has been the passivity and sense of "blank page" that overwhelms anyone trying to write about what is being read. Unless people read actively, there is no way they can be expected to respond to what they are reading actively on paper. Reading experts and literary critics are now beginning to talk about reading "skills" (an activity) and are apt to worry a bit less about exactly what a reader absorbs and more about how a reader *is absorbed in* a good book. Even the titles of many studies reflect reading as an ongoing response that will give the reader in the dual role as audience and writer something personal to communicate about what has been read. We are now beginning to look at what the following titles describe: *Literature as*

1

Exploration, The Dynamics of Literary Response, Poems in Persons, Self-Consuming Artifacts—and we are doing it all *With Respect to Readers*.[1]

Readers who wish to write about what they have read must first become *actively engaged* readers. In other words, they must develop ways to record and preserve their responses in order to use them to communicate effectively with an audience. Potential writers are also busy working, studying, and living in an environment that is often distracting. They therefore need systematic ways to read actively and to translate reactions to what they read into what they write. Students who participate in a variety of seemingly contradictory educational experiences need to develop ways of recording and studying their day-to-day responses to what they can otherwise get unconsciously caught up in. Most people *could* write well but *don't* because when the time for writing is upon them, they seemingly have nothing to say.

If you have ever been disillusioned or puzzled by the disparity between a good experience you've had in reading something and the uninspiring string of commonplaces you're able to get together on paper or in class discussion, you know that you may like *and* understand what you read without having much to say about it to anyone. Starting is often more of a problem than keeping things going. Getting something on paper requires that one first supply the missing link between the private experience of reading and the public discussion of that experience in written form, in the classroom, or even in ordinary conversation. The problem is to bring two often unrelated experiences (further separated by time and a montage of intervening experiences) closer together. One solution to this problem is the creation of a system for recording one's response in all its complexity immediately. In addition to capturing the moment, this record itself becomes a part of one's further response to the work when one returns to it later.

Let's reconstruct an all too familiar frustration, its implications, and a possible solution to the problem of getting started on paper. When you read a book or an essay and then have "nothing to say" in class, in a paper, or when someone just asks you about it, how are you to know whether (a) you really have no response, (b) you just don't want to share your real response in that particular setting, or (c) you had a response but because you have no record as you experienced the work, you are now facing the impossible task of reconstructing an immensely complex experience with no resources to draw on. Thus, "I read it, but I just can't remember much about it" no doubt means that memory *unaided* cannot re-create your immediate reactions to the work in a situation that calls as much for re-creating the past as it does for creating the present. In short, you go into a conversation or a test or you begin writing *cold*.

---

1. Louise M. Rosenblatt, *Literature as Exploration* (New York: Noble & Noble, 1968; orig. publ. 1938); Norman N. Holland, *The Dynamics of Literary Response* (New York: Oxford University Press, 1968) and *Poems in Persons: An Introduction to the Psychoanalysis of Literature* (New York: Norton, 1973); Stanley E. Fish, *Self-Consuming Artifacts* (Berkeley: University of California Press, 1972); Walter J. Slatoff, *With Respect to Readers* (Ithaca, N.Y.: Cornell University Press, 1970).

Of course a writer needs more than mere warmup sessions. But the many devices one can use effectively to preserve original responses to an essay can serve as a resource center to draw upon when the blank page, the early hour in class, or simply the distractions of a busy life cause frustration. Although the procedure for creating a personal record of a personal response must necessarily vary from individual to individual, the following outline might usefully survey the basics of what's needed:

1. Active response in reading.
2. Recording response through marginal comments or systematic note taking.
3. Developing a series of outlines inductively from the marginal comments.
4. Formalizing the margin-essay into a finished product—inductively.
5. The writer's critique of the finished product through marginal comments in which the writer becomes "his own best critic."

This process or one like it can effectively transfer a reader's involvement with a book into effective communication of his or her views on it. Once such a procedure is set in motion, it becomes ritualized self-education at its best. Writers train themselves to be responsive, and habitual ways of recording observations necessarily make them more observant. Most public figures, speakers, and teachers use some kind of marginal comments when they mark books, make notes, prepare lectures, and raise questions for further research and thought. If your favorite writers or instructors generally have more to say than you do, perhaps they have gotten started by recording what they think is worthwhile to preserve and you haven't.

The procedures for making active reading into effective writing should be kept simple. To begin, select an essay that makes a rather strong statement. Although the subject doesn't matter, the first few times try to work with inexpensive paperbacks or mimeographed materials that you can pass on to someone else in class easily (a sample chapter in a textbook, travel guide, or work manual would do, as long as you can be without it long enough for someone to see what comments you've made). Deliberately think about what you are doing when you read; remember that you are really entering into a creative involvement with a text and a full subjective exploration of your own feelings about what you read as you read it. With this in mind, force yourself to record responses through marginal notes, underlinings, questions, arrows for cross references, circling key words and phrases, exclamations, marks in the margin for emphasis, pictures, doodling, or any shorthand that can re-create your experience when you will need to have it fresh for later discussion. Of course if you borrow a book from the library, keep the same kind of marginalia in a notebook of your own.

This won't always be easy, but on psychological principles alone you will record more, think more, and hopefully synthesize more about what you're reading regardless of what you record at first or how you do it. But once the process is set in motion, conducting research and then writing about your discoveries will follow naturally from your increased sensitivity to what you read and from the systematic record of your reading response.

"Recipes" for creating nutritious marginal comments will not do. Like the cook who adds ingredients intuitively, each reader must develop individual techniques for recording individual reading experience. A set of devices that has worked for one professional writer is outlined by Mortimer Adler in his "How to Mark a Book."[2] Adler recommends several ways for the reader to intensify personal experience of a book as well as to record the experience in the process. His suggestions for a "personal index on the back-end papers" and an outline on scratch-pad inserts can be a valuable source for getting started on papers or discussions. While Adler's methods and any methods you devise for your own use will be time-consuming and restrict the material you can "cover," you'll probably agree with him that the point is not to see how many books you can get through, but rather "how many can get through you."

The first two stages of recording your responses—active reading and a keeping of records in the margin—serve at least two functions: A personal record on paper of a personal response to an essay is down in words concretely in front of you for reference after all the experiences that occur between your reading and the time when you are supposed to be able automatically to reproduce that experience in writing. Moreover, because the marginal comments necessarily follow the structure of what you were responding to, you have a start on organizing your "paper" on what you read while your thought is still in the framework your experience as reader created.

A workable system of marginal comments also gets a reader into the frame of mind necessary to be a writer. The process forces a writer to start thinking in words and, even more importantly, *on paper*. If you ask someone to write an essay, confusion sets in almost immediately. An essay is neither a learned dissertation nor the last word on a subject. It is an exploration of a writer's own thoughts and feelings on a topic. To "essay" an idea is to try it out, to test it, in a manner very like the chemist's testing hypotheses in the laboratory. The origin of our "essay" is the French *essayer:* to test or to try. A good essay is a logical extension of the marginal comments and rough drafts a writer uses to build it: personal, exploratory, lively, immediate, challenging, and almost always suggestive rather than conclusive. The reader of an essay expects to be talked to; the reader does not expect to read the encyclopedia.

As an extended exercise in becoming one who reads with a pen, try the following plan. As you record your reading experience and structure in the form in which it unfolds, you are already writing an essay. The marginal comments select details and structure them in such a way as to make a point. You will already, then, be "outlining" an essay in the traditional sense and

---

2. Mortimer Adler, *How to Read a Book* (New York: Simon & Schuster, 1940).

actually writing it as a self-contained piece of communication that comes into being with considerably more ease than what one might expect.

While some brief scanning of what you are about to read is always helpful, most productive marginal comments originate immediately when a reader begins to react. Usually this happens right away. Although these first impressions are invaluable, a reader who wants to write can't let the recording process stop there. As later responses become more complex, further marginal comments should precede any attempt to outline formally. Then look back once more to what you originally read and your own earlier marginal comments. On the basis of the original book or essay and with reference to an important comment on it (your own), you should be able to begin improving your reading of the work and to see a form in your reading response itself. You are now engaging in several activities at once. You are drawing upon your own reading experience for the form of your writing and you are providing empirical feedback on that experience. As a reader of the original and an "editor" of your own response to the original, you may wish to comment further in the margin (or use footnotes or some similar devices) so that the process repeats itself and serves as a check of its own effectiveness. The process thus stays loose because modification is built into your recorded views before they are formalized either in a final draft or even in class discussion. Much of the "warmups" and background hassles needed to precipitate your creating something are done. In both processes you can therefore begin sooner and get to the point more quickly and with greater effectiveness. You can now locate problems where they occur and either solve them yourself or know where to look for help. The blank page and the silent classroom regain possibilities in your eyes once more.

To write something meaningful, you need only transfer your personal responses onto paper and build your argument inductively. Similarly, to contribute to class discussion you need only take clues from your carefully controlled marginal comments and reenact the experience you had with the work based on your immediate record of it. Because you are using your own feedback as "sources" for the paper, if the process has not been short-circuited at any point, the finished product should be more closely anchored to the fullest possible reenactment of your actual reading experience. Even more importantly, if the process has either short-circuited or for any reason failed to work for you, you will be able to identify your problem for what it really is and deal with it where and when it occurs.

For example, if you "can't get anything out of" what you're reading, your problem will probably show up in the marginal-comments stage of the recording. There just may be none at all, bringing back memories of the blank page waiting to be filled. Or your marginal comments may reflect the confusion in your mind at the time. Such problems suggest again that learning to write means first learning to read actively. Often when you start dealing with your basic needs, you can then move with considerable ease into the effective expression of your new discoveries in papers and in class. Although you find "plenty to talk about" in what you read, perhaps you simply can't put your reading experience on paper. Similarly, if you read actively and respond fully but can't organize your responses effectively enough to communicate them, your problem will most likely show up in the transition from the record of your responses to the outlining process. While you may have worked on outlining in the past, you probably haven't used marginal comments as sources before. Or maybe you do actually need practice in outlining itself. This is the time to find out, and tracing the steps of your developing personal responses is one way to do so.

If your chief problem is making the finished product from the outline, this too will show up in the prewriting process. But then you're beginning to move beyond the prewriting stage. What is crucial is that you have begun and you have sufficient resources in your own recorded response to continue. Finally, problems that show up for the first time in the critique stage should be minimal if the earlier stages of the process are working. Because you are merely repeating the movement from response to recording in the margin to outline and finished product with increasing complexity, criticizing and editing your own material is only a matter of recording and thinking further about increasingly complex responses—all of which are *yours*. All these ways of getting off the track can be quickly spotted and corrected if you identify them for what they are. Although this may not always solve the problem, you can at least avoid channeling your energies into work you might not really need.

You'll find this process is flexible also because there are many options built into it. As further exercises in structure, argument, and critical evaluation, you can repeat the process by marking your finished product in a manner very like your essay in the margin. While these further stages in the process are the topic of discussion later in this book, it is worth noting here that your response to your own essay in the margin is actually a first step toward editing and revising your finished product. Because you are improving upon essentially the same process you used to write your essay, revision will later extend what is basically the same process. Revision is "more of the same better" rather than a new and seemingly foreign effort. You are becoming, in short, that elusive "tyrant"—your own best critic. Finally, beyond the individual instance of one better paper, you are now teaching yourself writing and revising. And when you have the opportunity to discuss your writing with others, you can profit from their reactions as well as from your own. You will seek out the responses of instructors and other students and writers and include their advice in your growing marginal comments and revisions on your own work.

Marshall McLuhan has provided much insight on why reading is seldom viewed as an *activity*. According to McLuhan, print is itself a nonparticipatory medium in which the reader is presented with prepackaged linear sequences. Print is uniform and repeatable. Unlike mosaic patterns calling for audience involvement in television and other electronic media, print leaves its audience nothing to fill in and hence creates the kind of detached reading and nonresponse this book will encourage you to overcome.

How many times have you caught yourself "plowing through" page after page (in sequence), line by line (lineal), generally unaware of what you were reading (disinterested response)? How often do you "read" without thinking about what you are doing *or* thinking? When you catch yourself in this trance of spectator reading, you experience the impersonal noninvolvement that nonparticipatory print fosters. This state of unawareness is a chief cause of the split between reading response and responding in writing. Marginal comments can counteract the uniformity and impersonality of print and help restore continuity between reading actively and thinking on paper.

But McLuhan also shows how this triumph of the disinterested noninvolvement with the linear developed gradually rather than all at once. In the days of the first printed books, he notes, it was not unusual for the owner of a printed volume "to take it to a scribe to have it copied and illustrated."[3] The uniqueness of the scribe's variations brought the reader back *into contact* once more with the *previously* uniform print. McLuhan cites the *Oxford English Dictionary* on the meaning of *textbook* even on into the early eighteenth century: "Classick author written very wide by the students, to give room for an interpretation dictated by the Master, etc., to be inserted in the interlines." What is called for in the scribe's transmission and in this interlinear note taking is precisely the subject of this book. To engage oneself fully in the active and responsive reading, however, more than the master's (or teacher's or critic's) comments are necessary. "In the interlines" and in the margin readers must record and develop *their own* thinking as well.

McLuhan notes that, before printing, students made "texts" by copying an essential passage and notating it with the teacher's interpretations. Although this sounds like a standard reading–lecture–note-taking format, the activity that went into the making of such "texts" is worth considering. Thinking on paper and through detailed annotations of one's own reading and building such active response into effective writing will be the chief subjects of this book.

The coming of the paperback has once again made the reader's in-depth participation in reading possible. Large, immobile, and expensive hard-bound books discouraged contact between reader and page typical in less uniform written manuscripts. Size, mobility, and expense are easy to see as differences between traditional books and paperbacks. But the ability to buy, own, and carry around what had previously existed only in libraries or on prominent shelves in the home also influences *the way people read.*

Readers can read paperbacks actively because they can pace themselves, think about what they read, and annotate their books accordingly. McLuhan notes that "the paperback reader has discovered that he can enjoy Aristotle or Confucius by simply slowing down" (p. 283). What follows from this slowing

---

3. *Understanding Media* (New York: Signet, 1964), p. 158.

down are the arguments of this book. "Slowing down" means reading actively and participating by responding in the margin. Reading "in depth" is thinking in the margin and in words on paper. Reading actively *is* writing because genuine response translates into effective communication.

As an extended preview of the exercises in chapters 2 through 12, create your own "text" or scrapbook of your work. Include copies of several readings you found most challenging or enjoyable as well as your own annotations and essays developed from the annotations. Photographs and excerpts from paperbacks and magazine and newspaper articles should be especially good material. But the emphasis should be on your own written responses to what you include. You are reader, writer, editor, and book-maker. Throughout the Exercises in this book you will be able to draw upon the material you have collected for your scrapbook.

Summary / Review

To write about something you have read is often difficult even when you have understood and even enjoyed it. There seems at times to be no connection between the two distinct processes of reading and responding to what you have read. This separation of the activities of reading and writing is a major cause of reading problems among many people. One way to close the gap is to record your initial responses to what you read in marginal notations *while you are responding*. Such marginal notations are a way of thinking on paper and become, at the same time, the starting points for an essay on what you have read. From active reading and marginal comments you can develop organizational outlines and a finished product inductively, creating order from within rather than as an imposition from outside. Marginal comments guide you through a process in which you discover, record, and draw upon your own responses. Such a systematic record of responses can help you get started and keep you going when you have begun. Marginal comments are also a way of counteracting the uniformity and linearity of print which discourages participation. What goes in the margins is a record of the slowing down and depth reading that are especially crucial for anyone in the dual role of reader-writer.

2 / Marginal Comments and Point of View: Persona as Organization from Within

A man should learn to detect and watch that gleam of light which flashes across his mind from within, more than the lustre of the firmament of bards and sages. Yet he dismisses without notice his thought, because it is his. In every work of genius we recognize our own rejected thoughts; they come back to us with a certain alienated majesty. Great works of art have no more affecting lesson for us than this. They teach us to abide by our spontaneous impression with good-humored inflexibility then most when the whole cry of voices is on the other side. Else tomorrow a stranger will say with masterly good sense *precisely what we have thought and felt all the time,* and we shall be forced *to take with shame our own opinion from another.*

—Emerson, "Self Reliance"; italics added

A loose paraphrase of Emerson might easily be the theme of this book. To be "self-reliant," you as a writer must "detect and watch" your own inner thoughts and feelings. You must examine the light which "flashes" through your mind and takes form in your reactions to, among other things, what you read. Too often, you as a reader or writer will instead "dismiss" your own thinking, only to recognize it later in the "approved" thoughts of an acclaimed genius. Everyone has listened to or read brilliant insights only to react in amazement with some form of "I wish I had said that." Or more to the point, a great writer of the past or that "stranger" will confront a reader with gems that he or she had "thought and felt all the time."

The "shame" Emerson refers to shows up most often in timid persons who don't trust—and therefore never examine—their own reactions to their world. This shyness and distrust of oneself has everything to do with marginal

9

comments as they take shape and grow in the writer's projection of voice or *persona* on paper. Emerson's constant refrain is "trust thyself." He warns that "nothing is at last sacred but the integrity of your own mind." In order *even to begin* to react in the margin, you as a reader must trust your own integrity. You must be convinced that your opinions matter, and you must want to study—and in the process to develop—your own reactions to what you are reading. Chapter 1 suggested a system of marginal notations to set in motion this process of growth through self-exploration. Chapters 2 and 3 examine how marginal comments begin to organize themselves on paper. In this chapter, the emphasis is on the concepts of point of view and persona as organizing mechanisms built into one's thinking out of ideas on paper. The following chapter looks in detail at examples of marginal notations primarily from notebooks to illustrate how great writers read other famous writers.

Emerson's "Self Reliance" is filled with quotable passages. Some of his advice is controversial, as one would expect: "Whoso would be a man, must be a nonconformist." Again, "A foolish consistency is the hobgoblin of little minds, adored by little statesmen and philosophers, and divines." And finally, "To be great is to be misunderstood." In the privacy of his or her own marginal comments, every reader can and *must* be a "nonconformist." Every reader can risk "greatness" and set aside a "foolish consistency." Creative thinking arises only from such daring. An "educated" response is not only "self-reliant" but also "self-critical" because it develops in the process of its expression. To quote Emerson one last time:

> There is a time in every man's education when he arrives at the conviction that envy is ignorance; that imitation is suicide; that he must take himself for better or for worse as his portion; that though the wide universe is full of good, no kernel of nourishing corn can come to him but through his toil bestowed on that plot of ground which is given to him to till.
>
> The power which resides in him is new in nature, and none but he knows what that is which he can do, nor does he know until he has tried. Not for nothing one face, one character, one fact, makes much impression on him, and another none. . . . We but half express ourselves, and are ashamed of that divine idea which each of us represents.

This passage is more than a "pep talk" for original thinking and growth through responsiveness. Emerson also describes what happens when such responses are set in motion. Initiative and trust in self nourish the seed, which is the human mind itself. Every unique response must be tried and thereby "known." When you as a reader "try out" your own responses, you can "know" your thinking as it grows. The ways in which writers' reactions grow can be seen in their careful control of point of view. One measure of writers' confidence in their own thinking can be seen in their ability to speak through a variety of voices and assume more than one point of view on a subject.

A chief indication of a person's security is the willingness and ability to understand opposing positions. In marginal comments differences of opinion show up first in contrasting points of view. Building on what is unique in their own thinking, writers study and develop their own position. As they study their own thinking, writers come to hear their own "voice." They then project that voice confidently through the careful choice of a *persona*—a concept that deserves detailed attention in the rest of this chapter.

A reader becomes a writer as soon as he or she begins to explore personal thinking on paper. As marginal comments take shape, they reflect his or her point of view. Structure develops as the writer enriches, clarifies, and expands on that unique point of view. The writer's first job is, therefore, to discover and develop the organization within his or her own material. Whenever two or more parties relate the details of any event, drastic discrepancies can result from shifts in the storytellers' point of view. The speakers' position in relation to what they see, their selection of details, their choice of language in describing those details, and their own beliefs and attitudes—all contribute to the shaping of what they communicate. The transmission of rumors dramatizes how content is reshaped whenever it is filtered through yet another point of view. Several more or less extreme examples are nonetheless familiar enough to illustrate the significance of a writer's perspective. Take the old parlor game in which each person passes on a story along a line. When the circuit is complete, the first and last person in the series compare the story as it was first told and last heard. The almost total lack of resemblance is usually funny, though significant. Or consider various short stories and films in which the same story is told several times from varying viewpoints. Crucial differences range from disagreements in fact to nuances of tone shift and often create the aura of a detective story.

Your point of view as a reader determines what you see and influences the organization or patterns in which you see it. Differences in point of view between author and reader are often the first step in the reader's rebuttal or counter-thinking. When you as the reader then write about what you have read, your tone and the voice you project in what you say create what we ordinarily think of as style. Every statement reflects the attitudes of its speaker, thereby communicating the information *and* tone of the message. Quite simply, every statement is either serious or humorous, literal or figurative, straight or satirical. (It is not usually difficult to hear the tone of a statement. "Lovely weather we're having," "She's beautiful," "I'd love to," or the simplest "Yes" or "No" can mean anything and everything depending on tone. Context and pitch of voice determine when the most flattering comment becomes the bitterest lament or when genuine friendliness is only time-filling chatter or even sarcasm.) The tone of readers' marginal comments reproduce their attitudes as they read. Writers' choice of diction, sentence structure, and imagery emerge from how they feel about their subject as well as what they have to say about it. Marginal comments allow writers to vent their emotions and at the same time look critically at those emotions as they captured them in language in the margins. By first recording and then carefully studying their responses as they develop, they can turn haphazard accidental projection of self into deliberately planned perspective.

Point of view organizes almost everything we do and all of what we perceive. In a short story or film, shifts in point of view can change what actually happens in the eyes of the reader or audience. So also differences in the way details are selected and put together can change what a speaker of an essay actually says to a reader. Being aware of one's point of view and its effects on one's marginal comments allows the writer consciously to control ideas and to keep a check on what might go wrong in the recording and communicating of meaningful responses.

Most of us are now exposed to enough popular psychology to be familiar with role playing in our day-to-day affairs. But the way writers also play roles when they communicate is a little harder to see. The link between role playing that comes naturally and acting out a role through words on a page is easy to see as a reader's marginal comments develop. The writer's point of view and the voice he or she projects become clearer as personal responses take form in words in the margin. When the writer can stand back and watch personal thinking develop, he or she is better able to see writing as a series of choices and strategies for communicating.

Playing a role day to day is much like performing. So also, reading and writing are performances. Readers perform an interpretive act on what they perceive; writers choose a role as speaker and perform for their audience. In marginal comments you as a writer explore your own range of responses and then choose ways in which you can best reach your audience. As in Greek tragedy where the actors used masks to more fully create roles, so you as a writer assume a mask or *persona* through which you communicate your own responses. Thus, the "I" in your essay can be no more than a part of "you"—that part you project through your conscious choices in vocabulary, tone, and style. Choices about whether to be serious or humorous, "straight" or satirical, simple or sophisticated, formal or informal must continue to be made all throughout the various stages of marginal comments.

It is a recurring argument of this book that lack of substance often results from a lack of preserved personal responses and hence lack of the structure and style your responses had while they were still alive in marginal comments. Letting your responses follow their own structure and style—while enriching both in the process—is an essential step in discovering and clarifying what you genuinely want to say. Writers often discover what they have to say in the process of saying it. The use of a *persona* is an important part of that discovery.

The *persona* that a writer creates on paper means quite literally the person through whom the writer speaks to an audience. The *persona* is the personality or role, the voice or mouthpiece which the reader is able to identify from the written communication. Our terms *person, personal, personality,* and other derivatives originate in the Latin verb *personāre,* meaning "to sound through." In Greek drama, the *persona* was a mask used by an actor or a "personage," "role," or "character" played by an actor who was then referred to as a "person." "Personality" or "personage" on paper designates the role or mask in which a writer is best able "to sound through" ideas. The notions of "sounding out" one's ideas as a way of measuring their clarity or "sounding out" a person to determine that person's opinions or feelings survive in our everyday speech. We speak also of a "sounding board" as a listener or reader who will be in some sense critical audience as well as attentive listener; "hear me out" means, in effect, "listen to or read my ideas as I 'sound them through' for you" by presenting them through a "personage" or "persona." The meaning of "sound out" as a measuring device derives from the French verb *sonder,* "to sound the depth of." In many of its earliest forms, to "sound" meant to measure the depth of water; for an actor, the role he creates measures or "sounds through" for his audience the character he portrays. So also, a writer measures material as he or she presents it through a mouthpiece or persona.

The writer's projection of voice through a persona is obviously somewhat artificial. After all, the printed page cannot capture all the nuances of "personality" that are possible in the gestures and intonations of face-to-face conversation. Neither can the written word compete for vitality and explicitness with the electronic media. But the built-in limitations of communication in writing should alert the reader or writer to the necessity to compensate through an even more deliberate attempt to be in control of his or her projection of voice. The *artificiality* of the written persona is, in fact, also its chief source of *artistry.* Because writers create written personas from the resources of their language, they can achieve their desired goals through the special effects of the style and voice they use to "sound through" their ideas. The selection of a particular persona and the consistent control of point of view allow a writer to develop fully the thinking expressed in initial marginal comments. Several examples of the effects of a writer's decision to take a point of view and to "sound" ideas "through" a persona seem in order.

Suppose a student or worker discusses difficulties he or she is experiencing in a course or on the job with anyone from the following six groups: (1) casual friends or acquaintances; (2) parents; (3) an instructor or present employer; (4) a prospective employer; (5) a *close* friend, wife, or husband; (6) a total stranger. Obviously, what someone discusses depends on to whom the person is talking. But even when the *same* issues or problems arise, the "mask" or "role" will shift depending on the audience. Rather than pausing to consider someone else's example here, play the role of that student or worker and project yourself into these six different settings. Write out your statements exactly as you would realistically make them to different people in your lives. Notice how the same "context" produces different effects according to the image you choose to project through the persona you create. No one would accuse you of being a "fraud" because you project different voices to each of these six groups. No one can or wants to be the same person at all times in all company. Part of what defines one's relationships with others depends on how one acts and talks with different audiences. Just as everyday roles are accepted as a part of one's total personality, so also the writer plays out roles on paper.

Consider someone who wishes to criticize a matter of public policy or social custom. The person has a "bitch" and, through marginal comments, begins to see what it is and how it can be expressed best on paper. But before the argument can develop, the writer must consider the persona that will be appropriate in terms of the subject *and* audience. Decisions about the best formats for different audiences are a chief subject of later chapters in this book. For now, the choice of a point of view and the persona through which that point of view will develop are crucial. Examples from media other than writing support the importance of controlled point of view in all forms of communication.

In film, point of view is the angle from which the camera "sees" what it communicates to an audience. Whatever "content" is filmed on any particular camera shot is determined by camera perspective, duration of shots, and juxtaposition of scenes in a progression to a whole. Although we shall come back to this later in discussing the importance of detailed description (chapter 8), try playing the role of a camera spanning a room to see how point of view structures the form and content of your responses. It is at first extremely difficult to confine yourself to camera-angle perceptions. But this kind of "limitation" in point of view also intensifies what you see and opens up new relationships between seemingly unrelated perceptions. Similarly, careful attention to the unique point of view in your marginal comments illustrates that what you see can be limited or expanded depending on the particular angle of your vision.

Perhaps you have also been told at one time or another that the good writer never uses "I" in writing essays. According to this view "objective fact" is prefered to opinion, evidence to speculative "feeling." While it is of course tiresome to read a page full of unrelieved "I ____," elimination of the self from prose entirely is an impossible and clearly undesirable overreaction. In the essay especially, taking your "self" out of your writing weakens your control of the point of view that gives writing meaning and style. Although the advice may be well intentioned, "Never use I in formal writing" confuses a desired objectivity with what really can turn out to be bland impersonality. Such a pursuit of "objectivity" often produces uniformly dull or inconsistent prose with little if anything to say.

Examples of well-known projections of the "subjective" in literature help explain how the discovery of self can often be a strategy for exploring "objective" reality. Often accused of being egomaniacs, Romantic poets such as Wordsworth, Coleridge, and Whitman wrote about themselves so that, as Coleridge says, they might "steal/from my own nature all the natural man/This was my sole resource, my only plan." In this view, concentrating on one's own experiences enables writers to explore humanity and the world through an intense self-awareness. Thus the writers' concern is with objective truth as they know it best in their subjective self. Looked at in this way, the "I" in poetry and essays is the chief organizer and creator of the reality the writer communicates to an audience. In short, Whitman's "myself" is "large and contains multitudes" because his own "self" is where he finds an ability to make sense out of the kaleidoscopic world before him. Whitman therefore sang about himself in order to learn about his own reactions to the world and to clarify and enrich his own perspective.

But full exploration of "self" in order to understand the world outside the self does not mean "anything goes." Even though emphasis on the subjective "I" in writing does call for personal reactions, those reactions can and must be evaluated in terms of their intensity *and* complexity. What makes a personal reaction effective or ineffective *as communication* will depend on your ability to be understandable and persuasive and to hold the interest of your audience. You can express a personal reaction well only if you can express it in language complex enough to reproduce its full meaning. All this means simply that you must experience fully what you want to say and shape language so as to capture rather than obscure your experience as you lived through it. Only an "I" that expresses the intensity and complexity of a speaker's subjective experiences can say something interesting, significant, and maybe even new to an audience. The job of the writer, then, is not to be something other than himself or herself, but to be an interesting self that has worked to get personal responses into effective language.

One very common persona used in developing a written argument is the ironic stance toward a subject. Irony means saying one thing and meaning another. "I loved the movie" when it was an utter bore is sarcasm. A proud master might affectionately refer to his dog as "stupid" when he is really boasting about the beast's astute thinking. Irony is usually lighter in tone than sarcasm, and it is often a good deal more subtle. Often one's intent to praise is expressed in blame, and the assigning of blame is camouflaged by praise. An understated compliment is an example of the former; Antony's "Brutus is an honorable man" illustrates the latter. We often refer to an ironic statement as one that is made "tongue in cheek." Orally, irony is detected primarily through tone of voice and gestures. In writing, a reader must rely heavily on stylistic techniques and predictable forms to determine when the persona is being ironic. Examples of such techniques are the overstatement of hyperbole, the subtlety of understatement, and dramatic irony in which the character speaking is less aware than the audience of the meaning of statements. Our saying "he didn't know how right he was" identifies dramatic irony in speech. All writing handbooks explain these and other techniques for "saying one thing and meaning another" with varying degrees of complexity. "A Modest Proposal" by Jonathan Swift is one of the great examples of irony in the English language. The speaker "proposes" that the poor "overcome" their poverty by selling or eating their children—thus at once gaining monetary compensation and reducing the population problem. As the "modest" proposal becomes increasingly hideous, Swift gets the maximum effects from the ironic persona. The syndicated columnist Art Buchwald and many others often use what can be called "modest proposer" irony. "A Modest Proposal" is reprinted with several other essays following chapter 5. Look ahead for a classic example of the ironic persona.

Perhaps you hold to the true but somewhat obscure old adage that "there's nothing new under the sun." But there may not be anything at all under the sun—new or old—until there is an "I" to experience it. In a sense, everything under the sun is as old and new as each "I" perceives it to be. The responsibility of the writer becomes an exploration of the world through a fresh "I" who can communicate the newness of his or her experience from the particular angle of vision that is the writer's alone. What a writer's audience looks for in this case is not "objective" truth, but rather a sufficiently intense and complex "subjective" exploration of that truth available to the "I" who is speaking.

What you are asked to write in "objective" essays sometimes appears to leave no room for self-exploration. Talking about ourselves is often thought to be distracting to clear perception of the issue under discussion. But we do not experience the world in any way other than through the *self* that such objective analysis insists we avoid. Similarly, because what a reader reads can be real to him or her only in the way it is subjectively experienced, what a reader has to say in writing must be based on a subjective response. A writer is first of all a creative audience perceiving what he or she is writing about. This perception—these personal reactions—is what makes meaning for the writer. In this sense a writer's personal reactions are the subject and style of his or her writing.

Because readers must always draw upon their own previous experiences, their responses on the whole depend greatly on what they know about themselves and their habits of response. If the essay you are assigned to read is really a transaction between you and what is on the page, then presumably to make any meaningful responses in a paper or in class, you need to explore your own subjectivity, research yourself as well as the topic at hand, and write about both your topic and your self. Only then can you respond fully as creative participant in a process in which active reading is one important part. One reason for not enjoying reading—and one reason for especially disliking writing about what we read—may be that we don't even try to understand our fullest personal responses in the process of reading itself.

While you draw upon your own reactions, you must—as we have seen—avoid the temptation to think that "anything goes." To reach an audience you have to get beyond the "my responses are as good as your responses" dead end. Learning to evaluate personal response as it develops is not easy, but is an important part of self-awareness. What we need—and shall try to develop throughout this book—are standards that can help each subjective reader develop potential from within rather than imposing rules from outside. As exercises in personal response, in awareness of personal response as it develops, and in studying personal response to structure point of view, try the following.

Exercises

1. Take a strong stand in expressing an argument you believe. Select a "pet peeve" or support a position that puts you in the minority. Write a letter to the editor of a paper attempting to convince an antagonistic audience of your point. Identify your specific audience, your exact argument, and the role you are assuming as the speaker of that argument.

2. Repeat exercise #1 now arguing the other side of the question to an audience who thinks as your speaker of #1 thought. Or perhaps write a response to the speaker of #1.

3. Assume the personalities and viewpoints of the following speakers on the following questions:

> (a) an inner-city apartment dweller on busing
> (b) a suburban homeowner on busing
> (c) a friend back home who asks, "Why are you in college?"
> (d) a college student who asks a friend back home, "Why *aren't* you in college?"
> (e) Emerson asks Thoreau why he is in jail
> (f) Thoreau asks Emerson why he isn't in jail

4. Repeat exercise #3 by treating each speaker ironically. Then contrast your direct and ironic treatment of the same persona.

5. Devise a variety of *role-playing* exercises. For example, write a speech or an essay in the voice of a dead historical figure on some contemporary subject.

6. Contruct a dialogue between two prominent figures on some contemporary issue.

7. Consider the different voices projected by various newscasters— (Walter Cronkite vs. Eric Sevareid?). Compare and contrast two or three well-known sportscasters. Describe the different viewpoints and styles prevalent in different sections of any newspaper.

8. Discuss persona in music. Study different renditions of the same song by two or three different groups. Compare the effects of different styles in terms of the musical persona created.

9. How does camera as persona create the reality of any given film? Discuss the function of the camera perspective in defining tone, point of view, and selection of details in the rhetoric of any currently popular film.

10. Select a series of essays (musical arrangements, paintings, or photographs) by the same artist and discuss differences in the various personas used. Make a list of factors which account for the differences.

11. Study the shaping influences of persona and voice in collage making. Assemble a collage on a bulletin board or some other flexible backing. Then rearrange the same material into another collage—illustrating shifts created by change of rhetorical stance or point of view.

12. Discuss the various personas used in television commercials. Use some of their techniques in creating a persuasive essay. How does persona and manipulation of audience operate in advertising?

13. Write a script for a short film or videotape television scene. Describe action, setting, costuming, and point of view for the camera. In short, create the persona of the film through the camera's eye.

14. Write a letter to yourself from any famous person saying whatever you want to hear. Then write an interview with yourself. Notice the effects of the persona you assign to the letter writer or interviewer.

15. Recalling Emerson's advice "trust thyself," write an essay entitled "I am the most fascinating person I know."

16. To be successful, writers must not only trust themselves but also take "gutsy" stands on issues important to them. Make a list of paper topics in answer to the following proposition: "_____ is a significant question facing people today. _____ and _____ have taken the following stand, which is generally accepted. But no one has considered _____ and I think they should. By looking carefully at what has been slighted or misinterpreted I shall argue _____."

17. Rewrite a famous story from the Bible or Shakespeare, or a children's story in a "modern" version. Carefully select the point of view or persona from which you relate the tale. Keep the same details as in the original version, but notice how shifts in persona change the story.

18. Write an essay in which your persona "plays dumb" when he or she actually understands what he or she is talking about. Then write a reply from one who pretends to be "in the know" without knowing much at all. Play the characters straight to achieve a "bluff." Then reverse the process on the same issues.

19. Study the persona projected by each of five or six popular magazines. Pay special attention to their advertising.

Summary / Review

A first step in working with one's own marginal comments is gaining self-confidence. Writers develop what Emerson calls "self-reliance" by trusting their own impressions and then studying the growth of their thinking as it takes shape before them on the page. A reader's reactions begin to organize themselves in an observable point of view. In the margin you as a writer can "try out" your thinking and develop a unique perspective and tone which you can build on, modify, or otherwise react to. The mask or *persona* is the role or voice in which the writer "sounds through" ideas. The artistry of a writer's projection of "personality" through careful control of point of view derives from stylistic techniques and compensates in part for the deficiencies of writing as opposed to speech. The roles a writer plays on paper thus involve a series of choices in which he or she selects and arranges details to achieve effects consistent with the subject and audience. Particularly effective in constructing argument is the ironic persona in which a writer says one thing while meaning another. Persona is a fundamental organizing principle of all communication—as demonstrated in nonprint media such as film, music, and advertising.

3 / Marginal Comments and Source Study: Writer as Reader and Annotator

In *The Annotator,* a combined research study and detective story, Alan Keen and Roger Lubbock have documented their "investigations into the mystery of *who wrote in the margin.*" The book is subtitled *The Pursuit of an Elizabethan Reader of Halle's Chronicle Involving Some Surmises About the Early Life of William Shakespeare* (London: Putnam, 1954). The mystery is the identity of the annotator of the volume in question. The intrigue surrounds the chief "surmise"—that the author of the marginal comments was Shakespeare. Owing not only to Shakespeare's fame but also to the fact that so little is known for sure about his life, any clues provided in marginal sources would be of the utmost value. Such annotations—like the notebooks and letters of famous writers—quickly become valuable historical and literary sources, once their authenticity is established. The marginal comments of famous writers, speakers, or statesmen are always looked upon as a valuable source in the study of their life and works. Even in the sketchiest of notes in the margin are the germinal insights developed more fully later or the special burst of spontaneity unavailable in any other form.

The way famous people in history react to what they read has always been a subject of endless fascination. Many libraries contain entire collections belonging at one time to philosophers, writers, or Presidents of the United States. Often volumes that contain extensive annotation are housed in special research rooms or exhibited under glass. Interest in the annotation varies depending on the fame of the annotator. Similarly, libraries collect the journals and notebooks of well-known figures. At times such notebooks are published—along with collected correspondence—to become a part of the body of material available to historians and literary critics. Occasionally marginal comments or private letters themselves become a significant part of an author's works. The "Annotations" of William Blake, Emerson's *Journals*, and the letters of John Keats are only three examples. In the study of the history of literature, the influence of writers upon each other is becoming a subject of increasing complexity. In identifying an influence, notes in the margin often provide clues available nowhere else.

Much more could be said about the uses of marginal comments as historical sources or as evidence about the personality—or what in chapter 2 was called the persona—of the annotator. Read any biography and watch for the biographer's remarks on the reading habits of his or her subject. Often in autobiographies, authors discuss at length their own reading habits or the special influence of certain books or authors on their thinking. If you have access to a large library with special collections, ask if they have books from the private collections of deceased writers or public figures. Often published biographies will include plates illustrating several pages from books annotated in the subject's own hand. Compare your own habits as "annotator" with techniques you observe in others. Study carefully the extensive examples below from the personal reactions in William Blake's "Annotations to Sir Joshua Reynolds' *Discourses*." Three of Reynolds' lectures are reprinted, and explanatory headnotes lead into the selections. Notice especially the development of persona and the control of point of view in Blake's marginal notations.

William Blake on Sir Joshua Reynolds

Blake's reactions to Reynolds' lectures are among the world's most famous marginal comments. Both men are major figures in the history of art, and the sweeping contrasts in their views stand out sharply in Blake's pointed annotations. In the brief excerpts reprinted here, notice particularly how Blake's ideas and feelings develop as he expresses them in the margin. As a fiercely active reader, Blake measured his thinking alongside what he read. As a result, his responses often grew *in the process* of his thinking on paper.

Sir Joshua Reynolds (1723–92) was England's most accomplished creator of renowned portraits. But he is also famous for his lectures and writing on art and as a teacher of painting. For about twenty years beginning in 1769, he delivered a series of fifteen lectures on art before the newly formed British Royal Academy. Though his subjects varied widely, his chief concern was the discovery of the best methods for training an artist.

William Blake (1757–1827) was a poet, an engraver, and a painter. He combined his talents by "publishing" his poems not in print form but in pages illuminated in watercolors and with illustrations engraved in copper plates. Blake wrote lyric songs as well as prophetic and mythic poems. His painting and his poetry rejected excessive rationalism and proposed entirely new symbols and mythologies based on the importance of imagination. Throughout his life he was engaged in reinterpreting the meaning of human thinking and sensibility.

These rapid summaries are certainly oversimplified. But such sweeping generalizations are intended to place in context the selections that follow here. The *Discourses* and marginal comments will themselves create a fuller picture of Reynolds' and Blake's thinking.

In Discourse One, Reynolds explains the workings of the Royal Academy and previews his insistence on the importance of Rules of Art. He also points to the dangers faced by students of art and urges the cultivation of habits of "scrupulous exactness." Blake's reactions follow the reprinting of Discourse Six, as they appear in the margins of his copy of the *Discourses*. After initial comments that capture his general impressions, he continues his notations alongside passages throughout the book. Blake's reactions to Reynolds' methods are volatile. He objects to the whole of the Discourse, selecting for special attack Reynolds' views on imitation. But Blake also praises what he regularly calls "Excellent" in Reynolds' insights. The "Annotations" convey a sense of dialogue between two stimulating artists.

Discourse Two is given to what Reynolds calls "The Course and Order of Study" as well as to "the different stages of art." He explores in detail "Invention," or the complex processes through which the artist creates. His curriculum includes the combining of "genius" and "industry" or innate talent and hard work. Discourse Two continues to speak to writers and artists today who seek to *develop* what is "given" in their seemingly unexplainable talent. Blake's reactions vary from "True" to "Nonsense," and he is primarily concerned with the dangers of underestimating imagination and overplaying the values of copying. Again their interaction is a brilliant exchange on the artist's development and exercise of his creative powers.

Discourse Six extends the exploration of the seeming opposition between Genius and Rules. Reynolds explores the artist's "inspiration" and what he calls "the true method of imitating" wherein the writer borrows and yet develops his own style in the process. Paradoxically, the artist imitates in order to become truly original. Discourse Six is perhaps the most concise statement of the English neoclassical theory of converting the riches and substance of classical models to one's own purpose. Blake's reactions are predictably vociferous. As his marginal comments quickly show, Blake feels that Reynolds has missed the point. His quarrel is not with minute details in the Discourse but with the whole philosophy of art and really the entire world view that Reynolds presents. The three selections reprinted here (followed by Blake's commentary) are representative of the views of a major figure in the history of art. The clashes that resound in Blake's "Annotations" express as well representative conflicts about what art is and how the artist creates.

Sir Joshua Reynolds, Discourses on Art*

DISCOURSE ONE

GENTLEMEN,

An Academy, in which the Polite Arts may be regularly cultivated, is at last opened among us by Royal Munificence. This must appear an event in the highest degree interesting, not only to the Artists, but to the whole nation.

It is indeed difficult to give any other reason, why an empire like that of Britain, should so long have wanted an ornament so suitable to its greatness, than that slow progression of things, which naturally makes elegance and refinement the last effect of opulence and power.

An Institution like this has often been recommended upon considerations merely mercantile; but an Academy, founded upon such principles, can never effect even its own narrow purposes. If it has an origin no higher, no taste can ever be formed in manufactures; but if the higher Arts of Design flourish, these inferior ends will be answered of course.

We are happy in having a Prince, who has conceived the design of such an Institution, according to its true dignity; and who promotes the Arts, as the head of a great, a learned, a polite, and a commercial nation, and I can now congratulate you, Gentlemen, on the accomplishment of your long and ardent wishes.

The numberless and ineffectual consultations which I have had with many in this assembly, to form plans and concert schemes for an Academy, afford a sufficient proof of the impossibility of succeeding but by the influence of Majesty. But there have, perhaps, been times, when even the influence of Majesty would have been ineffectual; and it is pleasing to reflect, that we are thus embodied, when every circumstance seems to concur from which honour and prosperity can probably arise.

There are, at this time, a greater number of excellent

---

*Reproduced by permission of The Huntington Library, San Marino, California.

Artists than were ever known before at one period in this nation; there is a general desire among our Nobility to be distinguished as lovers and judges of the Arts; there is a greater superfluity of wealth among the people to reward the professors; and, above all, we are patronized by a Monarch, who, knowing the value of science and of elegance, thinks every Art worthy of his notice, that tends to soften and humanise the mind.

After so much has been done by His Majesty, it will be wholly our fault, if our progress is not in some degree correspondent to the wisdom and generosity of the Institution: let us show our gratitude in our diligence, that, though our merit may not answer his expectations, yet, at least, our industry may deserve his protection.

But whatever may be our proportion of success, of this we may be sure, that the present Institution will at least contribute to advance our knowledge of the Arts, and bring us nearer to that ideal excellence, which it is the lot of genius always to contemplate and never to attain.

The principal advantage of an Academy is, that, beside furnishing able men to direct the Student, it will be a repository for the great examples of the Art. These are the materials on which Genius is to work, and without which the strongest intellect may be fruitlesly or deviously employed. By studying these authentick models, that idea of excellence which is the result of the accumulated experience of past ages, may be at once acquired; and the tardy and obstructed progress of our predecessors may teach us a shorter and easier way. The Student receives, at one glance, the principles which many Artists have spent their whole lives in ascertaining; and, satisfied with their effect, is spared the painful investigation by which they came to be known and fixed. How many men of great natural abilities have been lost to this nation, for want of these advantages! They never had an opportunity of seeing those masterly efforts of genius, which at once kindle the whole soul, and force it into sudden and irresistible approbation.

Raffaelle, it is true, had not the advantage of studying in an Academy; but all Rome, and the works of Michael Angelo in particular, were to him an Academy. On the sight of the Capella Sistina, he immediately from a dry, Gothick, and even insipid manner, which attends to the minute accidental discriminations of particular and individual objects, assumed that grand style of painting, which improves partial representation by the general and invariable ideas of nature.

Every seminary of learning may be said to be surrounded with an atmosphere of floating knowledge, where every mind may imbibe somewhat congenial to its own original conceptions. Knowledge, thus obtained, has always something more popular and useful than that which is forced upon the mind by private precepts, or solitary meditation. Besides, it is generally found, that a youth more easily receives instruction from the companions of his studies, whose minds are nearly on a level with his own, than from those who are much his superiors; and it is from his equals only that he catches the fire of emulation.

One advantage, I will venture to affirm, we shall have in our Academy, which no other nation can boast. We shall have nothing to unlearn. To this praise the present race of Artists have a just claim. As far as they have yet proceeded, they are right. With us the exertions of genius will henceforward be directed to their proper objects. It will not be as it has been in other schools, where he that travelled fastest, only wandered farthest from the right way.

Impressed, as I am, therefore, with such a favourable opinion of my associates in this undertaking, it would ill become me to dictate to any of them. But as these Institutions have so often failed in other nations; and as it is natural to think with regret, how much might have been done, I must take leave to offer a few hints, by which those errors may be rectified, and those defects supplied. These the Professors and Visitors may reject or adopt as they shall think proper.

I would chiefly recommend, that an implicit obedience to the *Rules of Art,* as established by the practice of the great Masters, should be exacted from the *young* Students. That those models, which have passed through the approbation of ages, should be considered by them as perfect and infallible guides; as subjects for their imitation, not their criticism.

I am confident, that this is the only efficacious method of making progress in the Arts; and that he who sets out with doubting, will find life finished before he becomes master of the rudiments. For it may be laid down as a maxim, that he who begins by presuming on his own sense, has ended his studies as soon as he has commenced them. Every opportunity, therefore, should be taken to discountenance that false and vulgar opinion, that rules are the fetters of genius. They are fetters only to men of no genius; as that armour, which upon the strong is an ornament and a defence, upon the weak and mis-shapen becomes a load, and cripples the body which it was made to protect.

How much liberty may be taken to break through these rules, and, as the Poet expresses it,

To snatch a grace beyond the reach of art,

may be a subsequent consideration, when the pupils become masters themselves. It is then, when their genius has received its utmost improvement, that rules may possibly be dispensed with. But let us not destroy the scaffold, until we have raised the building.

The Directors ought more particularly to watch over the genius of those Students, who, being more advanced, are arrived at that critical period of study, on the nice management of which their future turn of taste depends. At that age it is natural for them to be more captivated with what is brilliant than with what is solid, and to prefer splendid negligence to painful and humiliating exactness.

A facility in composing,—a lively, and what is called a masterly, handling of the chalk or pencil, are, it must be confessed, captivating qualities to young minds, and become of course the objects of their ambition. They endeavour to imitate those dazzling excellencies, which they will find no great labour in attaining. After much time spent in these frivolous pursuits, the difficulty will be to retreat; but it will be then too late; and there is scarce an instance of return to scrupulous labour, after the mind has been debauched and deceived by this fallacious mastery.

By this useless industry they are excluded from all power of advancing in real excellence. Whilst boys, they are arrived at their utmost perfection; they have taken the shadow for the substance; and make the mechanical felicity, the chief excellence of the art, which is only an ornament, and of the merit of which few but painters themselves are judges.

This seems to me to be one of the most dangerous sources of corruption; and I speak of it from experience, not as an error which may possibly happen, but which has actually infected all foreign Academies. The directors were probably pleased with this premature dexterity in their pupils, and praised their dispatch at the expence of their correctness.

But young men have not only this frivolous ambition of being thought masters of execution, inciting them on one hand, but also their natural sloth tempting them on the other. They are terrified at the prospect before them, of the toil required to attain exactness. The impetuousity of youth is disgusted at the slow approaches of a regular siege, and desires, from mere impatience of labour, to take the citadel by storm. They wish to find some shorter path to excellence, and hope to obtain the reward of eminence by other means, than those which the indispensible rules of art have prescribed. They must therefore be told again and again, that labour is the only price of solid fame, and that whatever their force of genius may be, there is no easy method of becoming a good Painter.

When we read the lives of the most eminent Painters, every page informs us, that no part of their time was spent in dissipation. Even an increase of fame served only to augment their industry. To be convinced with what persevering assiduity they pursued their studies, we need only reflect on their method of proceeding in their most celebrated works. When they conceived a subject, they first made a variety of sketches; then a finished drawing of the whole; after that a more correct drawing of every separate part,—heads, hands, feet, and pieces of drapery; they then painted the picture, and after all re-touched it from the life. The pictures, thus wrought with such pains, now appear like the effect of enchantment, and as if some mighty Genius had struck them off at a blow.

But, whilst diligence is thus recommended to the Students, the Visitors will take care that their diligence be effectual; that it be well directed, and employed on the proper object. A Student is not always advancing because he is employed; he must apply his strength to that part of the art where the real difficulties lie; to that part which distinguishes it as a liberal art; and not by mistaken industry lose his time in that which is merely ornamental. The Students, instead of vying with each other which shall have the readiest hand, should be taught to contend who shall have the purest and most correct out line; instead of striving which shall produce the brightest tint, or, curiously trifling, shall give the gloss of stuffs, so as to appear real, let their ambition be directed to contend, which shall dispose his drapery in the most graceful folds, which shall give the most grace and dignity to the human figure.

I must beg leave to submit one thing more to the consideration of the Visitors, which appears to me a matter of very great consequence, and the omission of which I think a principal defect in the method of education pursued in all the Academies I have ever visited. The error I mean is, that the Students never draw exactly from the living models which they have before them. It is not indeed their intention; nor are they directed to do it. Their drawings resemble the model only in the attitude. They change the form according to their vague and uncertain ideas of beauty, and make a drawing rather of what they think the figure ought to be, than of what it appears. I have thought this the obstacle, that has stopped the progress of many young men of real genius; and I very much doubt, whether a habit of drawing correctly what we see, will not give a proportionable power of drawing correctly what we imagine. He who endeavours to copy nicely the figure before him, not only acquires a habit of exactness and precision, but is continually advancing in his knowledge of the human figure; and though he seems to superficial observers to make a slower progress, he will be found at last capable of adding (without running into capricious wildness) that grace and beauty, which is necessary to be given to his more finished works, and which cannot be got by the moderns, as it was not acquired by the ancients, but by an attentive and well compared study of the human form.

What I think ought to enforce this method is, that it has been the practice (as may be seen by their drawings) of the great Masters in the Art. I will mention a drawing of Raffaelle, *The Dispute of the Sacrament*, the print of which, by Count Cailus, is in every hand. It appears, that he made his sketch from one model; and the habit he had of drawing exactly from the form before him appears by his making all the figures with the same cap, such as his model then happened to wear; so servile a copyist was this great man, even at a time when he was allowed to be at his highest pitch of excellence.

I have seen also Academy figures by Annibale Caracci, though he was often sufficiently licentious in his finished works, drawn with all the peculiarities of an individual model.

This scrupulous exactness is so contrary to the practice of the Academies, that it is not without great deference, that I beg leave to recommend it to the consideration of the Visitors; and submit to them, whether the neglect of this method is not one of the reasons why Students so often disappoint expectation, and, being more than boys at sixteen, become less than men at thirty.

In short, the method I recommend can only be detrimental when there are but few living forms to copy; for then Students, by always drawing from one alone, will by habit be taught to overlook defects, and mistake deformity for beauty. But of this there is no danger; since the Council has determined to supply the Academy with a variety of subjects; and indeed those laws which they have drawn up, and which the Secretary will presently read for your confirmation, have in some measure precluded me from saying more upon this occasion. Instead, therefore, of offering my advice, permit me to indulge my wishes, and express my hope, that this institution may answer the expectations of its Royal Founder; that the present age may vie in Arts with that of Leo the Tenth; and that *the dignity of the dying Art* (to make use of an expression of Pliny) may be revived under the Reign of GEORGE THE THIRD.

DISCOURSE TWO

GENTLEMEN,

I congratulate you on the honour which you have just received. I have the highest opinion of your merits, and could wish to show my sense of them in something which possibly may be more useful to you than barren praise. I could wish to lead you into such a course of study as may render your future progress answerable to your past improvement; and, whilst I applaud you for what has been done, remind you how much yet remains to attain perfection.

I flatter myself, that from the long experience I have had, and the unceasing assiduity with which I have pursued those studies, in which, like you, I have been engaged, I shall be acquitted of vanity in offering some hints to your consideration. They are indeed in a great degree founded upon my own mistakes in the same pursuit. But the history of errors, properly managed, often shortens the road to truth. And although no method of study that I can offer, will of itself conduct to excellence, yet it may preserve industry from being misapplied.

In speaking to you of the Theory of the Art, I shall only consider it as it has a relation to the *method* of your studies.

Dividing the study of painting into three distinct periods, I shall address you as having passed through the first of them, which is confined to the rudiments; including a facility of drawing any object that presents itself, a tolerable readiness in the management of colours, and an acquaintance with the most simple and obvious rules of composition.

This first degree of proficiency is, in painting, what grammar is in literature, a general preparation for whatever species of the art the student may afterwards choose for his more particular application. The power of drawing, modelling, and using colours, is very properly called the Language of the art: and in this language, the honours you have just received, prove you to have made no inconsiderable progress.

When the Artist is once enabled to express himself with some degree of correctness, he must then endeavour to collect subjects for expression; to amass a stock of ideas, to be combined and varied as occasion may require. He is now in the second period of study, in which his business is to learn all that has been known and done before his own time. Having hitherto received instructions from a particular master, he is now to consider the Art itself as his master. He must extend his capacity to more sublime and general instructions. Those perfections which lie scattered among various masters, are now united in one general idea, which is henceforth to regulate his taste, and enlarge his imagination. With a variety of models thus before him, he will avoid that narrowness and poverty of conception which attends a bigotted admiration of a single master, and will cease to follow any favourite where he ceases to excel. This period is, however, still a time of subjection and discipline. Though the Student will not resign himself blindly to any single authority, when he may have the advantage of consulting many, he must still be afraid of trusting his own judgment, and of deviating into any track where he cannot find the footsteps of some former master.

The third and last period emancipates the Student from subjection to any authority, but what he shall himself judge to be supported by reason. Confiding now in his own judgment, he will consider and separate those different principles to which different modes of beauty owe their original. In the former period he sought only to know and combine excellence, wherever it was to be found, into one idea of perfection: in this, he learns, what requires the most attentive survey and the most subtle disquisition, to discriminate perfections that are incompatible with each other.

He is from this time to regard himself as holding the same rank with those masters whom he before obeyed as teachers, and as exercising a sort of sovereignty over those rules which have hitherto restrained him. Comparing now no longer the performances of Art with each other, but examining the Art itself by the standard of Nature, he corrects what is erroneous, supplies what is scanty, and adds by his own observation what the industry of his predecessors may have yet left wanting to perfection. Having well established his judgment, and stored his memory, he may now without fear try the power of his imagination. The mind that has been thus disciplined, may be indulged in the warmest enthusiasm, and venture to play on the borders of the wildest extravagance. The habitual dignity which long converse with the greatest minds has imparted to him, will display itself in all his attempts; and he will stand among his instructors, not as an imitator, but a rival.

These are the different stages of the Art. But as I now address myself particularly to those Students who have been this day rewarded for their happy passage through the first period, I can with no propriety suppose they want any help in the initiatory studies. My present design is to direct your view to distant excellence, and to show you the readiest path that leads to it. Of this I shall speak with such latitude, as may leave the province of the professor uninvaded; and shall not anticipate those precepts, which it is his business to give, and your duty to understand.

It is indisputably evident that a great part of every man's life must be employed in collecting materials for the exercise of genius. Invention, strictly speaking, is little more than a new combination of those images which have been previously gathered and deposited in the memory: nothing can come of nothing: he who has laid up no materials, can produce no combinations.

A Student unacquainted with the attempts of former adventurers, is always apt to over-rate his own abilities; to mistake the most trifling excursions for discoveries of moment, and every coast new to him, for a new-found country. If by chance he passes beyond his usual limits, he congratulates his own arrival at those regions which they who have steered a better course have long left behind them.

The productions of such minds are seldom distinguished by an air of originality: they are anticipated in their happiest efforts; and if they are found to differ in any thing from their predecessors, it is only in irregular sallies, and trifling conceits. The more extensive therefore your acquaintance is with the works of those who have excelled, the more extensive will be your powers of invention; and what may appear still more like a paradox, the more original will be your conceptions. But the difficulty on this occasion is to determine who ought to be proposed as models of excellence, and who ought to be considered as the properest guides.

To a young man just arrived in *Italy*, many of the present painters of that country are ready enough to obtrude their precepts, and to offer their own performances as examples of that perfection which they affect to recommend. The Modern, however, who recommends *himself* as a standard, may justly be suspected as ignorant of the true end, and unacquainted with the proper object, of the art which he professes. To follow such a guide, will not only retard the Student, but mislead him.

On whom then can he rely, or who shall show him the path that leads to excellence? the answer is obvious: those great masters who have travelled the same road with success, are the most likely to conduct others. The works of those who have stood the test of ages, have a claim to that respect and veneration to which no modern can pretend. The duration and stability of their fame, is sufficient to evince that it has not been suspended upon the slender thread of fashion and ca- price, but bound to the human heart by every tie of sym- pathetick approbation.

There is no danger of studying too much the works of those great men; but how they may be studied to advantage is an enquiry of great importance.

Some who have never raised their minds to the considera- tion of the real dignity of the Art, and who rate the works of an Artist in proportion as they excel or are defective in the mechanical parts, look on theory as something that may enable them to talk but not to paint better; and confining themselves entirely to mechanical practice, very assiduously toil on in the drudgery of copying; and think they make a rapid progress while they faithfully exhibit the minutest part of a favourite picture. This appears to me a very tedious, and I think a very erroneous method of proceeding. Of every large composition, even of those which are most admired, a great part may be truly said to be *common-place*. This, though it takes up much time in copying, conduces little to improvement. I consider general copying as a delusive kind of industry; the Student satisfies himself with the appearance of doing something; he falls into the dangerous habit of imitating without selecting, and of labouring without any determinate object; as it requires no effort of the mind, he sleeps over his work; and those pow- ers of invention and composition which ought particularly to be called out, and put in action, lie torpid, and lose their energy for want of exercise.

How incapable those are of producing any thing of their own, who have spent much of their time in making finished copies, is well known to all who are conversant with our art.

To suppose that the complication of powers, and variety of ideas necessary to that mind which aspires to the first honours in the art of Painting, can be obtained by the frigid contempla- tion of a few single models, is no less absurd, than it would be in him who wishes to be a Poet, to imagine that by translating a tragedy he can acquire to himself sufficient knowledge of the appearances of nature, the operations of the passions, and the incidents of life.

The great use in copying, if it be at all useful, should seem to be in learning to colour; yet even colouring will never be perfectly attained by servilely copying the model before you. An eye critically nice can only be formed by observing well-coloured pictures with attention: and by close inspection, and minute examination, you will discover, at last, the manner of handling, the artifices of contrast, glazing, and other expedients, by which good colourists have raised the value of their tints, and by which nature has been so happily imitated.

I must inform you, however, that old pictures deservedly celebrated for their colouring, are often so changed by dirt and varnish, that we ought not to wonder if they do not appear equal to their reputation in the eyes of unexperienced painters, or young students. An artist whose judgment is matured by long observation, considers rather what the picture once was, than what it is at present. He has by habit acquired a power of seeing the brilliancy of tints through the cloud by which it is obscured. An exact imitation, therefore, of those pictures, is likely to fill the student's mind with false opinions; and to send him back a colourist of his own formation, with ideas equally remote from nature and from art, from the genuine practice of the masters, and the real appearances of things.

Following these rules, and using these precautions, when you have clearly and distinctly learned in what good colouring consists, you cannot do better than have recourse to nature herself, who is always at hand, and in comparison of whose true splendour the best coloured pictures are but faint and feeble.

However, as the practice of copying is not entirely to be excluded, since the mechanical practice of painting is learned in some measure by it, let those choice parts only be selected which have recommended the work to notice. If its excellence consists in its general effect, it would be proper to make slight sketches of the machinery and general management of the picture. Those sketches should be kept always by you for the regulation of your stile. Instead of copying the touches of those great masters, copy only their conceptions. Instead of treading in their footsteps, endeavour only to keep the same road. Labour to invent on their general principles and way of thinking. Possess yourself with their spirit. Consider with yourself how a Michael Angelo or a Raffaelle would have treated this subject: and work yourself into a belief that your picture is to be seen and criticised by them when completed. Even an attempt of this kind will rouse your powers.

But as mere enthusiasm will carry you but a little way, let me recommend a practice that may be equivalent to and will perhaps more efficaciously contribute to your advancement, than even the verbal corrections of those masters themselves, could they be obtained. What I would propose is, that you should enter into a kind of competition, by painting a similar subject, and making a companion to any picture that you consider as a model. After you have finished your work, place it near the model, and compare them carefully together. You will then not only see, but feel your own deficiencies more sensibly than by precepts, or any other means of instruction. The true principles of painting will mingle with your thoughts. Ideas thus fixed by sensible objects, will be certain and definitive; and sinking deep into the mind, will not only be more just, but more lasting than those presented to you by precepts only; which will always be fleeting, variable, and undetermined.

This method of comparing your own efforts with those of some great master, is indeed a severe and mortifying task, to which none will submit, but such as have great views, with fortitude sufficient to forego the gratifications of present vanity for future honour. When the Student has succeeded in some measure to his own satisfaction, and has felicitated himself on his success, to go voluntarily to a tribunal where he knows his vanity must be humbled, and all self-approbation must vanish, requires not only great resolution, but great humility. To him, however, who has the ambition to be a real master, the solid satisfaction which proceeds from a consciousness of his advancement, (of which seeing his own faults is the first step,) will very abundantly compensate for the mortification of present disappointment. There is, besides, this alleviating circumstance. Every discovery he makes, every acquisition of knowledge he attains, seems to proceed from his own sagacity; and thus he acquires a confidence in himself sufficient to keep up the resolution of perseverance.

We all must have experienced how lazily, and consequently how ineffectually, instruction is received when forced upon the mind by others. Few have been taught to any purpose who have not been their own teachers. We prefer those instructions which we have given ourselves, from our affection to the instructor; and they are more effectual, from being received into the mind at the very time when it is most open and eager to receive them.

With respect to the pictures that you are to choose for your models, I could wish that you would take the world's opinion rather than your own. In other words, I would have you choose those of established reputation, rather than follow your own fancy. If you should not admire them at first, you will, by endeavouring to imitate them, find that the world has not been mistaken.

It is not an easy task to point out those various excellencies for your imitation which lie distributed amongst the various schools. An endeavour to do this may perhaps be the subject of some future discourse. I will, therefore, at present only recommend a model for Stile in Painting, which is a branch of the art more immediately necessary to the young student. Stile in painting is the same as in writing, a power over materials, whether words or colours, by which conceptions or sentiments are conveyed. And in this Lodovico Carrache (I mean in his best works) appears to me to approach the nearest to perfection. His unaffected breadth of light and shadow, the simplicity of colouring, which holding its proper rank, does not draw aside the least part of the attention from the subject, and the solemn effect of that twilight which seems diffused over his pictures, appear to me to correspond with grave and dignified subjects, better than the more artificial brilliancy of sunshine which enlightens the pictures of Titian: though Tintoret thought that Titian's colouring was the model of perfection, and would correspond even with the sublime of Michael Angelo; and that if Angelo had coloured like Titian, or Titian designed like Angelo, the world would once have had a perfect painter.

It is our misfortune, however, that those works of Carrache which I would recommend to the Student, are not often found out of *Bologna*. The *St. Francis in the midst of his Friars, The Transfiguration, The Birth of St. John the Baptist, The Calling of St. Matthew, The St. Jerome, The Fresco Paintings* in the Zampieri palace, are all worthy the attention of the student. And I think those who travel would do well to allot a much greater portion of their time to that city than it has been hitherto the custom to bestow.

In this art, as in others, there are many teachers who profess to shew the nearest way to excellence; and many expedients have been invented by which the toil of study might be saved. But let no man be seduced to idleness by specious promises. Excellence is never granted to man, but as the reward of labour. It argues indeed no small strength of mind to persevere in habits of industry, without the pleasure of perceiving those advances; which, like the hand of a clock, whilst they make hourly approaches to their point, yet proceed so slowly as to escape observation. A facility of drawing, like that of playing upon a musical instrument, cannot be acquired but by an infinite number of acts. I need not, therefore, enforce by many words the necessity of continual application; nor tell you that the porte-crayon ought to be for ever in your hands. Various methods will occur to you by which this power may be acquired. I would particularly recommend, that after your return from the Academy (where I suppose your attendance to be constant) you would endeavour to draw the figure by memory. I will even venture to add, that by perseverance in this custom, you will become able to draw the human figure tolerably correct, with as little effort of the mind as is required to trace with a pen the letters of the alphabet.

That this facility is not unattainable, some members in this Academy give a sufficient proof. And be assured, that if this power is not acquired whilst you are young, there will be no time for it afterwards: at least the attempt will be attended with as much difficulty as those experience who learn to read or write after they have arrived to the age of maturity.

But while I mention the porte-crayon as the student's constant companion, he must still remember, that the pencil is the instrument by which he must hope to obtain eminence. What, therefore, I wish to impress upon you is, that whenever an opportunity offers, you paint your studies instead of drawing them. This will give you such a facility in using colours, that in time they will arrange themselves under the pencil, even without the attention of the hand that conducts it. If one act excluded the other, this advice could not with any propriety be given. But if Painting comprises both drawing and colouring, and if by a short struggle of resolute industry, the same expedition is attainable in painting as in drawing on paper, I cannot see what objection can justly be made to the practice; or why that should be done by parts, which may be done all together.

If we turn our eyes to the several Schools of Painting, and consider their respective excellencies, we shall find that those who excel most in colouring, pursued this method. The *Venetian* and *Flemish* schools, which owe much of their fame to colouring, have enriched the cabinets of the collectors of drawings, with very few examples. Those of Titian, Paul Veronese, Tintoret, and the Bassans, are in general slight and undetermined. Their sketches on paper are as rude as their pictures are excellent in regard to harmony of colouring. Correggio and Barocci have left few, if any finished drawings behind them. And in the *Flemish* school, Rubens and Vandyck made their designs for the most part either in colours, or in chiaro oscuro. It is as common to find studies of the *Venetian* and *Flemish*

Painters on canvass, as of the schools of *Rome* and *Florence* on paper. Not but that many finished drawings are sold under the names of those masters. Those, however, are undoubtedly the productions either of engravers or of their scholars, who copied their works.

These instructions I have ventured to offer from my own experience; but as they deviate widely from received opinions, I offer them with diffidence; and when better are suggested, shall retract them without regret.

There is one precept, however, in which I shall only be opposed by the vain, the ignorant, and the idle. I am not afraid that I shall repeat it too often. You must have no dependence on your own genius. If you have great talents, industry will improve them; if you have but moderate abilities, industry will supply their deficiency. Nothing is denied to well directed labour: nothing is to be obtained without it. Not to enter into metaphysical discussions on the nature or essence of genius, I will venture to assert, that assiduity unabated by difficulty, and a disposition eagerly directed to the object of its pursuit, will produce effects similar to those which some call the result of *natural powers.*

Though a man cannot at all times, and in all places, paint or draw, yet the mind can prepare itself by laying in proper materials, at all times, and in all places. Both Livy and Plutarch, in describing Philopoemen, one of the ablest generals of antiquity, have given us a striking picture of a mind always intent on its profession, and by assiduity obtaining those excellencies which some all their lives vainly expect from Nature. I shall quote the passage in Livy at length, as it runs parallel with the practice I would recommend to the Painter, Sculptor, and Architect.

"Philopoemen was a man eminent for his sagacity and experience in choosing ground, and in leading armies; to which he formed his mind by perpetual meditation, in times of peace as well as war. When, in any occasional journey, he came to a strait difficult passage, if he was alone, he considered with himself, and if he was in company he asked his friends, what it would be best to do if in this place they had found an enemy, either in the front, or in the rear, on the one side, or on the other. 'It might happen,' says he, 'that the enemy to be opposed might come on drawn up in regular lines, or in a tumultuous body, formed only by the nature of the place.' He then considered a little what ground he should take; what number of soldiers he should use, and what arms he should give them; where he should lodge his carriages, his baggage, and the defenceless followers of his camp; how many guards, and of what kind, he should send to defend them; and whether it would be better to press forward along the pass, or recover by retreat his former station: he would consider likewise where his camp could most commodiously be formed; how much ground he should inclose within his trenches; where he should have the convenience of water, and where he might find plenty of wood and forage; and when he should break up his camp on the following day, through what road he could most safely pass, and in what form he should dispose his troops. With such thoughts and disquisitions he had from his early years so exercised his mind, that on these occasions nothing could happen which he had not been already accustomed to consider."

I cannot help imagining that I see a promising young painter, equally vigilant, whether at home, or abroad, in the streets, or in the fields. Every object that presents itself, is to him a lesson. He regards all Nature with a view to his profession; and combines the countenance of men under the influence of passion; and often catches the most pleasing hints from subjects of turbulence or deformity. Even bad pictures themselves supply him with useful documents; and as Leonardo da Vinci has observed, he improves upon the fanciful images that are sometimes seen in the fire, or are accidentally sketched upon a discoloured wall.

The artist who has his mind thus filled with ideas, and his hand made expert by practice, works with ease and readiness; whilst he who would have you believe that he is waiting for the inspirations of Genius, is in reality at a loss how to begin; and is at last delivered of his monsters, with difficulty and pain.

The well-grounded painter, on the contrary, has only maturely to consider his subject, and all the mechanical parts of his art follow without his exertion. Conscious of the difficulty of obtaining what he possesses, he makes no pretensions to secrets, except those of closer application. Without conceiving the smallest jealousy against others, he is contented that all shall be as great as himself, who have undergone the same fatigue; and as his pre-eminence depends not upon a trick, he is free from the painful suspicions of a juggler, who lives in perpetual fear lest his trick should be discovered.

DISCOURSE SIX

GENTLEMEN,

When I have taken the liberty of addressing you on the course and order of your studies, I never proposed to enter into a minute detail of the art. This I have always left to the several Professors, who pursue the end of our institution with the highest honour to themselves, and with the greatest advantage to the Students.

My purpose in the discourses I have held in the Academy has been, to lay down certain general positions, which seem to me proper for the formation of a sound taste: principles, necessary to guard the pupils against those errors, into which the sanguine temper common to their time of life has a tendency to lead them; and which have rendered abortive the hopes of so many successions of promising young men in all parts of Europe. I wished also, to intercept and suppress those prejudices which particularly prevail when the mechanism of painting is come to its perfection; and which, when they do prevail, are certain utterly to destroy the higher and more valuable parts of this literate and liberal profession.

These two have been my principal purposes; they are still as much my concern, as ever; and if I repeat my own notions on the subject, you who know how fast mistake and prejudice, when neglected, gain ground upon truth and reason, will easily excuse me. I only attempt to set the same thing in the greatest variety of lights.

The subject of this discourse will be *Imitation*, as far as a painter is concerned in it. By imitation I do not mean imitation in its largest sense, but simply the following of other masters, and the advantage to be drawn from the study of their works.

Those who have undertaken to write on our art, and have represented it as a kind of *inspiration*, as a *gift* bestowed upon peculiar favourites at their birth, seem to insure a much more favourable disposition from their readers, and have a much more captivating and liberal air, than he who attempts to examine, coldly, whether there are any means by which this art be acquired; how the mind may be strengthened and expanded, and what guides will shew the way to eminence.

It is very natural for those who are unacquainted with the *cause* of any thing extraordinary, to be astonished at the *effect*, and to consider it as a kind of magick. They, who have never observed the gradation by which art is acquired; who see only what is the full result of long labour and application of an infinite number and infinite variety of acts, are apt to conclude from their entire inability to do the same at once, that it is not only inaccessible to themselves, but can be done by those only, who have some gift of the nature of inspiration bestowed upon them.

The travellers into the East tell us, that when the ignorant inhabitants of those countries are asked concerning the ruins of stately edifices yet remaining amongst them, the melancholy monuments of their former grandeur and long-lost science, they always answer, that they were built by magicians. The untaught mind finds a vast gulph between its own powers, and those works of complicated art, which it is utterly unable to fathom; and it supposes that such a void can be passed only by supermatural powers.

And, as for artists themselves, it is by no means their interest to undeceive such judges, however conscious they may be of the very natural means by which their extraordinary powers were acquired; though our art, being intrinsically imitative, rejects this idea of inspiration, more perhaps than any other.

It is to avoid this plain confession of truth, as it should seem, that this imitation of masters, indeed almost all imitation, which implies a more regular and progressive method of attaining the ends of painting, has ever been particularly inveighed against with great keenness, both by ancient and modern writers.

To derive all from native power, to owe nothing to another, is the praise which men who do not much think on what they are saying, bestow sometimes upon others, and sometimes on themselves; and their imaginary dignity is naturally heightened by a supercilious censure of the low, the barren, the groveling, the servile imitator. It would be no wonder if a student, frightened by these terrifick and disgraceful epithets, with which the poor imitators are so often loaded, should let fall his pencil in mere despair; (conscious as he must be, how much he has been indebted to the labours of others, how little, how very little of his art was born with him;) and, consider it may as hopeless, to set about acquiring by the imitation of any human master, what he is taught to suppose is matter of inspiration from heaven.

Some allowance must be made for what is said in the gaiety or ambition of rhetorick. We cannot suppose that any one can really mean to exclude all imitation of others. A position so wild would scarce deserve a serious answer; for it is apparent, if we were forbid to make use of the advantages which our predecessors afford us, the art would be always to begin, and consequently remain always in its infant state; and it is a common observation, that no art was ever invented and carried to perfection at the same time.

But to bring us entirely to reason and sobriety, let it be observed, that a painter must not only be of necessity an imitator of the works of nature, which alone is sufficient to dispel this phantom of inspiration, but he must be as necessarily an imitator of the works of other painters: this appears more humiliating, but is equally true; and no man can be an artist, whatever he may suppose, upon any other terms.

However, those who appear more moderate and reasonable, allow, that our study is to begin by imitation; but maintain that we should no longer use the thoughts of our predecessors, when we are become able to think for ourselves. They hold that imitation is as hurtful to the more advanced student, as it was advantageous to the beginner.

For my own part, I confess, I am not only very much disposed to maintain the absolute necessity of imitation in the first stages of the art; but am of opinion, that the study of other masters, which I here call imitation, may be extended throughout our whole lives, without any danger of the inconveniencies with which it is charged, of enfeebling the mind, or preventing us from giving that original air which every work undoubtedly ought always to have.

I am on the contrary persuaded, that by imitation only, variety, and even originally of invention, is produced. I will go further; even genius, at least what generally is so called, is the child of imitation. But as this appears to be contrary to the general opinion, I must explain my position before I enforce it.

Genius is supposed to be a power of producing excellencies, which are out of the reach of the rules of art; a power which no precepts can teach, and which no industry can acquire.

This opinion of the impossibility of acquiring those beauties, which stamp the work with the character of genius, supposes, that it is something more fixed than in reality it is; and that we always do, and ever did agreee in opinion, with respect to what should be considered as the characteristick of genius. But the truth is, that the *degree* of excellence which proclaims *Genius* is different, in different times and different places; and what shews it to be so is, that mankind have often changed their opinion upon this matter.

When the arts were in their infancy, the power of merely drawing the likeness of any object, was considered as one of its greatest efforts. The common people, ignorant of the principles of art, talk the same language, even to this day. But when it was found that every man could be taught to do this, and a great deal more, merely by the observance of certain precepts; the name of Genius then shifted its application, and was given only to him who added the peculiar character of the object he represented; to him who had invention, expression, grace, or dignity; in short, those qualities, or excellencies, the power of producing which, could not *then* be taught by any known and promulgated rules.

We are very sure that the beauty of form, the expression of the passions, the art of composition, even the power of giving a general air of grandeur to a work, is at present very much under the dominion of rules. These excellencies were, heretofore, considered merely as the effects of genius; and justly, if genius is not taken for inspiration, but as the effect of close observation and experience.

He who first made any of these observations, and digested them, so as to form an invariable principle for himself to work by, had that merit, but probably no one went very far at once; and generally, the first who gave the hint, did not know how to pursue it steadily, and methodically; at least not in the beginning. He himself worked on it, and improved it; others worked more, and improved further; until the secret was discovered, and the practice made as general, as refined practice can be made. How many more principles may be fixed and ascertained, we cannot tell; but as criticism is likely to go hand in hand with the art which is its subject, we may venture to say, that as that art shall advance, its powers will be still more and more fixed by rules.

But by whatever strides criticism may gain ground, we need be under no apprehension, that invention will ever be annihilated, or subdued; or intellectual energy be brought entirely within the restraint of written law. Genius will still have room enough to expatiate, and keep always at the same distance from narrow comprehension and mechanical performance.

What we now call Genius, begins, not where rules, abstractedly taken, end; but where known vulgar and trite rules have no longer any place. It must of necessity be, that even works of Genius, like every other effect, as they must have their cause, must likewise have their rules; it cannot be by chance, that excellencies are produced with any constancy or any certainty, for this is not the nature of chance; but the rules by which men of extraordinary parts, and such as are called men of Genius work, are either such as they discover by their own peculiar observations, or of such a nice texture as not easily to admit being expressed in words; especially as artists are not very frequently skillful in that mode of communicating ideas. Unsubstantial, however, as these rules may seem, and difficult as it may be to convey them in writing, they are still seen and felt in the mind of the artist; and he works from them with as much certainty, as if they were embodied, as I may say, upon paper. It is true, these refined principles cannot be always made palpable, like the more gross rules of art; yet it does not follow, but that the mind may be put in such a train, that it shall perceive, by a kind of scientifick sense, that propriety, which words, particularly words of unpractised writers, such as we are, can but very feebly suggest.

Invention is one of the great marks of genius; but if we consult experience, we shall find, that it is by being conversant with the inventions of others, that we learn to invent; as by reading the thoughts of others we learn to think.

Whoever has so far formed his taste, as to be able to relish and feel the beauties of the great masters, has gone a great way in his study; for, merely from a consciousness of this relish of the right, the mind swells with an inward pride, and is almost as powerfully affected, as if it had itself produced what it admires. Our hearts frequently warmed in this manner by the contact of those whom we wish to resemble, will undoubtedly catch something of their way of thinking; and we shall receive in our own bosoms some radiation at least of their fire and splendour. That disposition, which is so strong in children, still continues with us, of catching involuntarily the general air and manner of those with whom we are most conversant; with this difference only, that a young mind is naturally pliable and imitative; but in a more advanced state it grows rigid, and must be warmed and softened, before it will receive a deep impression.

From these considerations, which a little of your own reflection will carry a great way further, it appears, of what great consequence it is, that our minds should be habituated to the contemplation of excellence; and that, far from being contented to make such habits the discipline of our youth only, we should, to the last moment of our lives, continue a settled intercourse with all the true examples of grandeur. Their inventions are not only the food of our infancy, but the substance which supplies the fullest maturity of our vigour.

The mind is but a barren soil; a soil which is soon exhausted, and will produce no crop, or only one, unless it be continually fertilized and enriched with foreign matter.

When we have had continually before us the great works of Art to impregnate our minds with kindred ideas, we are then, and not till then, fit to produce something of the same species. We behold all about us with the eyes of those penetrating observers whose works we contemplate; and our minds accustomed to think the thoughts of the noblest and brightest intellects, are prepared for the discovery and selection of all that is great and noble in nature. The greatest natural genius cannot subsist on its own stock: he who resolves never to ransack any mind but his own, will be soon reduced, from mere barrenness, to the poorest of all imitations; he will be obliged to imitate himself and to repeat what he has before often repeated. When we know the subject designed by such men, it will never be difficult to guess what kind of work is to be produced.

It is vain for painters or poets to endeavour to invent without materials on which the mind may work, and from which invention must originate. Nothing can come of nothing.

Homer is supposed to be possessed of all the learning of his time: and we are certain that Michael Angelo, and Raffaelle, were equally possessed of all the knowledge in the art which had been discovered in the works of their predecessors.

A mind enriched by an assemblage of all the treasures of ancient and modern art, will be more elevated and fruitful in resources in proportion to the number of ideas which have been carefully collected and thoroughly digested. There can be no doubt but that he who has the most materials has the greatest means of invention; and if he has not the power of using them, it must proceed from a feebleness of intellect; or from the confused manner in which those collections have been laid up in his mind.

The addition of other men's judgment is so far from weakening our own, as is the opinion of many, that it will fashion and consolidate those ideas of excellence which lay in embryo, feeble, ill-shaped, and confused, but which are finished and put in order by the authority and practice of those, whose works may be said to have been consecrated by having stood the test of ages.

The mind, or genius, has been compared to a spark of fire, which is smothered by a heap of fuel, and prevented from blazing into a flame: This simile, which is made use of by the younger Pliny, may be easily mistaken for argument or proof. But there is no danger of the mind's being over-burthened with knowledge, or the genius extinguished by any addition of images; on the contrary, these acquisitions may as well, perhaps better, be compared, if comparisons signified any thing in reasoning, to the supply of living embers, which will contribute to strengthen the spark, that without the association of more fuel would have died away. The truth is, he whose feebleness is such, as to make other men's thoughts an incumbrance to him, can have no very great strength of mind or genius of his own to be destroyed; so that not much harm will be done at worst.

We may oppose to Pliny the greater authority of Cicero, who is continually enforcing the necessity of this method of study. In his dialogue on Oratory, he makes Crassus say, that one of the first and most important precepts is, to choose a proper model for our imitation. *Hoc sit primum in praeceptis meis ut demonstremus quem imitemur.*

When I speak of the habitual imitation and continued study of masters, it is not to be understood, that I advise any endeavour to copy the exact peculiar colour and complexion of another man's mind; the success of such an attempt must always be like his, who imitates exactly the air, manner, and gestures, of him whom he admires. His model may be excellent, but the copy will be ridiculous; this ridicule does not arise from his having imitated, but from his not having chosen the right mode of imitation.

It is a necessary and warrantable pride to disdain to walk servilely behind any individual, however elevated his rank. The true and liberal ground of imitation is an open field; where, though he who precedes has had the advantage of starting before you, you may always propose to overtake him: it is enough however to pursue his course; you need not tread in his footseps; and you certainly have a right to outstrip him if you can.

Nor whilst I recommend studying the art from artists, can I be supposed to mean, that nature is to be neglected: I take this study in aid, and not in exclusion, of the other. Nature is, and must be the fountain which alone is inexhaustible; and from which all excellencies must originally flow.

The great use of studying our predecessors is, to open the mind, to shorten our labour, and to give us the result of the selection made by those great minds of what is grand or beautiful in nature: her rich stores are all spread out before us; but it is an art, and no easy art, to know how or what to choose, and how to attain and secure the object of our choice. Thus the highest beauty of form must be taken from nature; but it is an art of long deduction, and great experience, to know how to find it. We must not content ourselves with merely admiring and relishing; we must enter into the principles on which the work is wrought: these do not swim on the superficies, and consequently are not open to superficial observers.

Art in its perfection is not ostentatious; it lies hid, and works its effect, itself unseen. It is the proper study and labour of an artist to uncover and find out the latent cause of conspicuous beauties, and from thence form principles for his own conduct: such an examination is a continual exertion of the mind; as great, perhaps, as that of the artist whose works he is thus studying.

The sagacious imitator does not content himself with merely remarking what distinguishes the different manner or genius of each master; he enters into the contrivance in the composition, how the masses of lights are disposed, the means by which the effect is produced, how artfully some parts are lost in the ground, others boldly relieved, and how all these are mutually altered and interchanged according to the reason and scheme of the work. He admires not the harmony of colouring alone, but examines by what artifice one colour is a foil to its neighbour. He looks close into the tints, examines of what colours they are composed, till he has formed clear and distinct ideas, and has learnt to see in what harmony and good colouring consists. What is learned in this manner from the works of others becomes really our own, sinks deep, and is never forgotten, nay, it is by seizing on this clue that we proceed forward, and, get further and further in enlarging the principles and improving the practice of our art.

There can be no doubt, but the art is better learnt from the works themselves than from the precepts which are formed upon those works; but if it is difficult to choose proper models for imitation, it requires no less circumspection to separate and distinguish what in those models we ought to imitate.

I cannot avoid mentioning here, though it is not my intention at present to enter into the art and method of study, an error which students are too apt to fall into. He that is forming himself, must look with great caution and wariness on those peculiarities, or prominent parts, which at first force themselves upon view; and are the marks, or what is commonly called the manner, by which that individual artist is distinguished.

Peculiar marks, I hold to be, generally, if not always, defects; however difficult it may be wholly to escape them.

Peculiarities in the works of art, are like those in the human figure; it is by them that we are cognizable and distinguished one from another, but they are always so many blemishes; which, however, both in real life and in painting, cease to appear deformities, to those who have them continually before their eyes. In the works of art, even the most enlightened mind, when warmed by beauties of the highest kind, will by degrees find a repugnance within him to acknowledge any defects; nay, his enthusiasm will carry him so far, as to transform them into beauties, and objects of imitation.

It must be acknowledged, that a peculiarity of style, either from its novelty, or by seeming to proceed from a peculiar turn of mind, often escapes blame; on the contrary, it is sometimes striking and pleasing; but this it is a vain labour to endeavour to imitate; because novelty and peculiarity being its only merit, when it ceases to be new, it ceases to have value.

A manner therefore being a defect, and every painter, however excellent, having a manner, it seems to follow, that all kinds of faults, as well as beauties, may be learned under the sanction of the greatest authorities. Even the great name of Michael Angelo may be used, to keep in countenance a deficiency or rather neglect of colouring, and every other ornamental part of the art. If the young student is dry and hard, Poussin is the same. If his work has a careless and unfinished air, he has most of the Venetian school to support him. If he makes no selection of objects, but takes individual nature just as he finds it, he is like Rembrant. If he is incorrect in the proportions of his figures, Correggio was likewise incorrect. If his colours are not blended and united, Rubens was equally crude. In short, there is no defect that may not be excused, if it is a sufficient excuse that it can be imputed to considerable artists; but it must be remembered, that it was not by these defects they acquired their reputation; they have a right to our pardon, but not to our admiration.

However, to imitate peculiarities or mistake defects for beauties, that man will be most liable, who confines his imitation to one favourite master; and even though he chooses the best, and is capable of distinguishing the real excellencies of his model, it is not by such narrow practice, that a genius or mastery in the art is acquired. A man is as little likely to form a true idea of the perfection of the art, by studying a single artist, as he would be to produce a perfectly beautiful figure, by an exact imitation of any individual living model. And as the painter, by bringing together in one piece, those beauties which are dispersed among a great variety of individuals, produces a figure more beautiful than can be found in nature, so that artist who can unite in himself the excellencies of the various great painters, will approach nearer to perfection than any one of his masters. He, who confines himself to the imitation of an individual, as he never proposes to surpass, so he is not likely to equal, the object of his imitation. He professes only to follow; and he that follows must necessarily be behind.

We should imitate the conduct of the great artists in the course of their studies, as well as the works which they produced, when they were perfectly formed. Raffaelle began by imitating implicitly the manner of Pietro Perugino, under whom he studied; hence his first works are scarce to be distinguished from his master's; but soon forming higher and more extensive views, he imitated the grand outline of Michael Angelo; he learned the manner of using colours from the works of Leonardo da Vinci, and Fratre Bartolomeo: to all this he added the contemplation of all the remains of antiquity that were within his reach; and employed others to draw for him what was in Greece and distant places. And it is from his having taken so many models, that he became himself a model for all succeeding painters; always imitating, and always original.

If your ambition, therefore, be to equal Raffaelle, you must do as Raffaelle did; take many models, and not even *him* for your guide alone to the exclusion of others.* And yet the number is infinite of those who seem, if one may judge by their style, to have seen no other works but those of their master, or of some favourite, whose *manner* is their first wish, and their last.

I will mention a few that occur to me of this narrow, confined, illiberal, unscientifick, and servile kind of imitators. Guido was thus meanly copied by Elizabetta Sirani, and Simone Cantarini; Poussin, by Verdier, and Cheron; Parmeggiano, by Jeronimo Mazzuoli. Paolo Veronese, and Iacomo Bassan, had for their imitators their brothers and sons. Pietro de Cortona was followed by Ciro Ferri, and Romanelli; Rubens, by Jacques Jordans, and Diepenbeck; Guercino, by his own family, the Gennari. Carlo Maratti was imitated by Giuseppe Chiari, and Pietro da Pietri; and Rembrant, by Bramer, Eckhout, and Flink. All these, to whom may be added a much longer list of painters, whose works among the ignorant pass for those of their masters, are justly to be censured for barrenness and servility.

To oppose to this list a few that have adopted a more liberal style of imitation;—Pelegrino Tibaldi, Rosso, and Primaticcio, did not coldly imitate, but caught something of the fire that animates the works of Michael Angelo. The Caraccis formed their style from Pelegrino Tibaldi, Correggio, and the Venetian School. Domenichino, Guido, Lanfranco, Albano, Guercino, Cavidone, Schidone, Tiarini, though it is sufficiently apparent that they came from the school of the

---

*Sed non qui maxime imitandus, etiam solus imitandus est. Quintilian.

Caraccis, have yet the appearance of men who extended their views beyond the model that lay before them, and have shewn that they had opinions of their own, and thought for themselves, after they had made themselves masters of the general principles of their schools.

Le Sueur's first manner resembles very much that of his master Voüet: but as he soon excelled him, so he differed from him in every part of the art. Carlo Maratti succeeded better than those I have first named, and I think owes his superiority to the extension of his views; beside his master Andrea Sacchi, he imitated Raffaelle, Guido, and the Caraccis. It is true, there is nothing very captivating in Carlo Maratti; but this proceeded from a want which cannot be completely supplied; that is, want of strength of parts. In this certainly men are not equal; and a man can bring home wares only in proportion to the capital with which he goes to market. Carlo, by diligence, made the most of what he had; but there was undoubtedly a heaviness about him, which extended itself, uniformly, to his invention, expression, his drawing, colouring, and the general effect of his pictures. The truth is, he never equalled any of his patterns in any one thing, and he added little of his own.

But we must not rest contented even in this general study of the moderns; we must trace back the art to its fountainhead; to that source from whence they drew their principal excellencies, the monuments of pure antiquity. All the inventions and thoughts of the Antients, whether conveyed to us in statues, bas-reliefs, intaglios, cameos, or coins, are to be sought after and carefully studied: the genius that hovers over these venerable reliques, may be called the father of modern art.

From the remains of the works of the antients the modern arts were revived, and it is by their means that they must be restored a second time. However it may mortify our vanity, we must be forced to allow them our masters; and we may venture to prophecy, that when they shall cease to be studied, arts will no longer flourish, and we shall again relapse into barbarism.

The fire of the artist's own genius operating upon these materials which have been thus diligently collected, will enable him to make new combinations, perhaps, superior to what had ever before been in the possession of the art: as in the mixture of the variety of metals, which are said to have been melted and run together at the burning of Corinth, a new and till then unknown metal was produced, equal in value to any of those that had contributed to its composition. And though a curious refiner should come with his crucibles, analyse and separate its various component parts, yet Corinthian brass would still hold its rank amongst the most beautiful and valuable of metals.

We have hitherto considered the advantages of imitation as it tends to form the taste, and as a practice by which a spark of that genius may be caught, which illumines those noble works that ought always to be present to our thoughts.

We come now to speak of another kind of imitation; the borrowing a particular thought, an action, attitude, or figure, and transplanting it into your own work: this will either come under the charge of plagiarism, or be warrantable, and deserve commendation, according to the address with which it is performed. There is some difference likewise, whether it is upon the antients or the moderns that these depredations are made. It is generally allowed, that no man need be ashamed of copying the antients: their works are considered as a magazine of common property, always open to the publick, whence every man has a right to take what materials he pleases; and if he has the art of using them, they are supposed to become to all intents and purposes his own property. The collection of the thoughts of the antients, which Raffaelle made with so much trouble, is a proof of his opinion on this subject. Such collections may be made with much more ease, by means of an art scarce known in his time; I mean that of engraving; by which, at an easy rate, every man may now avail himself of the inventions of antiquity.

It must be acknowledged that the works of the moderns are more the property of their authors; he, who borrows an idea from an antient, or even from a modern artist not his contemporary, and so accommodates it to his own work, that it makes a part of it, with no seam or joining appearing, can hardly be charged with plagiarism: poets practise this kind of borrowing, without reserve. But an artist should not be contented with this only; he should enter into a competition with his original, and endeavour to improve what he is appropriating to his own work. Such imitation is so far from having any thing in it of the servility of plagiarism, that it is a perpetual exercise of the mind, a continual invention. Borrowing or stealing with such art and caution, will have a right to the same lenity as was used by the Lacedemonians; who did not punish theft, but the want of artifice to conceal it.

In order to encourage you to imitation, to the utmost extent, let me add, that very finished artists in the inferior branches of the art, will contribute to furnish the mind and give hints, of which a skilful painter, who is sensible of what he wants, and is in no danger of being infected by the contact of vicious models, will know how to avail himself. He will pick up from dunghills what by a nice chymistry, passing through his own mind, shall be converted into pure gold; and, under the rudeness of Gothick essays, he will find original, rational, and even sublime inventions.

The works of Albert Durer, Lucas Van Leyden, the numerous inventions of Tobias Stimer, and Jost Ammon, afford a rich mass of genuine materials, which wrought up and polished to elegance, will add copiousness to what, perhaps, without such aid, could have aspired only to justness and propriety.

In the luxuriant style of Paul Veronese, in the capricious compositions of Tintoret, he will find something, that will assist his invention, and give points, from which his own imagination shall rise and take flight, when the subject which he treats will with propriety admit of splendid effects.

In every school, whether Venetian, French, or Dutch, he will find, either ingenious compositions, extraordinary effects, some peculiar expressions, or some mechanical excellence, well worthy of his attention, and, in some measure, of his imitation. Even in the lower class of the French painters great beauties are often found united with great defects. Though Coypel wanted a simplicity of taste, and mistook a presumptuous and assuming air for what is grand and majestick; yet he frequently has good sense and judgment in his manner of telling his stories, great skill in his compositions, and is not without a considerable power of expressing the passions. The modern affectation of grace in his works, as well as in those of Bouche and Vatteau, may be said to be separated, by a very thin partition, from the more simple and pure grace of Correggio and Parmeggiano.

Among the Dutch painters, the correct, firm, and determined pencil, which was employed by Bamboccio and Jean Miel, on vulgar and mean subjects, might, without any change, be employed on the highest; to which, indeed, it seems more properly to belong. The greatest style, if that style is confined to small figures, such as Poussin generally painted, would receive an additional grace by the elegance and precision of pencil so admirable in the works of Teniers; and though the school to which he belonged more particularly excelled in the mechanism of painting, yet it produced many, who have shewn great abilities in expressing what must be ranked above mechanical excellencies. In the works of Frank Halls, the portrait-painter may observe the composition of a face, the features well put together, as the painters express it; from whence proceeds that strong-marked character of individual nature, which is so remarkable in his portraits, and is not found in an equal degree in any other painter. If he had joined to this most difficult part of the art, a patience finishing what he had so correctly planned, he might justly have claimed the place which Vandyck, all things considered, so justly holds as the first of portrait-painters.

Others of the same school have shewn great power in expressing the character and passions of those vulgar people, which were the subjects of their study and attention. Among those Jean Stein seems to be one of the most diligent and accurate observers of what passed in those scenes which he frequented, and which were to him an academy. I can easily imagine, that if this extraordinary man had had the good fortune to have been born in Italy, instead of Holland, had he lived in Rome instead of Leyden, and been blessed with Michael Angelo and Raffaelle for his masters, instead of Brower and Van Gowen; the same sagacity and penetration which distinguished so accurately the different characters and expression in his vulgar figures, would, when exerted in the selection and imitation of what was great and elevated in nature, have been equally successful; and he now would have ranged with the great pillars and supporters of our Art.

Men who although thus bound down by the almost invincible powers of early habits, have still exerted extraordinary abilities within their narrow and confined circle; and have, from the natural vigour of their mind, given a very interesting expression, and great force and energy to their works; though they cannot be recommended to be exactly imitated, may yet invite an artist to endeavour to transfer, by a kind of parody, their excellencies to his own performances. Whoever has acquired the power of making this use of the Flemish, Venetian, and French schools, is a real genius, and has sources of knowledge open to him which were wanting to the great artists who lived in the great age of painting.

To find excellencies, however dispersed, to discover beauties, however concealed by the multitude of defects with which they are surrounded, can be the work only of him, who having a mind always alive to his art, has extended his views to all ages and to all schools; and has acquired from that comprehensive mass which he has thus gathered to himself, a well-digested and perfect idea of his art, to which every thing is referred. Like a sovereign judge and arbiter of art, he is possessed of that presiding power which separates and attracts every excellence from every school; selects both from what is great, and what is little; brings home knowledge from the East and from the West; making the universe tributary towards furnishing his mind and enriching his works with originality, and variety of inventions.

Thus I have ventured to give my opinion of what appears to me the true and only method by which an artist makes himself master of his profession; which I hold ought to be one continued course of imitation that is not to cease but with his life.

Those, who either from their own engagements and hurry of business, or from indolence, or from conceit and vanity, have neglected looking out of themselves, as far as my experience and observation reaches, have from that time, not only ceased to advance, and improve in their performances, but have gone backward. They may be compared to men who have lived upon their principal till they are reduced to beggary, and left without resources.

I can recommend nothing better, therefore, than that you endeavour to infuse into your works what you learn from the contemplation of the works of others. To recommend this has the appearance of needless and superfluous advice; but it has fallen within my own knowledge, that artists, though they were not wanting in a sincere love for their art, though they had great pleasure in seeing good pictures, and were well skilled to distinguish what was excellent or defective in them, yet have gone on in their own manner, without any endeavour to give a little of those beauties, which they admired in others, to their own works. It is difficult to conceive how the present Italian painters, who live in the midst of the treasures of art, should be contented with their own style. They proceed in their common-place inventions, and never think it worth while to visit the works of those great artists with which they are surrounded.

I remember, several years ago, to have conversed at Rome with an artist of great fame throughout Europe; he was not without a considerable degree of abilities, but those abilities were by no means equal to his own opinion of them. From the reputation he had acquired, he too fondly concluded that he stood in the same rank, when compared with his predecessors, as he held with regard to his miserable contemporary rivals. In conversation about some particulars of the works of Raffaelle, he seemed to have, or to affect to have, a very obscure memory of them. He told me that he had not set his foot in the Vatican for fifteen years together; that indeed he had been in treaty to copy a capital picture of Raffaelle, but that the business had gone off; however, if the agreement had held, his copy would have greatly exceeded the original. The merit of this artist, however great we may suppose it, I am sure would have been far greater, and his presumption would have been far less, if he had visited the Vatican, as in reason he ought to have done, at least once every month of his life.

I address myself, Gentlemen, to you who have made some progress in the art, and are to be, for the future, under the guidance of your own judgment and discretion, I consider you as arrived to that period, when you have a right to think for yourselves, and to presume that every man is fallible; to study the masters with a suspicion, that great men are not always exempt from great faults; to criticise, compare, and rank their works in your own estimation, as they approach to, or recede from, that standard of perfection which you have formed in your own minds, but which those masters themselves, it must be remembered, have taught you to make; and which you will cease to make with correctness, when you cease to study them. It is their excellencies which have taught you their defects.

I would wish you to forget where you are, and who it is that speaks to you. I only direct you to higher models and better advisers. We can teach you here but very little; you are henceforth to be your own teachers. Do this justice, however, to the English Academy; to bear in mind, that in this place you contracted no narrow habits, no false ideas, nothing that could lead you to the imitation of any living master, who may be the fashionable darling of the day. As you have not been taught to flatter us, do not learn to flatter yourselves. We have endeavoured to lead you to the admiration of nothing but what is truly admirable. If you choose inferior patterns, or if you make your own *former* works your patterns for your *latter*, it is your own fault.

The purport of this discourse, and, indeed, of most of my other discourses, is, to caution you against that false opinion, but too prevalent among artists, of the imaginary power of native genius, and its sufficiency in great works. This opinion, according to the temper of mind it meets with, almost always produces, either a vain confidence, or a sluggish despair, both equally fatal to all proficiency.

Study therefore the great works of the great masters, for ever. Study as nearly as you can, in the order, in the manner, and on the principles, on which they studied. Study nature attentively, but always with those masters in your company; consider them as models which you are to imitate, and at the same time as rivals with whom you are to contend.

Exercises

1. Write your own "Annotations to Sir Joshua Reynolds' *Discourses*" in the margins. Use the method you found successful following the exercises in chapter 2. Then trace the major patterns you notice in your reactions. Complete your marginal comments on Reynolds *before* you read Blake's "Annotations." Prepare notes for an essay on the relevance of Reynolds' advice for today's artists.

2. A genius presumably creates through inspiration. On the other hand, a skillful artist may create while feeling no flow of inspired genius. Is it possible to be a great artist and *not* be a genius? Or is it possible for a genius to be a *poor* craftsman? Has Reynolds successfully dealt with these dilemmas in your view?

3. How does one decide where the riches of the masters leave off and slavish imitation begins? Explore carefully Reynolds' discussion of "imitation" in Discourse Six and explain in detail the differences between productive and unproductive uses of "the past." Offer examples from your own experience and reading.

William Blake
Annotations to
*Sir Joshua Reynolds' Discourses**

DISCOURSE ONE

Page 24

I consider Reynolds's Discourses to the Royal Academy as the Simulations of the Hypocrite who smiles particularly where he means to Betray. His Praise of Rafael is like the Hysteric Smile of Revenge. His Softness & Candour, the hidden trap & the poisoned feast. He praises Michel Angelo for Qualities which Michel Angelo abhorr'd, & He blames Rafael for the only Qualities which Rafael Valued. Whether Reynolds knew what he was doing is nothing to me: the Mischief is just the same whether a Man does it Ignorantly or Knowingly. I always consider'd True Art & True Artists to be particularly Insulted & Degraded by the Reputation of these Discourses, As much as they were Degraded by the Reputation of Reynolds's Paintings, & that Such Artists as Reynolds are at all times Hired by the Satans for the Depression of Art—A Pretence of Art, To destroy Art.

Page 24

The Neglect of Fuseli's Milton in a Country pretending to the Encouragement of Art is a Sufficient Apology for My Vigorous Indignation, if indeed the Neglect of My own Powers had not been. Ought not the Employers of Fools to be Execrated in future Ages? They Will and Shall! Foolish Men, your own real Greatness depends on your Encouragement of the Arts, & your Fall will depend on [your *del.*] their Neglect & Depression. What you Fear is your true Interest. Leo X was advised not to Encourage the Arts; he was too Wise to take this Advice.

Page 24

The Rich Men of England form themselves into a Society to Sell & Not to Buy Pictures. The Artist who does not throw his

---

*From *The Complete Writings of William Blake* by William Blake (Ed. by Sir Geoffrey Keynes), published by Oxford University Press.

Contempt on such Trading Exhibitions, does not know either his own Interest or his Duty.

> *When Nations grow Old, The Arts grow Cold*
> *And Commerce settles on every Tree,*
> *And the Poor & the Old can live upon Gold,*
> *For all are Born Poor, Aged Sixty three.*

Page 24

Reynolds's Opinion was that Genius May be Taught & that all Pretence to Inspiration is a Lie & a Deceit, to say the least of it. For if it is a Deceit, the whole Bible is Madness. This Opinion originates in the Greeks' Calling the Muses Daughters of Memory.

The Enquiry in England is not whether a Man has Talents & Genius, But whether he is Passive & Polite & a Virtuous Ass & obedient to Noblemen's Opinions in Art & Science. If he is, he is a Good Man. If Not, he must be Starved.

Page 24

After so much has been done by His Majesty. . . .

3 Farthings!

Page 24

Raffaelle, it is true, had not the advantage of studying in an Academy; but all Rome, and the works of Michael Angelo in particular, were to him an Academy. On the sight of the Capella Sistina, he immediately from a dry, Gothick, and even insipid manner, which attends to the minute accidental discriminations of particular and individual objects, assumed that grand style of painting which improves partial representation by the general and invariable ideas of nature.

Minute Discrimination is Not Accidental. All Sublimity is founded on Minute Discrimination.

I do not believe that Rafael taught Mich. Angelo, or that Mich. Angelo taught Rafael, any more than I believe that the Rose teaches the Lilly how to grow, or the Apple tree teaches the Pear tree how to bear Fruit. I do not believe the tales of Anecdote writers when they militate against Individual Character.

Page 25

I would chiefly recommend that an implicit obedience to the Rules of Art, as established by the practice of the great Masters should be exacted from the young Students. That those models, which have passed through the approbation of ages, should be considered by them as perfect and infallible guides; as subjects for their imitation, not their criticism.

Imitation is Criticism.

Page 26
A facility in composing—a lively, and what is called a masterly handling of the chalk or pencil are . . . captivating qualities to young
minds.

I consider The Following sentence is Supremely Insolent for
the following Reasons:—Why this Sentence should be begun
by the Words "A Facility in Composing" I cannot tell, unless it
was to cast a stigma upon Real Facility in Composition by As-
similating it with a Pretence to, & Imitation of, Facility in
Execution; or are we to understand him to mean that Facility
in Composing is a Frivolous pursuit? A Facility in Composing
is the Greatest Power of Art, & Belongs to None but the
Greatest Artists and the Most Minutely Discriminating & Determinate.

Page 26
By this useless industry they are excluded from all power of advancing in real excellence. Whilst boys, they are arrived at their utmost
perfection; . . . and make the mechanical felicity the chief excellence
of the art, which is only an ornament.

Mechanical Excellence is the Only Vehicle of Genius.

This seems to me to be one of the most dangerous sources of corruption . . . which has actually infected all foreign Academies. The directors . . . praised their dispatch at the expence of their correctness.

This is all False & Self-Contradictory.

But young men have not only this frivolous ambition of being thought
masters of execution, inciting them on one hand, but also their
natural sloth tempting them on the other.

Execution is the Chariot of Genius.

Pages 26-27
They wish to find some shorter path to excellence, . . . They must
therefore be told again and again, that labour is the only price of solid
fame, . . .

This is All Self-Contradictory, Truth & Falsehood Jumbled
Together.

When we read the lives of the most eminent Painters, every page informs us that no part of their time was spent in dissipation . . . They
pursued their studies . . .

The Lives of Painters say that Rafael Died of Dissipation.
Idleness is one Thing & Dissipation Another. He who has
Nothing to Dissipate Cannot Dissipate; the Weak Man may be

Virtuous Enough, but will Never be an Artist.
Painters are noted for being Dissipated & Wild.

Page 27
When they [the old masters] conceived a subject, they first made a
variety of sketches, then a finished drawing of the whole; after that a
more correct drawing of every separate part—heads, hands, feet, and
pieces of drapery; they then painted the picture, *and after all re-
touched it from life.*

This is False.

The Students instead of vying with each other which shall have the
readiest hand, should be taught to contend who shall have the purest
and most correct outline.

Excellent!

Page 27
The error I mean is, that the students never draw exactly from the
living models which they have before them. They make a drawing
rather of what they think the figure ought to be, than of what it appears. I have thought this the obstacle that has stopped the progress
of many young men . . . I very much doubt whether a habit of drawing correctly what we see, will not give a proportionable power of
drawing correctly what we imagine.

This is Admirably Said. Why does he not always allow as
much?

Page 28
He who endeavours to copy nicely the figure before him, not only
acquires a habit of exactness and precision, but is continually
advancing in his knowledge of the human figure.

Excellent!

Page 28
The Labour'd Works of Journeymen employ'd by Correggio,
Titian, Veronese & all the Venetians, ought not to be shewn to
the Young Artist as the Works of original Conception any more
than the Engravings of Strange, Bartollozzi, or Wollett. They
are Works of Manual Labour.

DISCOURSE TWO

Page 29
The course and order of Study.—The different Stages of Art.—Much
copying discountenanced.—The artist at all times and in all places
should be employ'd in laying up materials for the exercise of his art.

What is Laying up materials but Copying?

Page 29

When the Artist is once enabled to express himself . . . he must then endeavour to collect subjects for expression; to amass a stock of ideas . . . to learn all that has been known and done before . . .

After having been a Fool, a Student is to amass a Stock of Ideas, &, knowing himself to be a Fool, he is to assume the Right to put other Men's Ideas into his Foolery.

Page 30

Though the Student will not resign himself blindly to any single authority, when he may have the advantage of consulting many, he must still be afraid of trusting to his own judgment, and of deviating into any track where he cannot find the footsteps of some former master.

Instead of Following One Great Master he is to follow a Great Many Fools.

Page 31

A Student unacquainted with the attempts of former adventurers, is always apt to over-rate his own abilities; to mistake the most trifling excursions for discoveries of moment, and every coast new to him, for a new-found country.

Contemptible Mocks!

The productions of such minds are seldom distinguished by an air of originality; they are anticipated in their happiest efforts; and if they are found to differ in anything from their predecessors, it is only in irregular sallies and trifling conceits.

Thus Reynolds Depreciates the Efforts of Inventive Genius. Trifling Conceits are better than Colouring without any meaning at all.

Page 32

How incapable those are of producing anything of their own, who have spent much of their time in making finished copies, is well known to all who are conversant with our art.

This is most False, for no one can ever Design till he has learn'd the Language of Art by making many Finish'd Copies both of Nature & Art & of whatever comes in his way from Earliest Childhood. The difference between a bad Artist & a Good Artist is: the Bad Artist Seems to Copy a Great deal. The Good one Really Does Copy a Great deal.

Page 32

The great use in copying, if it be at all useful, should seem to be in learning to colour; yet even colouring will never be perfectly attained by servilely copying the model before you.

Contemptible! Servile Copying is the Great Merit of Copying.

Page 33

Following these rules, and using these precautions, when you have clearly and distinctly learned in what good colouring consists, you cannot do better than have recourse to nature herself, who is always at hand, and in comparison of whose true splendour the best coloured pictures are but faint and feeble.

Nonsense! Every Eye Sees differently. As the Eye, Such the Object.

Page 33

Instead of copying the touches of those great masters, copy only their conceptions . . . Labour to invent on their general principles and way of thinking.

General Principles Again! Unless you Consult Particulars You Cannot even Know or See Mich. Ang°. or Rafael or any Thing Else.

But as mere enthusiasm will carry you but a little way . . .

Meer Enthusiasm is the All in All! Bacon's Philosophy has Ruin'd England. Bacon is only Epicurus over again.

Page 34

Few have been taught to any purpose who have not been their own teachers.

True!

Page 35

A facility of drawing, like that of playing upon a musical instrument, cannot be acquired but an infinite number of acts.

True!

Page 36

I would particularly recommend that after your return from the Academy . . . you would endeavour to draw the figure by memory.

Good advice!

But while I mention the port-crayon as the student's constant companion, he must still remember that the pencil is the instrument by which he must hope to obtain eminence.

Nonsense!

Page 36

The Venetian and Flemish schools, which owe much of their fame to colouring, have enriched the cabinets of the collectors of drawings with very few examples.

—because they could not draw.

Page 36
Those of Titian, Paul Veronese, Tintoret, and the Bassans are in general slight and undetermined. Their sketches on paper are as rude as their pictures are excellent in regard to harmony of colouring. Correggio and Baroccio have left few, if any finished drawings behind them. And in the Flemish school, Rubens and Vandyck made their drawings for the most part in colour or in chiaro oscuro.

All the Pictures said to be by these Men are the Laboured fabrications of Journey-work. They could not draw.

Page 38
He who would have you believe that he is waiting for the inspiration of Genius, is in reality at a loss how to begin, and is at last delivered of his monsters, with difficulty and pain.

A Stroke at Mortimer!

Page 38
He regards all Nature with a view to his profession; and combines her beauties, or corrects her defects. . . .
The well-grounded painter . . . is contented that all shall be as great as himself, who have undergone the same fatigue . . .

The Man who asserts that there is no Such Thing as Softness in Art, & that everything in Art is Definite & Determinate, has not been told this by Practise, but by Inspiration & Vision, because Vision is Determinate & Perfect, & he Copies That without Fatigue, Everything being Definite & determinate. Softness is Produced alone by Comparative Strength & Weakness in the Marking out of the Forms. I say These Principles could never be found out by the Study of Nature without Con—or Innate Science.

DISCOURSE SIX

Page 38
Imitation.—Genius begins where rules end.—Invention;— Acquired by being conversant with the inventions of others.—The true method of imitating . . .

When a Man talks of Acquiring Invention & of learning how to produce Original Conception, he must expect to be call'd a Fool by Men of Understanding; but such a Hired Knave cares not for the Few. His Eye is on the Many, or, rather, on the Money.

Page 39
Those who have undertaken to write on our art, and have represented it as a kind of inspiration . . . seem to insure a much more favourable disposition from their readers . . . than he who attempts

to examine, coldly, whether there are any means by which this art may be acquired . . .

Bacon's Philosophy has Destroy'd [*word cut away*] Art & Science. The Man who says that the Genius is not Born, but Taught—Is a Knave.

> *O Reader, behold the Philosopher's Grave!*
> *He was born quite a Fool, but he died quite a Knave.*

Page 40
. . . to owe nothing to another, is the praise which men . . . bestow sometimes upon others; and sometimes on themselves; and their imaginary dignity is naturally heightened by a supercilious censure of . . . the servile imitator.

How ridiculous it would be to see the Sheep Endeavouring to walk like the Dog, or the Ox striving to trot like the Horse; just as Ridiculous it is to see One Man Striving to Imitate Another. Man varies from Man more than Animal from Animal of different Species.

Page 41
But the truth is, that the degree of excellence which proclaims Genius is different, in different times and different places; and what shews it to be so is, that mankind have often changed their opinion upon this matter.

Never, Never!

Page 42
These excellencies were, heretofore, considered merely as the effects of genius; and justly, if genius is not taken for inspiration, but as the effect of close observation and experience.

Damn'd Fool!

Page 42
He who first made any of these observations . . . had that merit, but probably no one went very far at once . . . others worked more and improved further . . .

If Art was Progressive We should have had Mich. Angelos & Rafaels to Succeed & to Improve upon each other. But it is not so. Genius dies with its Possessor & comes not again till Another is Born with It.

Page 42
It must of necessity be, that even works of Genius, like every other effect, as they must have their cause, must likewise have their rules.

Identities or Things are Neither Cause nor Effect. They are Eternal.

Page 43

. . . our minds should be habituated to the contemplation of excellence . . .we should to the last moment of our lives continue a settled
intercourse with all the true examples of grandeur. Their inventions
are not only the food of our infancy, but the substance which supplies
the fullest maturity of our vigour.

Reynolds Thinks that Man Learns all that he knows. I say on
the Contrary that Man Brings All that he has or can have Into
the World with him. Man is Born Like a Garden ready Planted
& Sown. This World is too poor to produce one Seed.

The mind is but a barren soil; a soil which is soon exhausted, and will
produce no crop, . . .

The mind that could have produced this Sentence must have
been a Pitiful, a Pitiable Imbecillity. I always thought that the
Human Mind was the most Prolific of All Things & Inexhaustible. I certainly do Thank God that I am not like Reynolds.

Page 43

. . . or only one, unless it be continually fertilized and enriched with
foreign matter.

Nonsense!

Page 44

It is vain for painters or poets to endeavour to invent without materials on which the mind may work. . . . Nothing can come of nothing.

Is the Mind Nothing?

. . . . we are certain that Michael Angelo, and Raffaelle, were equally
possessed of all the knowledge in the art which had been discovered
in the works of their predecessors.

If so they knew all that Titian & Correggio knew. Correggio
was two years older than Mich. Angelo. Correggio born 1472,
Mich. Angelo born 1474.

Page 45

. . . . it is not to be understood, that I advise any endeavour to copy
the exact peculiar colour and complexion of another man's
mind. . . . His model may be excellent but the copy will be ridiculous.

Why then Imitate at all?

Page 45

Art in its perfection is not ostentatious; it lies hid, and works its effect,
itself unseen. It is the proper study and labour of an artist to uncover
and find out the latent cause of conspicuous beauties . . .

This is a Very Clever Sentence; who wrote it, God knows.

Page 46
Peculiar marks, I hold to be, generally, if not always, defects; . . .

Peculiar Marks are the Only Merit.

Peculiarities in the works of art, are like those in the human figure . . . they are always so many blemishes;

Infernal Falshood!

Page 47
Even the great name of Michael Angelo may be used, to keep in countenance a deficiency or rather neglect of colouring, and every other ornamental part of the art.

No Man who can see Michael Angelo can say that he wants either Colouring or Ornamental parts of Art in the highest degree, for he has Every Thing of Both.

Page 47
. . . . there is no defect that may not be excused, if it is a sufficient excuse that it can be imputed to considerable artists; . . .

He who Admires Rafael Must admire Rafael's Execution. He who does not admire Rafael's Execution Cannot Admire Rafael.

Page 49
. . . want of strength of parts. In this certainly men are not equal . . .

A Confession!

Pages 50-51
In order to encourage you to imitation, to the utmost extent, let me add, that the very finished artists in the inferior branches of the art, will contribute to furnish the mind and give hints . . .

This Sentence is to Introduce another in Condemnation & Contempt of Alb. Durer.

The works of Albert Durer, Lucas Van Leyden, the numerous inventions of Tobias Stimmer, and Jost Ammon, afford a rich mass of genuine materials . . .

A Polish'd Villain who Robs & Murders!

Page 51
The greatest style, if that style is confined to small figures, . . . would receive an additional grace by the elegance and precision of pencil so admirable in the works of Teniers . . .

What does Precision of Pencil mean? If it does not mean Outline, it means Nothing.

Page 52

Jan Steen seems to be one of the most diligent and accurate observers . . . if [he] . . . had been blessed with Michael Angelo and Raffaelle for his masters . . . he now would have ranged with the great pillars and supporters of our Art.

Jan Steen was a Boor, & neither Rafael nor Mich. Ang. could have made him any better.

Page 52

Men who although thus bound down by the almost invincible powers of early habits have still exerted extraordinary abilities . . . and have . . . given . . . great force and energy to their works . . .

He who can be bound down is No Genius. Genius cannot be Bound; it may be Render'd Indignant & Outrageous.
"Opression makes the Wise Man Mad."
SOLOMON.

Exercises

1. To what extent does your reading of Blake's "Annotations" affect your ideas on Reynolds? What are some of the important similarities and differences between Blake's marginal comments and your own?

2. What are Blake's basic objections to Reynolds' theories? What issues does he emphasize repeatedly? When does he become most vehement? Make detailed notes on Blake's comments and write a description of his major quarrels with Reynolds. Show how Blake's use of marginal comments helped him develop and clarify his own thinking.

3. Based on your reading of his marginalia, what sort of character would you say Blake was? Describe his attitudes and values based on the statements reprinted here. Examine carefully the differences in point of view between Reynolds and Blake. What are the distinguishing features of the personas or voices projected in the *Discourses* and the "Annotations"?

4. Now annotate your copy of Blake's "Annotations." Examine carefully your own marginal comments on Reynolds and Blake. From your own point of view (and after reading both writers carefully), decide to what extent Blake's objections are valid. Prepare notes for an essay in which you will take a stand with one or the other. Describe in detail your own point of view on the issues they raise. Apply their questions to the problems of artistic creation today. To what extent does the point of view from which you raise the questions determine your position on the issues?

5. How do you suppose Reynolds would respond to Blake's objections? Create a set of notes on Blake's "Annotations" from the point of view of Reynolds. Write a dialogue or debate between the two figures on the issues you feel are most crucial. Include your own analysis of the debate in a separate set of notes, and then write an essay in which you take a stand and "settle" the questions you are exploring in their debate.

Summary/Review

Marginal comments are often valuable sources for the study of a writer's thinking in its germinal stages. Insights found in the margin can predict later writings and provide clues about an author's habits and the influences on his development. Marginal annotations also allow the writer to discover the persona in which he or she can best "sound through" ideas. Among many famous examples of published marginal comments in history are the "Annotations" of English poet and painter William Blake. Close reading of Sir Joshua Reynolds' *Discourses on Art* alongside Blake's "Annotations" on the *Discourses* illustrates how the form of the marginal comment not only records but also stimulates Blake's responses. Similarly, a writer can record, study, and develop personal thoughts by reading actively and developing his or her own voice in the margin.

4/Marginal Comments and Organization from Within

Once you are recording your responses systematically in marginal comments, you should then begin to decide what you want to say *specifically* to an audience. This decision to choose from the growing list of what you *could* say creates boundaries and places restrictions on the shape and range of your responses. You therefore limit your topic by creating structure *from within*. Effective ways to structure your thoughts begin in marginal comments and take shape formally as you become aware of your purpose for writing to a particular audience.

When readers look for only certain things, chances are they'll find little else. In this sense writers who "limit their subject" too severely when responding in the margin risk choking off the vitality and the full development of their own thinking. At the same time, "gut-level" responses may go in too many directions at once, resulting in no focus at all or a focus requiring the length of a book rather than an essay for adequate development. When beginning an essay, a writer generally has some idea of the questions that might be pursued. A tentative organizational plan allows a writer to begin and sets some directions in which to keep going. While you should not block out seemingly "irrelevant" reactions, developing a focus *as your reactions grow* will actually allow you to sharpen your own thoughts, raise further questions for yourself, and discover a pattern in your own characteristic way of approaching issues. The discipline of your response derives, then, from a form emerging within rather than from an imposed set of rules. To trust yourself is also to study yourself as you think through your ideas.

Establishing focus is not necessarily a narrowing of range but entails often a broadening out that enables the writer to discuss larger patterns more clearly. As a preliminary means of seeing focus take shape even in your earliest reactions, try posing several questions for yourself at the outset of your marginal comments. Stand back from your own reactions and watch them develop in the same way in which you might watch yourself on videotape. Then apply these questions to what you have already written:

1. "So what?" Anticipate this response from your audience, propose tentative answers to questions, and point out the implications of your comments as you present them.

2. "How did you come to think this way?" Your audience wants to know how your personal reactions add up. What emotionally, intellectually, and procedurally led you to such conclusions?

3. "Do you know what you're talking about?" Establishing credibility in this sense lends support to your personal reactions without stifling their range.

4. "How are you going to work it out for us?" Demonstrate contact with your audience by structuring your responses step by step for their understanding. Emphasize focus with a purpose, not just limitation for lack of space.

With these preliminary considerations in mind, the most important part of the writing process itself begins: your marginal comments take shape. Later chapters consider more thoroughly the ways initial responses add up to a finished product in inductive outlines and through devices such as transitions and paragraphing. But for now, study the examples in this chapter and develop your own system as suggested in chapter 1.

Immediately the need for selective note taking becomes obvious. Readers cannot annotate everything interesting to them, and deciding what they are looking for or what they want to emphasize can save valuable time. Responsive readers are open to everything that moves them in their reading. But underlining or otherwise marking everything on a page will confuse essential and incidental points and diminish your ability to clarify your thinking or emphasize what is especially significant to you. A systematic plan for thinking in the margin often heads off wasteful excess and at the same time suggests direction for the reading process itself.

As an active reader you will generally find yourself using three basic kinds of marginal notations. Simply to clarify and better understand what you are reading, you will circle words you wish to "look up" and write in the margin questions you can explore by reading further and through class discussion. Before going much beyond this simple question-and-answer stage about basic meanings, you should skim the whole selection and then mark key words and phrases and label major sections for easier recall. When you have a sense of the overall meaning, you can then summarize and digest smaller units in order to capture the ways in which the author develops his meaning. In the margin a broad outline will emerge that follows the pattern of the material itself. Finally, when you have answered your initial questions and moved closer to the meaning and organization of a selection, you can then more effectively react by voicing your opinion. Agreements or disagreements can then include further suggestions as counterproposals—all recorded in the margin where they can be studied alongside the passages that prompted the reactions.

These various kinds of marginal comments might seem obvious. But important differences between reading for "facts" and reading for "ideas" can be overlooked with disastrous results. Reading to find out "information" requires little "thinking in the margin." One merely finds what one is looking for and marks it accordingly. But most of the reading and writing referred to in this book requires that the reader or writer understand his or her own reactions. Recording not only facts or the author's position but also the reader's own responses is the first step in understanding one's own thinking.

Read the essay reprinted below, and study the sample marginal comments. To develop your own techniques for recording your active reading in marginal comments, you will find it necessary to establish some ground rules beforehand: a notation symbol system such as left-side margin for following major "headings" and the movement of the essay, the use of short titles to name things for yourself as you follow the writer's arguments, "X" used merely for emphasis or to call attention to underlined sentences, "?" to note confusion or objectionable points, "cf." to relate one point to another, cite contradictions, or argue back and forth. Read through the essay once, recording any initial questions that seem to call for study and discussion. Use a notation system that is uniquely yours. Then repeat the procedure a second time as you become more familiar with both the essay and your own immediate impressions of it. Include your own responses to the arguments of the essay. You will no doubt discover that some of your later responses are reactions to your own earlier responses as well as to the original essay. For purposes of illustration here, use different-colored pens each time you read the essay to sort out *what* you're responding to and *when*.

Once started, your chief problem will soon be to limit the comments so they stay intelligible and record something real. As you will see in the sample essay and notations, you must be prepared to use a mixture of symbols to reflect all kinds of comments, questions, and feelings. Your notation system must allow for increasing complexity as you mix first reactions with later, more informed responses. Finally, you must be able to live with uncertainty, undeveloped strands of reactions, and even contradictions as you "think out" the essay while responding to it in the margin. The markings are intended to create not prepackaged stock responses but rather an organic process. Study the examples with your own process in mind, remembering that your primary purpose is to discover a flexible procedure for recording the workings of your own creative mind in its various stages of activity.

Notice that in the annotated "To Abolish Children" (pp. 81–90) there are again three basic kinds of marginal notations. In the left-hand margin are the summary labels that "digest" and outline the essay. In both margins and between the lines are (1) simple questions about meaning and (2) forceful reactions to Shapiro's statements. The selection follows first unmarked for your own annotations and then again with sample marginal comments.

To Abolish Children
by Karl Shapiro*

Betrayal is an act of vengeance obviously. But in an age of betrayal, when men of authority traduce their office and violate the trust placed in their hands, betrayal becomes the official morality. "Official morality" shortly becomes "public immorality"; whereupon the fabric of a society rots before one's eyes. In the years since the end of the Second World War, announced by the drop of the first Ultimate Weapon, the world has been stunned, horrified, and ultimately cajoled and won over to the official morality of America and its corollary of public immorality and anarchy. Hardly a leader, whether president, general, public relations man, professor, publisher, or poet, can be held to be honorable in his intentions. Everywhere lies the hidden premise and the calculated betrayal, the secret and chauvinistic lie.

To what end? Who is the betrayer, and why? Who are the betrayed? In a pyramidal society, a hierarchy, one would know the answers. But in a jungle there are no answers, only cries of victory or death. In the modern American jungle there are no answers.

Must America give birth to fascism? Or can it survive its pristine Constitution? Both issues seem doubtful. Can the economic motive live with the mass monster it has created? Can the poor white who has sacrificed his brain to television, or the poor Negro who loots a TV set from the store, ever again cross the line from somnambulism to wakeful joy? Can only the modern artist discover beauty in the twentieth century?

The entire world has become aware of the pervasiveness of American violence. The Americans were the last to discover it. This is as it should be. A betrayed husband is the last to know his situation. America is shocked at itself; someone has handed it a mirror. Instead of the young and handsome heir of all the ages, with his bathing-beauty consort, winners of

Olympic Games, we see the soft and rotten killer (almost Hemingway style) with his call-girl WASP girlfriend, wearing a tiny crucifix between her scientifically measured bosoms. Wars are staged and televised on the battlefield; all sports are openly and avowedly big business; all books sell according to the amount of money deposited for advertising; countries are bought and sold in the stock market like cattle. Not that any of this is particularly new. What is new is that it is all now *public* knowledge. And what is awesome is that nobody cares. Everyone wants a share of the rot, the *faisandage*. Ours is a gamy culture from top to bottom. Books about the gaminess are best-sellers.

The goal of any writer or professor nowadays is to defend his—there is an old-fashioned word—honor. Can a writer write what he wants and in his manner? Can a teacher teach what he was hired to teach, in his own manner? Or must he give way to some form of blackmail from above or below, some Big Brother, who reinterprets his role for him. But we have heard enough of this structural mechanism from the time of Aldous Huxley, Orwell, McLuhan, and so forth.

At the bottom of the spectrum of betrayal are the "Movements," the pseudo-revolutionary insurrections without goals. The purest of these aim at simple theft and sabotage, such as occur during and after hurricanes. The more complicated are identified with civil rights and sex, freedom of drugs and pills of various forms, the right to unlimited travel vouchers and hospitalization. These are the heirs to the kingdom of Wall Street—the latest generation of betrayers and destroyers. This is the generation that uses the word Love as a synonym for Hate, that practices infantilism on a scale which has never been seen.

In between are the always duped Bourgeoisie, playing both ends against the middle. The bourgeois pays his children off to stay away, horrified at his mistake of educating these free-wheeling organisms equipped with electric guitars.

Possibly because the economic structure has reached the saturation point, the old order of social development is defunct. The pattern roughly used to be immigrant (or settler), bourgeois, professional man, and artist (or patron). The child enacts the pattern in reverse; the young man or woman aspires to be artist first, deploring professionalism and education itself, condemning the standards of safety of the bourgeois (while exploiting the material wealth of the bourgeois exchequer), and eventually achieving the role of pseudo-immigrant or "native." The Beats and Hippies are products of the American aesthetic which has always preached disaffiliation and single combat with the forces of nature and of society. All American dissident movements tend to fall apart as soon as they are organized. Each artist and pseudo-artist is his own Huckleberry Finn, a moral expatriate. All of our best artists have been recluses of one kind or another, Melville, Faulkner, Hemingway, Cummings. The American artist who does not shun the Center is suspect. The dissident, however, misunderstands the commitment of the artist and thinks of this commitment only in terms of rebellion. The failure of the masses of dissidents to evolve a politic is inherent in the national aesthetic of individualism. And because the dissidents offer no organized threat to the existing order, the existing order continues to consolidate its gains and to ignore the threat of blackmail. The dissidents simply supply additional dry rot to the cultural fabric. The burning and looting of slums signify the abysmal failure of imagination of the would-be revolutionaries, who in fact have no goals. Their only goals are pillage and revenge. The intellectual infantilism of the American radical makes him a figure of fun or of affection (or disaffection, as the case may be). The most one can say of an Allen Ginsberg or a Timothy Leary or a LeRoi Jones is that they are sincere. Children are always sincere.

Dissidence spread to the professoriat with the installation of artists and writers on the campuses of the nation. (I am one of the writer-professors who encouraged the moral-intellectual drop-out philosophy for about a decade.) It was easy and sometimes necessary to equate the mass university with other forms of the bureaucratic organism, but the vagueness of the issues involved and the failure to clarify them simply added up to an abstract dissent. That a university can be a democracy is patently absurd. The prattle about Free Speech at Berkeley which thrilled the sophomores of all ages served simply to debase whatever issues were at hand. Professors such as myself had already fought this issue in the courts, and won. The campus rioters were betraying these gains and taking a little private revenge on the side.

Vietnam itself is a falsified issue in the dissident "revolutions." The war is one of the most evil adventures in our history and its evil effects on the American character are incalculable, but the dissent is largely hypocritical. The "Underground" did not raise its voice against the Russian suppression of Hungary; it pursues a hands-off policy vis-à-vis Castro, even to the endorsement of antique Marxist slogans; it does not agitate for the overthrow of the last big brother of the

Axis, Francisco Franco. On the contrary, the dissidents are to be found disporting themselves as frequently in Spain as in other exotic places, pursuing their careers and brushing up on the guitar. If it is laudable to avoid a draft, it is despicable to moralize about it.

The importation of mysticism and pseudo-mysticism into the West was an early stratagem of withdrawal from the known modes of communication. Mysticism is simultaneously an insult and a threat to communal behavior. Mystical evidence is by definition hearsay and inhibits communication. The conveniences of Zen and the Sutras to the dissidents (who were rarely if ever "believers") were that they opened the door to a counter-culture, one in which consciousness was superseded by unconsciousness, and provisioned their minds with a counter-literature. The literature of the Orient has never been and cannot be naturalized in the West, but the stratagem of the haiku, for instance, is supposed to put the quietus on Western poetry.

But neither poetry nor any of the other arts are essential to the existence and furtherance of the "Movement," as its members refer to it with typical mystification. The Beat poets were the only dissidents who maintained even diplomatic relations with poetry, but their poetry was openly propaganda for the Movement. The planks of the primitive dissident platform were simple and narcissistic: pot, homosexuality, and doom-prophecy, a tame and almost Baptist program. The poetry lacked ambition to rise above these themes.

Because poetry was meaningless as a vehicle or an aesthetic to the Movement, the early Beat poetry took to the drum and trumpet (nineteenth-century symbols of slave revolt). The mixture of jazz and verse laid the groundwork for the dissident aesthetic: volume of noise, mass hypnotism, pure size, all canceled out the possibility of dialogue or even thought. Nor did hatred of the electronic world preclude the utmost exploitation of the amplifier. Herewith began the invasion of parks.

The deliberate and mischievous inversion of modes (anything "adult" was proscribed) opened a Pandora's box for the child mentality which would have driven Lewis Carroll to suicide. The wave of male and female hysterics with guitars and brotherhood lyrics turned into a mass industry, on the one hand, and, on the other, a generation of *révoltés* without goals. The dissident music is verbal—both the music and the language descend to levels of callousness and insensitivity heretofore unknown—but the contents are those of the infant

banging its fists on the highchair. It is an amazing phenomenon that this art, pitched directly to the level of the five- or
six-year-old, should also be the level of the college student.
(Dissidence appears to taper off thereafter.) Dissident sartorial
fashion also abolishes distinctions between the sexes; the not
very subtle transvestism of the dissident costume situates the
Movement in the years prior to puberty. The burlesque
Edwardianism of the Beatles expresses a nostalgia for the age
of aristocracy and unlimited wealth.

Throughout human history the fine arts have provided
the nexus between intuitional insight and civilized hindsight.
That is what the arts have been for. But at times when
intuition usurps the more wakeful states of mind, the arts
plunge into the playpen and the cry of "immediacy" fills the
air. Immediacy (as in D. H. Lawrence's "immediate present"
or the Zen Now!) cripples hindsight and deliberation and
prevents criteria from coming into existence. The failure of the
Beat community to create poetry or any of the other arts is the
most significant fact about the Movement. The hidden
aesthetic premise of the Movement is that art is evil and must
be hamstrung. Only states of unconsciousness are valid:
drug-states, violence in bed and on the street, secret
languages, political nihilism. These are the lingua franca of the
Movement.

The drug agitprop of the Movement is widely misinterpreted. The Movement does not want drugs to be legalized for
their own use; it wants to convert others to drugs. The drug
propaganda is entirely evangelistic: take acid and you will be
saved is the same message as Jesus Saves. The counterviolence of the police and the drug authorities is not so much
opposed by the drug propagandists as it is courted. Legalization of the drugs would remove the thrill; without the official
opposition and the melodrama of rebellion, LSD would be
about as attractive as ice cream. But the uses of hallucinogenic
materials also provide the necessary escape from creativity,
from the action of writing a poem or painting a picture. If you
have been to the artificial paradise, why write about it? There
all the poems and paintings and music are readymade. There
everyone is a Michelangelo, a Mozart, and a Shakespeare. The
Movement maintains its puritanical aversion to alcohol
("Scotch is for fathers"), for alcohol confers only a temporary
nonactivity upon the psyche. Hallucinogens show you the
Promised Land.

As the students of medieval and Oriental mysticism know,
only about one in a hundred thousand mystics has ever

recorded his or her "trip" in even mildly impressive prose or
poetry. The jottings of drug-takers are even less engaging. The
taker of drugs may be trying to force the gates of the
imagination, as perhaps was the case with Coleridge, but the
mass movement for freedom of unconsciousness is clearly an
aesthetic draft-dodge. The aesthetic arrogance of the drug user
in any case lacks the substantiation of visible works. Pothead,
show me your book!

The nihilistic mind is a runaway horse. The Movement
blots out literature without ever having cracked a book. Or
rather, it burns all literature to the ground. The Movement
cultivates cultural brainwashing; even advanced university
students pretend to be ignorant of what they know. The fear of
cultural infection and the demand for "immediacy" immunize
their minds to any responses except to the latest fad or artifact.
Their speech and writing degenerate into code (at the moment
it is the underworld argot of the slum Negro, a genuine
proletarian dialect for him which is, however, awkward and
inapplicable to well-wishers and fellow-travelers). The
Movement's adulation of the Negro slum-dweller as hero-
victim leads it with characteristic naiveté to adopt his
sublanguage as a generalized medium of communication. The
very mystery of this language gives it credence: the terminol-
ogy and metaphors of jazz, sex, drugs, double-speak, and
revenge supply the necessary circuits of sympathy to the
adolescent of the upper worlds. You dig?

The jazz put-on is a major form of cultural blackmail by
the Movement. Anyone not "with" the jazz is a marked man.
The hagiography of jazz is as immense as the Vatican Library.
It is all phony, a conglomeration of the Music Corporation of
America and the masses of delayed and permanent adolescents. Jazz is only a minor facet of modern folk music. What is
beatified about jazz is that it is Negro. The Negro, as the most
obvious victim of society since the latest massacre of the Jews,
is thought to be universalizing about the human condition in
jazz. Nothing could be further from reality. Negro jazz
is—Negro jazz: charming, entertaining, hot, cool, abstract,
evangelistic, white, black, blue, but never revolutionary.
Negro jazz is masochistic; and that is precisely its failure and
its appeal to the adolescent. What it lacks in content it makes
up for in sentimentality, sexuality, and volume.

The blotting-out of language in jazz lyrics, the accommo-
dation by skillful musical improvisers to cranked-out dollar-
making stanzas, many of them half a century old, attests to the
deliberate destruction of language as a medium. The nostalgia

of the horn takes over; there is a vague reminiscence of language, unbelievably debased to begin with, whether it came from Tin Pan Alley or from Hollywood. The insistence on jazz, as taken over by the Movement, is the insistence on hysteria as a Way of Life. As such it appeals to the American joy in violence.

The Movement nominates Bob Dylan as great poet. The whining puerilities of this phenomenon are not to be taken lightly in the stock market or in the hearts of millions of children bursting with vitamins and cash. Is he the Leader?

The open release of violence is always a surprise to intellectuals. Rebellion without goals is the most fascinating spectacle of all. The Media intone with relentless stupidity: Why? Why? Congresses mourn. Whole cities are put to the torch while children dance and scream as at a jazz festival or an ice capade. Yet violence is inculcated by the elders and is exactly predictable. Violence is the answer to the question, Why?

It is quite natural and expectable in psycho-politics that Negro looters should espouse white genocide and Nazi anti-semitism. It is quite natural that WASP children in posh suburbs should play Nazi, instead of Cowboy and Indian. In a child society the only authentic emotion is hate. In Hippy language Hate is spelled Love; any four-letter word will suffice.

America is the child society *par excellence*, and possibly the only one ever politically arrived at. It is the society of all rights and no obligations, the society of deliberate wreckage and waste, the only society that ever raised gangsterism to the status of myth, and murder to the status of tragedy or politics. The American adulation of the child mentality leads to an industrialized hedonism, on the one hand, and a chauvinistic psychology of greed, on the other. In advertising, anyone over the age of twenty-one or twenty-five is portrayed as an idiot who has got behind in the science and commerce of rejuvenation. This "adult" is appealed to by an almost invisible Big Brother (Mad-Ave or the Executive in the White House) because the "adult" has made the mistake of legal and contractual obligation. Therefore he is an idiot. The costuming of the so-called radical population is a form of jeering: the beard is not only a red flag with certain flickering political messages; it is also the ultimate taunt at the man in the suit. Arson, looting, and murder are also gentle reminders to the fathers that the tumbrils are rolling. (In many of my creative writing classes the students sit in judgment on their parents and make specific judgments about which of the elders will be allowed to live. Confronted with the fact that the elders and the state are paying their way through education, the students snort and sneer at the stupidity of authorities.)

Humanities departments, notoriously the most deprived segment of the American university system, have been powerless to halt the invasion of the child psychosis in higher education. The effeminate backstairs aggressiveness of the Humanities gives way to the Creative Writing Gestalt. "Creative Writing" is to the Humanities as strychnine is to the horse. Any symptom of guilt discerned by the undergraduate on the part of its elders is parlayed into immediate sabotage—a sabotage which stops short of the curtailment of personal benefits, however. The gangsterism of the American youth mind makes it as easy a prey to the Marine recruiter as it does to the Creative Writing instructor. The goals are not education but theft, generally theft of scholarships and undeserved preferment. As American literature heroizes the outlaw, so the outlaw student gains advantage over his more serious companions; the style of contempt, the "cool," determines to a large extent the amount of loot acquired and the length of absolution from the institutions which threaten his freedom of operation.

The cultivation of Youth with a capital Y has kept the growth of the American mind off balance since perhaps the early nineteenth century. The trashy frontier mythology, hand-to-hand combat, Horatio Alger, Alger Hiss, spy-psychology, advertising, Hell's Angels, Beats, Hippies, Beatles, dropouts, assassins, amnesiac mass murders, pseudo-mystics lately from Kyoto or Benares, CIA, Black Muslims and Black Nazis, these are all part and parcel of the American dream of Youth. The dream was dreamed by the fathers, now on the proscribed list.

As Negro antisemitism is Christian (the only political training the Negro was ever given was the flaming cross), so anti-adultism is American flag-waving in reverse. For this state of affairs there would seem to be no remedy. And indeed there is not. Should one suggest a program to slow down or stop the strangulation of American life by children, it might read:

1. Cut off all sources of economic supply to Youth except what they earn by physical or observable mental labor.

2. Deny all higher education except on absolute proof of ability. No student should be admitted to a college or university unless he or she has earned a scholarship or has otherwise demonstrated unusual ability. Public universities

should be more stringent in this respect than private, rich universities (the private school is unsupervisable).

3. Deny free travel privileges to children. For instance, raise the age minimum of drivers' licenses to thirty or forty. Deny foreign travel except to those who have been granted the privilege from their school.

4. Set aside a large land area for all dissidents to reside in, with ingress but no egress. As children think the world is their personal property, give them their acre of personal property. Keep them there.

5. Discourage the cowardice and intimidation of parents and "authorities" by re-educating them to the nature of the Yahoo. Encourage construction of housing, especially suburban housing, to delimit or exclude the child, and to suit the needs and requirements of adults.

6. Disenfranchise those who reject military service, male and female. Why does conscription legislation apply only to make Youth?

7. Abolish the child. Deliberate the intelligent society in which the infant is loved and cared for and controlled until he is ready to be shipped to a place of education, should he be worthy. Consider two types of human beings: the infant and the adult. Destroy all concepts of the adolescent.

Whereupon his "literature" will wither away, his "music," his drugs, his revolutions and murders, his terrorism of everything he lacks the understanding and knowledge to comprehend.

The power-shift lies in this direction. Man is an aesthetic animal. His greatest works are slashed to ribbons by "youth" and will continue to be until Grown Man relinquishes his image of the advertised profile of Youth. As long as Grown Man apes Youth, he will remain the victim of his seed.

The American adult must battle "youth" to the death. "Youth" is a figment of the American imagination which is destroying America itself.

The essays that follow should be read as a documentary. All of them lie in another dimension from the preceding note. For instance, a few years ago I delivered a lecture at a Negro university in Atlanta in which I stated that "retribution is not Negro." Not long after, the Negro youth blew the lid off all over the U.S.A. Here was illiteracy in action, television come to life, Nazism being born in full view. The tendency of American politicians and journalists to look for the "cause" is inherent in the myopia of the American mythologists and opportunists who imagine that the status quo is verbalized in the eighteenth-century Constitution. Yet no generation of Americans since the signing of that document has regarded it as the rock of ages. Only politicans and law-makers perpetuate this document in bad faith, encouraging the unconscionable materialism of the people and inflating the images of gangster, murderer, and thief. Little wonder that some of the greatest presidents have fallen to the youthful assassin, trained in histrionics and expert in shooting in the back. . . .

To
Abolish
Children
by Karl Shapiro

Betrayal is an act of vengeance obviously. But in an age of betrayal, when men of authority traduce their office and violate the trust placed in their hands, betrayal becomes the official morality. "Official morality" shortly becomes "public immorality"; whereupon the fabric of a society rots before one's eyes. In the years since the end of the Second World War, announced by the drop of the first Ultimate Weapon, the world has been stunned, horrified, and ultimately cajoled and won over to the official morality of America and its corollary of public immorality and anarchy. Hardly a leader, whether president, general, public relations man, professor, publisher, or poet, can be held to be honorable in his intentions. Everywhere lies the hidden premise and the calculated betrayal, the secret and chauvinistic lie.

To what end? Who is the betrayer, and why? Who are the betrayed? In a pyramidal society, a hierarchy, one would know the answers. But in a jungle there are no answers, only cries of victory or death. In the modern American jungle there are no answers.

Must America give birth to fascism? Or can it survive its pristine Constitution? Both issues seem doubtful. Can the economic motive live with the mass monster it has created? Can the poor white who has sacrificed his brain to television, or the poor Negro who loots a TV set from the store, ever again cross the line from somnambulism to wakeful joy? Can only the modern artist discover beauty in the twentieth century?

The entire world has become aware of the pervasiveness of American violence. The Americans were the last to discover it. This is as it should be. A betrayed husband is the last to know his situation. America is shocked at itself; someone has handed it a mirror. Instead of the young and handsome heir of all the ages, with his bathing-beauty consort, winners of Olympic Games, we see the soft and rotten killer (almost Hemingway style) with his call-girl WASP girlfriend, wearing a tiny crucifix between her scientifically measured bosoms.

Wars are staged and televised on the battlefield; all sports are openly and avowedly big business; all books sell according to the amount of money deposited for advertising; countries are bought and sold in the stock market like cattle. Not that any of this is particularly new. What is new is that it is all now *public* knowledge. And what is awesome is that nobody cares. Everyone wants a share of the rot, the *faisandage.* Ours is a gamy culture from top to bottom. Books about the gaminess are best-sellers.

The goal of any writer or professor nowadays is to defend his—there is an old-fashioned word—honor. Can a writer write what he wants and in his manner? Can a teacher teach what he was hired to teach, in his own manner? Or must he give way to some form of blackmail from above or below, some Big Brother, who reinterprets his role for him. But we have heard enough of this structural mechanism from the time of Aldous Huxley, Orwell, McLuhan, and so forth.

At the bottom of the spectrum of betrayal are the "Movements," the pseudo-revolutionary insurrections without goals. The purest of these aim at simple theft and sabotage, such as occur during and after hurricanes. The more complicated are identified with civil rights and sex, freedom of drugs and pills of various forms, the right to unlimited travel vouchers and hospitalization. These are the heirs to the kingdom of Wall Street—the latest generation of betrayers and destroyers. This is the generation that uses the word Love as a synonym for Hate, that practices infantilism on a scale which has never been seen.

In between are the always duped Bourgeoisie, playing both ends against the middle. The bourgeois pays his children off to stay away, horrified at his mistake of educating these free-wheeling organisms equipped with electric guitars.

Possibly because the economic structure has reached the saturation point, the old order of social development is defunct. The pattern roughly used to be immigrant (or settler), bourgeois professional man, and artist (or patron). The child enacts the pattern in reverse; the young man or woman aspires to be artist first, deploring professionalism and education itself, condemning the standards of safety of the bourgeois (while exploiting the material wealth of the bourgeois exchequer), and eventually achieving the role of pseudo-immigrant or "native." The Beats and Hippies are products of the American aesthetic which has always preached disaffiliation and single combat with the forces of nature and of society. All American dissident movements tend to fall apart as soon as they are organized. Each artist and pseudo-artist is his own Huckleberry Finn, a moral expatriate. All of our best artists have been recluses of one kind or another, Melville, Faulkner, Hemingway, Cummings. The American artist who does not shun the Center is suspect. The dissident, however, misunderstands the commitment of the artist and thinks of this commitment only in terms of rebellion. The failure of the masses of dissidents to evolve a politic is inherent in the national aesthetic of individualism. And because the dissidents offer no organized threat to the existing order, the existing order continues to consolidate its gains and to ignore the threat of blackmail. The dissidents simply supply additional dry rot to the cultural fabric. The burning and looting of slums signify the abysmal failure of imagination of the would-be revolutionaries, who in fact have no goals. Their only goals are pillage and revenge. The intellectual infantilism of the American radical makes him a figure of fun or of affection (or disaffection, as the case may be). The most one can say of an Allen Ginsberg or a Timothy Leary or a LeRoi Jones is that they are sincere. Children are always sincere.

Dissidence spread to the professoriat with the installation of artists and writers on the campuses of the nation. (I am one of the writer-professors who encouraged the moral-intellectual drop-out philosophy for about a decade.) It was easy and sometimes necessary to equate the mass university with other forms of the bureaucratic organism, but the vagueness of the issues involved and the failure to clarify them simply added up to an abstract dissent. That a university can be a democracy is patently absurd. The prattle about Free Speech at Berkeley which thrilled the sophomores of all ages served simply to debase whatever issues were at hand. Professors such as myself had already fought this issue in the courts, and won. The campus rioters were betraying these gains and taking a little private revenge on the side.

Vietnam itself is a falsified issue in the dissident "revolutions." The war is one of the most evil adventures in our history and its evil effects on the American character are incalculable, but the dissent is largely hypocritical. The "Underground" did not raise its voice against the Russian suppression of Hungary; it pursues a hands-off policy vis-à-vis Castro, even to the endorsement of antique Marxist slogans; it does not agitate for the overthrow of the last big brother of the Axis, Francisco Franco. On the contrary, the dissidents are to be found disporting themselves as frequently in Spain as in other exotic places, pursuing their careers and brushing up on the guitar. If it is laudable to avoid a draft, it is despicable to moralize about it.

The importation of mysticism and pseudo-mysticism into the West was an early stratagem of withdrawal from the known modes of communication. Mysticism is simultaneously an insult and a threat to communal behavior. Mystical evidence is by definition hearsay and inhibits communication. The conveniences of Zen and the Sutras to the dissidents (who were rarely if ever "believers") were that they opened the door to a counter-culture, one in which consciousness was superseded by unconsciousness, and provisioned their minds with a counter-literature. The literature of the Orient has never been and cannot be naturalized in the West, but the stratagem of the haiku, for instance, is supposed to put the quietus on Western poetry.

But neither poetry nor any of the other arts are essential to the existence and furtherance of the "Movement," as its members refer to it with typical mystification. The Beat poets were the only dissidents who maintained even diplomatic relations with poetry, but their poetry was openly propaganda for the Movement. The planks of the primitive dissident platform were simple and narcissistic: pot, homosexuality, and doom-prophecy, a tame and almost Baptist program. The poetry lacked ambition to rise above these themes.

Because poetry was meaningless as a vehicle or an aesthetic to the Movement, the early Beat poetry took to the drum and trumpet (nineteenth-century symbols of slave revolt). The mixture of jazz and verse laid the groundwork for the dissident aesthetic: volume of noise, mass hypnotism, pure size, all canceled out the possibility of dialogue or even thought. Nor did hatred of the electronic world preclude the utmost exploitation of the amplifier. Herewith began the invasion of parks.

The deliberate and mischievous inversion of modes (anything "adult" was proscribed) opened a Pandora's box for the child mentality which would have driven Lewis Carroll to suicide. The wave of male and female hysterics with guitars and brotherhood lyrics turned into a mass industry, on the one hand, and, on the other, a generation of révoltés without goals. The dissident music is verbal—both the music and the language descend to levels of callousness and insensitivity heretofore unknown—but the contents are those of the infant banging its fists on the highchair. It is an amazing phenomenon that this art, pitched directly to the level of the five- or six-year-old, should also be the level of the college student. (Dissidence appears to taper off thereafter.) Dissident sartorial fashion also abolishes distinctions between the sexes; the not very subtle transvestism of the dissident costume situates the Movement in the years prior to puberty. The burlesque Edwardianism of the Beatles expresses a nostalgia for the age of aristocracy and unlimited wealth.

Throughout human history the fine arts have provided the nexus between intuitional insight and civilized hindsight. That is what the arts have been for. But at times when intuition usurps the more wakeful states of mind, the arts plunge into the playpen and the cry of "immediacy" fills the air. Immediacy (as in D. H. Lawrence's "immediate present" or the Zen Now!) cripples hindsight and deliberation and prevents criteria from coming into existence. The failure of the Beat community to create poetry or any of the other arts is the most significant fact about the Movement. The hidden aesthetic premise of the Movement is that art is evil and must be hamstrung. Only states of unconsciousness are valid: drug-states, violence in bed and on the street, secret languages, political nihilism. These are the lingua franca of the Movement.

The drug agitprop of the Movement is widely misinterpreted. The Movement does not want drugs to be legalized for their own use; it wants to convert others to drugs. The drug propaganda is entirely evangelistic: take acid and you will be saved is the same message as Jesus Saves. The counterviolence of the police and the drug authorities is not so much opposed by the drug propagandists as it is courted. Legalization of the drugs would remove the thrill; without the official opposition and the melodrama of rebellion, LSD would be about as attractive as ice cream. But the uses of hallucinogenic materials also provide the necessary escape from creativity, from the action of writing a poem or painting a picture. If you have been to the artificial paradise, why write about it? There all the poems and paintings and music are readymade. There everyone is a Michelangelo, a Mozart, and a Shakespeare. The Movement maintains its puritanical aversion to alcohol ("Scotch is for fathers"), for alcohol confers only a temporary nonactivity upon the psyche. Hallucinogens show you the Promised Land.

As the students of medieval and Oriental mysticism know, only about one in a hundred thousand mystics has ever recorded his or her "trip" in even mildly impressive prose or poetry. The jottings of drug-takers are even less engaging. The

---

Marginal handwritten notes:

put-on? hasn't a lot changed since he wrote this? (look up when written)

what's this about the Beatles?

overgeneralized!?

look up Zen — does he understand it?

meaning?

these are sheer escape, but they aren't the same! Perhaps they are the same!

mystical cop-out again But is it really mystical?

what does he say "art" is?

motives of the drug-user

a state of unconsciousness replaces difficulties

taker of drugs may be trying to force the gates of the
imagination, as perhaps was the case with Coleridge, but the
mass movement for freedom of unconsciousness is clearly an
aesthetic draft-dodge. The aesthetic arrogance of the drug user
in any case lacks the substantiation of visible works. Pothead,
show me your book!

The nihilistic mind is a runaway horse. The Movement
blots out literature without ever having cracked a book. Or
rather, it burns all literature to the ground. The Movement
cultivates cultural brainwashing; even advanced university
students pretend to be ignorant of what they know. The fear of
cultural infection and the demand for "immediacy" immunize
their minds to any responses except to the latest fad or artifact.
Their speech and writing degenerate into code (at the moment
it is the underworld argot of the slum Negro, a genuine
proletarian dialect for him which is, however, awkward and
inapplicable to well-wishers and fellow-travelers). The
Movement's adulation of the Negro slum-dweller as hero-
victim leads it with characteristic naiveté to adopt his
sublanguage as a generalized medium of communication. The
very mystery of this language gives it credence: the terminol-
ogy and metaphors of jazz, sex, drugs, double-speak, and
revenge supply the necessary circuits of sympathy to the
adolescent of the upper worlds. You dig?

The jazz put-on is a major form of cultural blackmail by
the Movement. Anyone not "with" the jazz is a marked man.
The hagiography of jazz is as immense as the Vatican Library.
It is all phony, a conglomeration of the Music Corporation of
America and the masses of delayed and permanent adolescents. Jazz is only a minor facet of modern folk music. What is
beatified about jazz is that it is Negro. The Negro, as the most
obvious victim of society since the latest massacre of the Jews,
is thought to be universalizing about the human condition in
jazz. Nothing could be further from reality. Negro jazz
is—Negro jazz: charming, entertaining, hot, cool, abstract,
evangelistic, white, black, blue, but never revolutionary.
Negro jazz is masochistic; and that is precisely its failure and its
appeal to the adolescent. What it lacks in content it makes up
for in sentimentality, sexuality, and volume.

The blotting-out of language in jazz lyrics, the accommo-
dation by skillful musical improvisers to cranked-out dollar-
making stanzas, many of them half a century old, attests to the
deliberate destruction of language as a medium. The nostalgia
of the horn takes over; there is a vague reminiscence of
language, unbelievably debased to begin with, whether it

came from Tin Pan Alley or from Hollywood. The insistence on jazz, as taken over by the Movement, is the insistence on hysteria as a Way of Life. As such it appeals to the American joy in violence.

The Movement nominates Bob Dylan as great poet. The whining puerilities of this phenomenon are not to be taken lightly in the stock market or in the hearts of millions of children bursting with vitamins and cash. Is he the Leader?

The open release of violence is always a surprise to intellectuals. Rebellion without goals is the most fascinating spectacle of all. The Media intone with relentless stupidity: Why? Why? Congresses mourn. Whole cities are put to the torch while children dance and scream as at a jazz festival or an ice capade. Yet violence is inculcated by the elders and is exactly predictable. Violence is the answer to the question, Why?

It is quite natural and expectable in psycho-politics that Negro looters should espouse white genocide and Nazi anti-semitism. It is quite natural that WASP children in posh suburbs should play Nazi, instead of Cowboy and Indian. In a child society the only authentic emotion is hate. In Hippy language Hate is spelled Love; any four-letter word will suffice.

America is the child society *par excellence*, and possibly the only one ever politically arrived at. It is the society of all rights and no obligations, the society of deliberate wreckage and waste, the only society that ever raised gangsterism to the status of myth, and murder to the status of tragedy or politics. The American adulation of the child mentality leads to an industrialized hedonism, on the one hand, and a chauvinistic psychology of greed, on the other. In advertising, anyone over the age of twenty-one or twenty-five is portrayed as an idiot who has got behind in the science and commerce of rejuvenation. This "adult" is appealed to by an almost invisible Big Brother (Mad-Ave or the Executive in the White House) because the "adult" has made the mistake of legal and contractual obligation. Therefore he is an idiot. The costuming of the so-called radical population is a form of jeering: the beard is not only a red flag with certain flickering political messages; it is also the ultimate taunt at the man in the suit. Arson, looting, and murder are also gentle reminders to the fathers that the tumbrils are rolling. (In many of my creative writing classes the students sit in judgment on their parents and make specific judgments about which of the elders will be allowed to live. Confronted with the fact that the elders and the state are paying their way through education, the students snort and sneer at the stupidity of authorities.)

Humanities departments, notoriously the most deprived segment of the American university system, have been powerless to halt the invasion of the child psychosis in higher education. The effeminate backstairs aggressiveness of the Humanities gives way to the Creative Writing Gestalt. "Creative Writing" is to the Humanities as strychnine is to the horse. Any symptom of guilt discerned by the undergraduate on the part of its elders is parlayed into immediate sabotage—a sabotage which stops short of the curtailment of personal benefits, however. The gangsterism of the American youth mind makes it as easy a prey to the Marine recruiter as it does to the Creative Writing instructor. The goals are not education but theft, generally theft of scholarships and undeserved preferment. As American literature heroizes the outlaw, so the outlaw student gains advantage over his more serious companions; the style of contempt, the "cool," determines to a large extent the amount of loot acquired and the length of absolution from the institutions which threaten his freedom of operation.

The cultivation of Youth with a capital Y has kept the growth of the American mind off balance since perhaps the early nineteenth century. The trashy frontier mythology, hand-to-hand combat, Horatio Alger, Alger Hiss, spy-psychology, advertising, Hell's Angels, Beats, Hippies, Beatles, dropouts, assassins, amnesiac mass murderers, pseudo-mystics lately from Kyoto or Benares, CIA, Black Muslims and Black Nazis, these are all part and parcel of the American dream of Youth. The dream was dreamed by the fathers, now on the proscribed list.

As Negro anti-semitism is Christian (the only political training the Negro was ever given was the flaming cross), so anti-adultism is American flag-waving in reverse. For this state of affairs there would seem to be no remedy. And indeed there is not. Should one suggest a program to slow down or stop the strangulation of American life by children, it might read:

1. Cut off all sources of economic supply to Youth except what they earn by physical or observable mental labor.

2. Deny all higher education except on absolute proof of ability. No student should be admitted to a college or university unless he or she has earned a scholarship or has otherwise demonstrated unusual ability. Public universities should be more stringent in this respect than private, rich universities (the private school is unsupervisable).

3. Deny free travel privileges to children. For instance, raise the age minimum of drivers' licenses to thirty or forty. Deny foreign travel except to those who have been granted the privilege from their school.

4. Set aside a large land area for all dissidents to reside in, with ingress but no egress. As children think the world is their personal property, give them their acre of personal property. Keep them there.

5. Discourage the cowardice and intimidation of parents and "authorities" by re-educating them to the nature of the Yahoo. Encourage construction of housing, especially suburban housing, to delimit or exclude the child, and to suit the needs and requirements of adults.

6. Disenfranchise those who reject military service, male and female. Why does conscription legislation apply only to male Youth?

7. Abolish the child. Deliberate the intelligent society in which the infant is loved and cared for and controlled until he is ready to be shipped to a place of education, should he be worthy. Consider two types of human beings: the infant and the adult. Destroy all concepts of the adolescent.

Whereupon his "literature" will wither away, his "music," his drugs, his revolutions and murders, his terrorism of everything he lacks the understanding and knowledge to comprehend.

The power-shift lies in this direction. Man is an aesthetic animal. His greatest works are slashed to ribbons by "youth" and will continue to be until Grown Man relinquishes his image of the advertised profile of Youth. As long as Grown Man apes Youth, he will remain the victim of his seed.

The American adult must battle "youth" to the death. "Youth" is a figment of the American imagination which is destroying America itself.

The essays that follow should be read as a documentary. All of them lie in another dimension from the preceding note. For instance, a few years ago I delivered a lecture at a Negro university in Atlanta in which I stated that "retribution is not Negro." Not long after, the Negro youth blew the lid off all over the U.S.A. Here was illiteracy in action, television come to life, Nazism being born in full view. The tendency of American politicians and journalists to look for the "cause" is inherent in the myopia of the American mythologists and opportunists who imagine that the status quo is verbalized in the eighteenth-century Constitution. Yet no generation of Americans since the signing of that document has regarded it as the rock of ages. Only politicians and lawmakers perpetuate this document in bad faith, encouraging the unconscionable materialism of the people and inflating the images of gangster, murderer, and thief. Little wonder that some of the greatest presidents have fallen to the youthful assassin, trained in histrionics and expert in shooting in the back. . . .

public officials and "the people" rather than "youth" are to blame.

The reader in this example read actively and his marginal comments helped to create and enrich, as well as to record, his responses. Some brief comments on the principles behind his markings should serve to lead into the outline stage and the final product. This reader-responder-recorder used the left-side margin to locate the structure and movement of the essay. He "made up" major headings and titles when needed, underlined "thesis" statements, and cross-referenced strands of the author's argument as it developed. This traditional summarizing activity occurred principally in the second stage of markings and grew out of his initial reactions that were predictably less structured. It is important to see, however, that these outlining devices did arise from the structure of the essay as modified by the effects of his experience in reading it. The reader simply followed along with the essay and took it apart to see how it worked. The summarizing activity in no way resulted from an imposition from outside.

The earliest stages of his response are mere circling of key words and phrases, questions to himself in the margin, allusions to something else the writer hasn't mentioned, brief notes that add something beyond summary, objections to what the author says, cross references to something else the responder has read or experienced lately, notations on the meaning of words unfamiliar at first, or doodlings as the reader pauses to think. Although he experienced many complex feelings at the time of this reading, without a way of recording them he could not re-create them tomorrow or in that tomorrow-on-paper. Then, too, some of the markings are merely X's or lines down the margin, arrows or variations of underlinings the recorder used to remind himself of something. Finally, a number of his comments appear to reach a dead end. Perhaps they record responses he had that were valuable to his thinking out the whole essay but will not fit into his major emphasis. As this reader develops a pattern inductively, such secondary material will assume a lesser role in his essay. In short, structure from within will help him get rid of material that could get in his way later.

To structure personal responses and still allow them range in which to develop, you need to discover an effective pattern inductively by working with sufficiently developed marginal comments. While no one wants to ramble on aimlessly or talk just to hear oneself talk, neither should we set arbitrary boundaries on self-exploration on paper at its earliest stages especially. Order from within answers the problem posed by the need for undistorted personal response as well as a structure that brings the communication of such response to its fullest potential.

Organization from within as opposed to an imposition from outside is as old as Aristotle and as individualized as your own reactions will allow. Aristotle found structure and order as causes within matter itself: potential developing into its realization, the plant actualizing itself from the seeds of order, structure, and growth within its own nature as a plant. Thus marginal comments become for the effective writer richer and more complex on their way to finding their own most effective order and structure. Assuming that potential is there if you don't stifle it, the end product can be actualized through full exploration of your ideas for what they are.

We have examined some of the possible ways in which personal responses come into being and actualize their potential in the writing process itself. Just as full exploration of self requires some kind of marginal comments or record of your response so that you can preserve it and enrich it by returning to it, so also choosing a topic and limiting the focus of that topic call for increasingly detailed exploration of personal reactions for what they are and for the potential they have within themselves to develop. We have also seen how the point of view one assumes begins the process of organization from within. In some ways a part of the point of view a writer takes—the writer's tone and voice—creates the style of the subjective response. The oft-quoted "style is the man" suggests much about realization of potential within one's own subjective responses. The degree to which all these separate parts of one's personal reactions interact provides the basis for a discussion of order from within. Drawing upon marginal comments and following the potential within emerging inductive outlines, the writer is actually developing in the finished product.

Following the prewriting stages, the next step of the process—the outline—can be sketched directly from the marginal comments. As in the more advanced stages of recording in the margin, you can now begin to recognize the organization of the original essay and to shape your own responses in accord with the original. But the outline, rather than an artificial imposition from outside, is an organic form that tries to capture as much as possible of your actual reading response as it occurred. The outline, too, becomes more complex as the reader's response does; but unlike imposed structures, it stays in contact with the experience it records. This stage also gives you the chance to work further on short-circuited steps of the process before the "unity" and "coherence" of your original reactions collapse. You can also discard unrelated materials and test things for workability by following the development already recorded through various kinds of marginal comments. The traditional summarizing and structuring work of the conventional outline is still important. But you'll see more reason for it and understand better where it's coming from when you can make it an integral part of what it's a record of—your response, which is ultimately what you have to say.

Exercises

1. As an exercise in discovery of order from within, look back to your own marginal comments on "To Abolish Children" and to the sample comments given as examples.

2. Try to project an inductive outline based on the sample marginal comments.

3. Then create an inductive outline for your own responses to the essay and compare the two sets of marginal comments and the two outlines.

4. Study the sample sections of the list below and the finished product developed from that list. Note the *grouping* of random marginal comments.

Betrayal as official morality. Problem—Symptom
Who has done the betraying? Objection
Breakdown of hierarchy. Problem—Cause
Failure of authority, not those under authority. Objection (Cause)
Confuses causes of the problem with its symptoms. Problem/
    Objection
Pervasiveness of violence. Problem—symptom
Intellectual infantilism. Problem—Cause
Movements at bottom of betrayal. Problem—Symptom and Cause?
Energy with no restraint. Problem—Cause
Reverse development. Problem—Cause
Dissidents supply dry rot. Problem—Symptom
Children are sincere. Problem—Symptom
Hasn't America always been violent? Objection (Cause)
All packaged for public consumption. Problem—Symptom
More than "gamy" culture; it's greed. Objection (Cause)
"Now" generation wants everything with no work. Problem—
    Cause
Mr. S. doesn't understand adolescent stages. Objection
Concept of Individuality not clear. Objection (more needed)
Generation gap overlooked here? Objection (more needed)
Mysticism as dropout. Problem—Cause
Drugs are escape. Problem—Cause
Overgeneralizes grouping things together. Style/Objection
"Pothead, show me your book." Objection (Style)
Function of artist; his is only one theory. Objection (more needed)
Phony culture and need for fad. Problem—Symptom
Speech code/"sincerity" replaces action. Problem—Symptom
Society as whole all rights, no obligations. Problem expanded
"Youth" as figment of Imagination Worshipped. Problem expanded
Growth arrested. Problem expanded

Seven-point program to abolish the child. Solutions?/Objection
Tone too glib/overstatement misses mark. Style/Objection
Overgeneralization a problem of logic, not style. Style/Objection
Vivid imagery. Style/Objection
His solutions are as simplistic as the copouts he rejects. Style/
    Objection

This sample list reflects the inductive strategy of the prewriting by recorded response process. Note how the list accumulates essential details from the marginal comments and then groups together related points inductively. This annotator thus developed the following major clusters of comments and subheadings:

I.   Depiction of the problem
      A. Symptoms
          1. Pervasiveness of violence
          2. Dissidents supply dry rot
      B. Causes
          1. Breakdown of hierarchy
          2. Intellectual infantilism
      C. Symptoms and causes in one
          1. Movements at bottom of betrayal
          2. Further subheadings in each category
              (a) mysticism
              (b) drugs
              (c) other

Other major headings emerge inductively from the list:

II.   Causes of the problem expanded
       A. Society on the whole works on all rights and no obligations
       B. "Youth"/a figment of Imagination Worshipped
           1. attempts to recapture an irresponsible past
           2. Rejuvenation as escape/destroying America
       C. Growth arrested by dream for instantaneous
III.   "Solutions" to the problem
       A. Implied in discussion of what's wrong
       B. Seven-point program to abolish the child
IV.   Style
       A. Overstatement—effective to a point
       B. Glibness—overdone
       C. Invective—misses the mark
       D. Imagery—vivid
       E. Tone—disparaging to the authority he is trying to show a
              need for
       F. Overgeneralizations—a problem of logic, not style
V.   Objections: Confusion of cause and symptoms, glib style, more
              evidence needed
       A. Placing of blame (cause)
       B. Economic motivation underlying (cause)

C.   Tradition of violence not new (more needed)

D.   Generation gap? (more needed)

E.   Function of an artist—his is only one view (more needed)

F.   Concept of Individuality not clear (more needed)

G.   Reactionaries are just as bad (more needed)

H.   Movement from babyhood to adulthood unrealistic—no initiation rite at all? (solution)

I.   Who has done the betraying? (cause)

J.   Overstated, glib . . . (style)

K.   Seven-point plan foolish (solution/style)

The original list thus clusters inductively into various headings and subheadings. And because some overlap, a structure for discussing interrelated points arises. Thus the problem divides into symptoms and causes, and each has its subheadings. Causes and solutions to the problem are expanded, and matters of style and structure are clarified. Running through each category are "objections" voiced by the reader. These objections then form a separate category, with causes, effects, solutions, style, and a "more needed" tag unifying the reader's response to the whole. Each major section is developed only briefly here—though a series of potential essays has been designed in the process.

At first, the outline seems a bit unruly. And it does start out that way. Because it is a record of a complex experience, the limitation of the subject arises in part through sorting out the marginal comments as the subject for a paper comes into focus. The student in this example could not write about everything in the outline. The summarizing activity reflected in his original list is compressed in accord with a more limited subject. The writer can assume also that his audience has read the essay and proceed to what he has to say about it. For purposes of the outline, this writer's parenthetical objections in the list are repeated to a degree in the "Issues Not Sufficiently Developed" heading later. Notes on solutions here are overly neat and brief because Shapiro's seven-point program need not be repeated in outline form. Since the reader had decided that the program would not be the subject of his paper, he did not engage in detailed analysis of each point. In fact, lack of comments in the margin would indicate that the program didn't interest him much in the first place. Finally, the reader includes a section on what he thought of the style of the essay as it bears on its overall effectiveness. This, in short, is the outline of the outline—a brief and simple process in which he codified his recorded response, reconstructed it even more thoroughly, and prepared it for presentation in the finished product.

Again you must devise your own system, and most any notation and form that are effective for you will do. To avoid imposing the order from outside your own response, keep it free and loose and begin the process of limiting the subject and focusing more sharply on what you choose to deal with *inductively*. The outline then becomes more than summary; it is actually a reaction, a record of responses you had at the time and still do, an analysis of style and effectiveness, and a positioning of your additions to the whole discussion in the framework in which they will make the most sense.

The revised sample outline that follows also operates inductively. Based on his original comments, the list, and his original outline, this student grouped his reactions, selected and ordered them, and created a structure inductively. He grouped his categories, analyzed his own views, and expanded individual sections. Note how he *grouped* his sortings of Shapiro's depiction of the problem into subheadings—each expanding into a potential outline of its own. Similarly, matters of style and technique as well as the reader's own additions and points of disagreement shaped themselves into a workable structure. His problem now was not getting started, but channeling what he had started into productive outlets. The revised outline thus emerges from a more limited focus and a further expansion of that workable subject. The new outline can then serve as the basis for one finished essay from the many potential essays implicit in this reader's responses.

Revised, Expanded Outline of Limited Subject

I. Objections to Mr. Shapiro's views: he confuses causes with symptoms of the problem
  A. Objections to his view of causes of the problem
    1. Placing of blame too limited
    2. Economic motivation underlying
    3. Who has betrayed whom?
  B. Objections to his solutions to the problem
    1. No concept of movement from babyhood to adulthood, no initiation rite at all?
    2. Seven-point plan foolish
  C. Mr. S.'s arguments rejected because more evidence is needed
    1. Tradition of violence not new
    2. Generation gap more important than Mr. S. seems to think
    3. Mr. S.'s view of the artist only one view
    4. Mr. S.'s concept of individuality not clear
    5. Reactionaries as bad as those in the "Movements"
  D. Objections to his style and presentations
    1. Seven-point plan foolish
    2. Overstatement effective only to a point
    3. Glibness overdone
    4. Invective misses mark
    5. Tone disparaging to authority he is trying to show a need for
    6. Overgeneralizations a problem of logic, not style

Exercises

1. Select an essay and record your responses to it: black ink for immediate reaction, blue ink for organizational and structural comments

(capital letters) red ink for further reading responses. Develop your own effective notation system.

2. List your marginal comments, analyzing and classifying the items on your list.

3. Develop an overall outline inductively—an outline of your total response to the essay.

4. Revise the original outline by limiting it and establishing a sharper focus. Compare the revised, limited outline to your original list and marginal comments to determine the context of your limited subject in relation to the whole.

Summary / Review

An effective system of marginal comments builds an internal organizational structure inductively. In preparing your personal reactions for an audience, you need to enrich your comments as you record them. It is useful at this stage to pose questions for yourself in anticipation of your audience's reception of your written views. Establishing your credibility, re-creating the steps of your developing thoughts, and pointing out the significance of what you're saying all help to reach an audience. The sample annotated essay "To Abolish Children" illustrates one student's system of marginal comments in operation. Studying your own marginal comments is a useful way to sort out, choose from, and organize your reactions as they develop. In sorting through the comments, form emerges as a discipline of materials from within rather than as an abstract imposition from outside. Rather than bringing what you have to say in accord with an outside order and thus often diminishing the intensity and complexity of your own voice, work on saying what you really feel in the form in which it can most effectively be said. Studying the various stages of inductive outlines illustrates how you can structure your own responses so as to enrich rather than stifle their potential for further development. The inductive outline thus further helps you to limit, organize, and expand your responses as you move toward the finished essay.

5/ From Outline to Finished Product

In the marginal notations and lists of chapter 4 the reader Actively read and began to write the at same time. With what is often the most difficult task (getting started) behind him, the writer now has material to build on. By working with his original marginal comments and lists of his responses, he has organized his thoughts into a coherent, manageable pattern. He has then selected the one limited unit of that overall outline he wishes to write a paper about. Although he is aiming toward a paper on "Objections to Mr. Shapiro," he will necessarily have to draw upon the other major headings to fill in the whole picture. That is, the limiting of the subject does not isolate that particular topic from the rest of his responses; rather, his expansion of the limited subject requires that he draw upon the whole preliminary outline at least for background information. A paper objecting to any of Mr. Shapiro's views must first describe briefly those views. In fact, in this case, one of the writer's chief objections to the paper is that Mr. Shapiro confused causes of the problem with the symptoms readily observable. The basic-framework outline for his paper, then, looks something like this:

A.   Mr. Shapiro's arguments in "To Abolish Children" are half right, half misguided.
   1. Objection to "causes."
   2. Objection to "symptoms."
B.   His solutions are inadequate.
C.   He ignores some important issues.
D.   His style and presentation are offensive and inadequate.

Based on this overall outline and the expanded section of the earlier outline, the writer created the following finished product:

Objections to Mr. Shapiro

In "To Abolish Children" Karl Shapiro describes the breakdown of the American Dream as an act of betrayal, a collapse of the societal hierarchy, and a worship of violence supported by various movements that are all escapes from reality. He traces America's ills to its "cultivation of youth" and its creation of "the child society par excellence," a society with "all rights and no obligations." But Mr. Shapiro's confusion of the causes and symptoms of the problem he raises together with his overlooking some crucial issues restrict the effectiveness of his arguments.

Even if Mr. Shapiro's picture of American society is accurate (and I think it is), he consistently identifies symptoms of the problems with causes and therefore provides an ineffective "solution." For example, he blames movements of all sorts for replacing responsibility with infantilism when the movements often arise to fill a void of irresponsibility already evident; he blames the pervasiveness of American violence on the collapse of American ideals when American society has always been one of violence; he blames the ills of society on the collapse of a hierarchy when the hierarchy collapsed because the ills of the society pointed to the uselessness of the hierarchy; in short, he either places the blame in the wrong place or doesn't go far enough in tracing the causes beyond the symptoms of the problem he discusses.

Similarly, Mr. Shapiro often over simplifies his explanations of a complex problem by failing to pursue some crucial issues further. He repeatedly discusses a movement from babyhood to adulthood with little appreciation of either the process of gradual maturing or the inevitable generation gap that occurs. Mr. Shapiro's theory of art as "disaffiliation" is only one view, and it doesn't seem to carry over to any understanding of the growth of the individual today. The result is a foolish seven-point program for abolishing the child that is as infantile as the events he says caused society's problems in the first place.

In addition to the confusion of cause and effect and the many undeveloped issues he raises, Mr. Shapiro's style diminishes the effectiveness of his argument. As an essayist, Mr. Shapiro uses a strong, forceful style which depends on

VERY BRIEF SUMMARY LEAD-IN BASED ON ORIGINAL LIST AND OUTLINE

SUBJECT LIMITED NOW WITH REFERENCE TO LIMITED OUTLINE.

STRAIGHT FROM THE LIST

EXAMPLES FROM THE LIST AND THE OUTLINE

READ FROM THE "MORE EVIDENCE NEEDED" SECTION OF THE OUTLINE

vivid imagery, deliberate overstatement, and a glibness that is sometimes humorous, sometimes just offensive. While his "the dissidents simply supply additional dry rot to the cultural fabric" makes its point, his "In Hippy Language Hate is Spelled Love" and "Pothead, Show me your book" simply miss the mark. Mr. Shapiro's style of excess reinforces his substantive confusions: overgeneralizations then become a problem of logic not style and his tone contradicts the authoritative hierarchy he is trying to show a need for.

My objections to Mr. Shapiro's views have little to do with his condemnation of young people. In fact, he goes beyond finding fault with young people in his attack on the whole society's desire for all rights and no obligations. And his depiction of America's worship of "youth" as a figment of its imagination and its attempts to recapture an irresponsible past seems sound. He is saying that Americans are destroying themselves by creating a rejuvenation of escape and a growth process that requires only dreaming of the instantaneous. It's too bad he chose the style he did because it perpetuates the very thing he is trying to reject—oversimplification and easy solutions in place of a more deliberate exploration of the complex problems we face today.

CONCLUSION DRAWS ON "PROBLEMS EXPANDED" SECTION OF THE ORIGINAL OUTLINE—THEN STATES BRIEFLY THE CONCLUSIONS

Of course, this essay is only one approach to "To Abolish Children." It grew out of one reader's lengthy marginal comments and outlines, which were presented in chapter 4. What follows is a response to "Objections to Mr. Shapiro" by a reader who takes a different approach and reaches sharply contrasting conclusions:

An Essay on the Attack (A Reply to "Objections to Mr. Shapiro")

The author of "Objections to Mr. Shapiro" is fair enough in his summary of content, and his distinctions between symptoms and causes of problems are important. But this author misses the point because he just doesn't catch on to Shapiro's tone. "To Abolish Children" is a lavish and effective put-on. It is a put-on with a point, a strong point that seems to have eluded the author of "Objections."

Shapiro doesn't "overlook crucial issues." He overlooks nothing. His medical encyclopedia of our sick society is kaleidoscopic and bludgeoning. "To Abolish Children" doesn't "solve" anything; that isn't its purpose. The essay explores and embellishes what it finds. Whenever anyone overstates a point for effect, there is always a "failing to pursue some crucial issues further." His seven-point "program" is most assuredly "foolish"—as are countless other generalizations proposed to solve the ills all around us. That is the point. Shapiro's program is very like Swift's "Modest Proposal" which also would not stand up to the literal readings that "Objections" tries to impose.

Far from "diminishing the effectiveness" of Shapiro's arguments, his style is a very part of those arguments. He often deliberately parrots what he is mocking, and he glibly attacks with outlandish humor. At its best, such a technique is *of course* offensive. Shapiro's careful use of strong and direct attacks is supposed to offend somebody. But his attacks are nothing like the sloppy and shallow whining which, as he demonstrates, attacks nothing because it believes in nothing.

The author of "Objections" is correct in his conclusions that Shapiro "goes beyond finding fault with young people in his attacks on the whole society's desire for all rights and no obligations." And that too is the point. While the style Shapiro chooses is not the only one in sight (and perhaps it's not even the best), it does not undermine his valuable ideas. That he so persistently angers his readers should show that his style is working. An essay on the attack is discomforting and does not call for comfortable responses.

Exercises

1. Select an essay and record your initial reactions to it using a system of marginal comments that you find effective. Reread the essay at least twice and carefully note the growth of your responses in the margin. Use different colors of ink to distinguish between your initial "gut" reactions, further expanded comments, and later more structured and organized notes. Explain the differences in the kind of thinking you record in each instance.

2. Drawing from your marginal comments, compile a list of what you consider to be your most important reactions. Then locate the organization suggested in the list itself and build an overall outline inductively.

3. Choose the subject that you would most like to write on in your overall outline. In other words, limit your range and then expand on your more focused subject. Draw upon the rest of the outline, but keep the subject focused.

4. With reference to the original essay and your notations, your original list and outline, and your revised and expanded outline, write an essay which is a finished product.

5. Find in your reading examples of essays written in response to a book or another essay. Magazines often choose a theme and then commission several essays on that topic. The editors sometimes give advanced copy to contributors so they can reply to one another in a type of published debate. Discuss the selections you have chosen and then try to reconstruct the marginal comments and outlines that the participants might reasonably have used.

6. Neither "Objections to Shapiro" nor the reply say the last word on "To Abolish Children" or the issues that essay raises. Do you agree or disagree with the conclusions reached by these authors? Are their methods appropriate for dealing with the questions Shapiro explores? To what extent does your approval or disapproval of "Objections to Shapiro" lead you back to the author's marginal notations? Stress wherever you are in strong agreement or disagreement with the author and then point to specific places in his marginal notations or outlines where he "went wrong" or "got it right." Compare your comments once again to Blake's "Annotations" in chapter 3.

7. Appoint yourself contributor to, and editor of, a magazine planning a special issue on a theme of current interest. After everyone in the class has read a good amount on the topic, call for a series of essays to be submitted for possible publication in the magazine. Plan the range of subjects to include a variety of approaches to the topic chosen.

8. Study the sample essays (reprinted below) written by students in response to "To Abolish Children." Fúrther reversing the process described here, try to reconstruct the general outline and marginal comments used by these students, and then comment at greater length on the ideas and techniques in these essays.

Who's to Blame?[*]

"To Abolish Children" is one of the most involved and involving essays I have ever read. Certainly no one could read this complicated work and not feel moved in some way by what Karl Shapiro is saying. It is not a paper which states the author's views coldly and calmly; instead, it thrusts ideas at the reader as a gun fires bullets at its victims . . . much with the same result. The ideas become lodged, like bullets, deep within the reader's mind and make him think about what the author is trying to get across to his audience.

In his essay, Shapiro discusses topics such as the rotting of America, various "Movements," jazz music, and the use of drugs, attacking each with equal vehemence. Though his knife-sharp views are often dulled by an over-use of hard-to-understand words ("the hagiography of jazz" or "industrialized hedonism"), and his complex sentence structure, Shapiro nevertheless makes many valid points. On page 3, he discusses the legalization of drugs and the outcome of such an act. He compares the legalized drug's attractiveness to that of a common everyday item—ice cream. What makes this such a good point is the truth behind his comparison. How many times have each of us found this to be true; if the danger and excitement are removed from doing something, much of the pleasure and fun gained from doing it is also taken away!

Another excellent point which Shapiro stresses can be found on the first page of his essay. In paragraph 3, the author speaks of a shocked America being handed a mirror and seeing its true self for the very first time. Instead of appearing as the dashing hero or the defender of everything that is good and fair, America sees itself, at last, as the "soft and rotten killer" which it actually is. Things that were once considered evil and un-American—such as the buying and selling of countries as though they were nothing more than prime cattle, or big business with its greedy fingers clutching at the uniforms of the sports world—are now public knowledge. And what's worse, Shapiro complains, people not only realize such events are going on all around them, they simply do not care! On the

---

[*]The following four essays were among those written in a composition class at Central Michigan University. The assignment was similar to the exercises in this chapter, and the students were given no opportunity to revise the essays then or now. The authors of these "first drafts" have graciously consented to my including them in this chapter.

contrary, everyone is more than happy to share in the rot and decay of our falling nation.

Shapiro could very easily have ended his essay at this point. It would have told of many of the well-known faults of America. And though the reader may have been moved by the power with which the author states his complaints, he probably would have agreed with Shapiro's views and thought little more about the work. But that is not what Shapiro wants. He has something vital to say, and he uses a method in his paper to make the reader take note of what is developing.

To catch and *hold* the reader's attention Shapiro selects a person or persons whom he can (and does) blame for all that is going wrong in America. The unsuspecting victims chosen are the "child" and "Youth." Throughout his entire essay, Shapiro relentlessly attacks Youth; he speaks of their music and language as "descending to levels of callousness and insensitivity heretofore unknown." And he goes further in insulting Youth by endlessly generalizing. It seems that to Shapiro Youth falls into one of two categories: the Beat Community or Hippies, neither of which he fully explains. Both, according to the author, are deeply involved in taking drugs, and other such abnormal, un-American pastimes— mysticism and pseudo-mysticism.

Making such statements and generalizations as these, Shapiro could not possibly have expected to avoid disagreeing with his audience—especially if his readers fall into the age group at which he is aiming such derogatory remarks. I feel that is exactly what the author is striving for. He wishes to get some *big* reaction from his audience!

When I first read this essay I was very angry. It surprised me how any intelligent person could suggest that Youth and the child were responsible for the horrible things which Shapiro was describing. I quickly lost all objectivity towards the essay. But the angrier I became at Shapiro's ideas, the more ridiculous some of his views became. They seemed to lose their credibility. At this point I realized that if the author had any intelligence at all there must be a point deeply hidden in his absurd suggestions and ideas. So I began searching for that hidden point.

Making the reader search is an accomplishment Karl Shapiro can be proud of. Few papers ask (in this case, force) the reader to think about not only what they are saying, but what they are *not* saying. Also, by having his reader look for what he is implying (instead of saying straight out), Shapiro is forcing his audience to form its own answers! When faced with the idea that "Youth" is to blame for the fall of America, the Youth themselves say, "Wait, we know we're not to blame; but then, who is?" Therefore, Youth begins to search for the real culprits!

No reader could accept the idea that the child is the cause of *all* that's happening. So, not only does Youth seek out those who are to blame, but others who read the essay also find themselves looking for answers which Shapiro has wisely avoided giving.

To understand another point which the author is getting at, an explanation is needed on how the words *child* and *Youth* could possibly have been used in the essay. When Shapiro speaks of the child, he never comes right out and describes a child as we know him. Instead, he speaks of "the child Mentality" or "the intellectual infantalism of America." In this way, Shapiro isn't really attacking the young child; he is hitting at that part in each of us (no matter what our age) which makes us behave in a childish way. Nothing is quite so impulsive or unthinking as that very young child, and because of this the child (or childish adult) often finds himself in some very unfortunate situations. Shapiro offers several examples: Movements with no aims, drug users, mystics, or Jesus freaks escaping from what they must face.

There are many more ideas presented in Shapiro's essay. The few I've chosen to write on seem to me the most important. One thing holds true no matter how you look at his work. Shapiro has created and developed in a few short pages enough material to fill hundreds of pages of explanation. At the same time, he presents his views (many stated before by others) in such a way as to make them appear totally unique. He has provided much thought-food for the gluttonous organ—the brain.

—GAIL GUENTHER

In Defense of Youth

Numerous essays have been written on and about our American way of life. They range from political and social epistemologies to what we do with our leisure time. "To Abolish Children" is an unusual essay concerned with youth, revolution, immorality, and the corruption of our society in general. Not only is the essay difficult to read, but to the average layman it is difficult to understand as well. A close examination of the work reveals that it is built primarily on a criticism of "youth." But the essay also finds fault with the larger society in America as well. Is American youth the root of this so called "rot"? Some people may believe so; however, if we are going to survive as a nation we are going to have to help our youth, guide them, support them, and give them our confidence. Karl Shapiro's essay is a false accusation about how American youth is unproductive.

The author, who is almost a muckraker in style, maintains that modern America is a jungle. From the standpoint of population, he may be correct. Yet he claims that there are no answers in a jungle, "only cries of victory or death." It has always been true that when a large group speaks, the voice of the majority is heard. But rarely are these voices so decisive as victory or death. Today we are becoming more cautious of snap judgments than we have been in the past.

It is true that America has blemished its reputation abroad through various criminal acts, most notably the assassinations of John and Robert Kennedy and Dr. Martin Luther King. This reflection has shocked America. But to say that nobody cares would be overlooking the views of many Americans. The mass media are playing a greater role than ever before to bring the daily bad news home. Children today are forced to grow up with it and consequently learn to live with it. We are not narcotized to the bad news, we simply are forced not to let it disturb us to an inordinate extent. If we did allow ourselves to become emotionally involved, the mental effects could be serious. This is a far cry from the fact that nobody cares.

To say that nobody cares is far from the truth. The energy of youth is awesome, flowing, beautiful. Adults must learn to recognize this potential and work to harness it toward everyone's benefit. The author speaks of "pseudo-revolutionary insurrections without goals." How many times have you attempted to perform a task that you didn't know exactly how to tackle? This is the position of youth today. They are not revolutionaries; they are simply expressing themselves in the best way they know, and that generally means getting out and demonstrating. And it has worked, because people are watching them now. They see a giant task in trying to correct so many of the injustices of the past, and react by calling the entire mess a shambles. Perhaps they have been a little too hasty in making their remarks, but with time and patience they will see a means to deal with each problem. What is important is that they are concerned.

The author finds great pleasure in mocking modern youth's musical tastes. He must have wasted (spent) considerable time in research, trying to correlate how loud rock music is a means of expressing revolution! Each generation in America has had its own music, games, pranks, cars, and dress, and each seems equally absurd at the time. The point is that youth today are more interested in the world around them and what happens to it than ever before. Were young people of the past demonstrating for world peace, ecology, and civil rights? No. This doesn't mean they didn't care. They probably didn't know or weren't informed as to how to help. The natural reaction when you see something wrong is to yell, demonstrate, strike. These are powerful actions appropriate for certain situations. Already students are learning that there are better ways of achieving favorable results.

Granted, this generation's drug culture has been a scar on its face. But look at what's happening. At the time "To Abolish Children" was written, drug use was on the rise and it looked like nothing could stop it. But with the help of doctors and interested people, a massive campaign to show how wasteful drugs really are has been effective in slowing the use of hard drugs. And what's fantastic is that kids have opened talk lines and help centers to give their fellow men assistance should trouble arise.

The author suggests a seven-point program to "stop the strangulation of American life by children." His plans are hardly feasible and the most violent radical might find them a bit hasty. What the author doesn't realize, or is afraid to realize, is that if he did "abolish children" he would strangle America. We need the vitality of youth to add spice to our society. If the youth of America are truly as revolutionary as the author claims, shipping them off to an area simply for children would result in a mass riot. This type of action isn't likely, however, because most Americans realize the importance of strong healthy youth.

America's strength in the years ahead lies in her youth. By understanding that even adults are merely grown up children and that our society is a child trying to grow up in the world, perhaps we can better our relationship with our youth.

—DAVID P. TOUTANT

Before and After: Shapiro Revisited

The pivotal word of this essay is "youth." To unlock Shapiro's meaning, the word "youth" must be defined.

When I read the essay for the first time, I was utterly confused by it. After reading it over and establishing the meaning of the word I find an interpretation that satisfies me. What I am going to do in this paper is present my interpretation both before I clearly defined the word "youth" and after I came up with an adequate definition. This is how the first version read:

"Karl Shapiro is definitely not my style writer. I can't see how he could actually appeal to anyone if this work is representative of his writing style. Throughout the entire essay he uses distorted images to try to prove his point; 'the soft rotten killer with his call-girl WASP girlfriend' and 'the wave of male and female hysterics with guitars and brotherhood lyrics' are two examples of his generalizations.

"He paints a very abstract picture of both the youth of today and the adults of yesterday. The youth of today are led about like sheep to the slaughter by any number of social deviates and lunatics, according to Mr. Shapiro. If our generation is so totally corrupt why is his generation so infallible? As the saying goes, 'As the twig is bent, so the tree will grow.' That is the reason we are supposedly the way we are, it is not our fault, it is your fault, Karl Shapiro—you and your generation!"

That's how my first reaction to Karl Shapiro and his essay sounded. It's a pretty shaky attempt at undercutting him, so I felt I should rethink the essay. Another point that made me review my thinking is that I looked into Karl Shapiro's background. He seems to be a man who had always sided with youth, and I cannot see a man changing his view that drastically. What did Shapiro mean by his essay then? Perhaps what we should ask is what does Shapiro mean by *youth?*

It seems that his statements "The American adult must battle 'youth' to the death! 'Youth' is a figment of the American imagination which is destroying America itself," are the most important of the paper. "Youth" does not mean here the age of a person; rather "youth" is a state of mind—an immature, self-centered state of mind.

For example, youth is not behind the drug movement—Shapiro's "youth" is. "Youth" in this case is the man who makes money. He is the pusher—the official who holds out his palm and turns his head, the man who has something to gain from the sale of drugs.

I've also changed by thinking about some images that Shapiro painted. Why is it we think of the "soft and rotten killer?" Because he is the "youth" in the news headlines. Charles Manson, Richard Speck, Sirhan Sirhan are in the newspaper banners across the nation. You don't hear about planes that don't crash. How many fit into this sleazy mold Shapiro has shaped? Not many, and he knows this. What Mr. Shapiro is showing us is the extreme end of the spectrum. There are no more "bad" children now than there were during his youthful days.

The opening sentence implies to me that Shapiro will not betray youth. The essay is merely pointing out the pitfalls that the real youth can fall into. Shapiro has written about the shortcomings of our generation knowing that this age has no more faults than his and that the future will be in the hands of this age's youth.

—DAVID J. RHODES

Interpretations of "Youth"

Each individual reader of Karl Shapiro's essay "To Abolish Children" will reach a new and different interpretation of what the author is trying to say. That there are so many possible ways in which this essay can be interpreted can be traced to the style the author uses. Throughout the essay the reader can detect satire, irony, and symbolism used effectively to make a point. As just one reader, I have derived several possible meanings from the title concerning the abolishment of children. Also the different meanings of the "youth" that Shapiro suggests ridding the world of include: radical adolescents, close-minded American adults, and on a broader scale, the entire "youth-oriented" society in which we live.

Perhaps the author was indirectly trying to represent (through the voice he uses in the essay) an attitude held by a large portion of American people. The pompous style of this essay, as exaggerated and over-generalized as it may seem, is merely another device used by Shapiro to emphasize that a great many people actually do see youth as the cause of all their problems. The purpose of this obviously one-sided and opinionated viewpoint is to put the reader on the defensive. The effect is to make him realize how childish this attitude really is. Therefore, when he recommends abolishing children in the title (and again in his seventh solution to America's problems) he is not speaking of literally ridding the country of youth. Rather, he suggests trying to heal the sick minds and childlike mentalities that (among other limitations) can see fault *only* in the "younger generation."

Another interpretation of this essay is that the author really believes in what he is saying and sees youth as the root of all the trouble in this country. If the essay is interpreted in this way, the author is not using satire or any other indirect method of expressing his ideas. Instead, he states his views with honesty and straightforwardness. The main problems that he sees youth responsible for are: the gradual breakdown of communication between people, the dissidence that is spreading throughout America, and the betrayal of the country. In order to reinforce his opinions concerning the corruptness of youth, he also takes a minority of America's youth and makes them into a majority. "These are the heirs to the kingdom of Wall Street—the latest generation of betrayers and destroyers."

Still another way in which this essay can be interpreted is to assume that there is some truth in what he is saying but that he purposely exaggerates and over-generalizes. This technique can be a means to several different ends. He overstates his points about the destructiveness of youth in order to reach conclusions about the over-emphasis put on "youth" in general. He examines youth-orientated commercials and the well-known concept "anyone over the age of twenty-one or twenty-five is portrayed as an idiot." These are just two examples of the "anti-adultist" society that is engulfing America. One result of the youth-mania in society is a stagnation of the American mind: "The cultivation of American Youth with a capital Y has kept the growth of the American mind off balance since perhaps the early nineteenth century." Too many people spend all their time trying to be or wishing that they were young. Instead of developing their minds, they are satisfied with the childlike mentality that seems to prevail. In proposing remedies for this anti-adultism he denies youth many of the privileges that they now enjoy. According to this interpretation of the essay, denials of the things that seem to make youth so "appealing" would make people less and less eager to search for the "fountain of youth" and much more satisfied with being who they are with what they have.

Considering all these different interpretations, the closing sentence ("Youth is a figment of the American imagination which is destroying America itself") means "youth" is the close-minded American who finds faults not within himself but only in the "younger generation." "Youth" finds fault with the radical adolescent who has only destructive criticisms to make about America and the "youth-oriented" society which is not satisfied with what they have. These are the "Youth" that "the American adult must battle to the death."

—KATHERINE KAISER

Further Selections for Annotation

The rather large amount of material presented here and in the previous chapter on Shapiro's "To Abolish Children" is an extensive exercise in the use of marginal comments applied to one central source. So that this discussion doesn't appear to be a commentary on one essay, three short selections follow. In addition to providing further material to annotate, each essay illustrates some of the key concepts discussed throughout this book. In "Reading"—a chapter from *Walden*—Thoreau explores the differences between "mindless" reading for information and the active reading of a "self-reliant" and probing mind. Thoreau describes reading "in a high sense, not that which lulls us as a luxury and suffers the noble faculties to sleep the while, but what we have to stand on tip-toe to read and devote our most alert and wakeful hours to." That alertness is stimulated by thinking in the margin. In "A Modest Proposal," Jonathan Swift creates one of the most famous examples in literature of the ironic persona (see chapter 2). Brief "starter" marginal comments accompany each selection for purposes of illustration. It is also interesting to read essays that grow directly out of underlinings and marginal notations. "Literature Is the 'Stuffy' Art" is a frivolous tour through a mass of reading. The essay is a "progress report" from a large collection of notes tracing the recurring use of one word in the history of literature.

Henry David Thoreau
Reading, from _Walden_

With a little more deliberation in the choice of their pursuits, all men would perhaps become essentially <u>students and observers</u>, for certainly their nature and destiny are interesting to all alike. In accumulating property for ourselves or our posterity, in founding a family or a state, or acquiring fame even, we are mortal; but <u>in dealing with truth we are immortal, and need fear no change nor accident.</u> The oldest Egyptian or Hindoo philosopher raised a corner of the veil from the statue of the divinity; and still the trembling robe remains raised, and I gaze upon as fresh a glory as he did, since <u>it was I in him that was then so bold, and it is he in me that now reviews the vision.</u> No dust has settled on that robe; no time has elapsed since that divinity was revealed. <u>That time which we really improve, or which is improvable, is neither past, present, nor future.</u>

My residence was more favorable, not only to thought, but to serious reading, than a university; and though I was beyond the range of the ordinary circulating library, I had <u>more than ever come within the influence of those books which circulate round the world,</u> whose sentences were first written on bark, and are now merely copied from time to time on to linen paper. Says the poet Mîr Camar Uddîn Mast, "Being seated to run through the region of the spiritual world; I have had this advantage in books. To be intoxicated by a single glass of wine; I have experienced this pleasure when I have drunk the liquor of the esoteric doctrines." I kept Homer's Iliad on my table through the summer, though I looked at his page only now and then. Incessant labor with my hands, at first, for I had my house to finish and my beans to hoe at the same time, made more study impossible. Yet I sustained myself by the prospect of such reading in future. I read one or two shallow books of travel in the intervals of my work, till that employment made me ashamed of myself, and I asked where it was then that _I_ lived.

The student may read Homer or Æschylus in the Greek without danger of dissipation or luxuriousness, for it implies that he in some measure emulate their heroes, and consecrate morning hours to their pages. The heroic books, even if

Emerson's "self-reliance"

links with the past

emphasis on the reader, on the self confronting books

printed in the character of our mother tongue, will always be in a language dead to degenerate times; and we must laboriously seek the meaning of each word and line, conjecturing a larger sense than common use permits out of what wisdom and valor and generosity we have. The modern cheap and fertile press, with all its translations, has done little to bring us nearer to the heroic writers of antiquity. They seem as solitary, and the letter in which they are printed as rare and curious, as ever. It is worth the expense of youthful days and costly hours, if you learn only some words of an ancient language, which are raised out of the trivialness of the street, to be perpetual suggestions and provocations. It is not in vain that the farmer remembers and repeats the few Latin words which he has heard. Men sometimes speak as if the study of the classics would at length make way for more modern and practical studies; but the adventurous student will always study classics, in whatever language they may be written and however ancient they may be. For what are the classics but the noblest recorded thoughts of man? They are the only oracles which are not decayed, and there are such answers to the most modern inquiry in them as Delphi and Dodona never gave. We might as well omit to study Nature because she is old. To read well, that is, to read true books in a true spirit, is a noble exercise, and one that will task the reader more than any exercise which the customs of the day esteem. It requires a training such as the athletes underwent, the steady intention almost of the whole life to this object. Books must be read as deliberately and reservedly as they were written. It is not enough even to be able to speak the language of that nation by which they are written, for there is a memorable interval between the spoken and the written language, the language heard and the language read. The one is commonly transitory, a sound, a tongue, a dialect merely, almost brutish, and we learn it unconsciously, like the brutes, of our mothers. The other is the maturity and experience of that; if that is our mother tongue, this is our father tongue, a reserved and select expression, too significant to be heard by the ear, which we must be born again in order to speak. The crowds of men who merely *spoke* the Greek and Latin tongues in the middle ages were not entitled by the accident of birth to *read* the works of genius written in those languages; for these were not written in that Greek or Latin which they knew, but in the select language of literature. They had not learned the nobler dialects of Greece and Rome, but the very materials on which they were written were waste paper to them, and they prized instead a cheap contemporary literature. But when the several nations of Europe had acquired distinct though rude written languages of their own, sufficient for the purposes of their rising literatures, then first learning revived, and scholars were enabled to discern from that remoteness the treasures of antiquity. What the Roman and Grecian multitude could not *hear*, after the lapse of ages a few scholars *read*, and a few scholars only are still reading it.

However much we may admire the orator's occasional bursts of eloquence, the noblest written words are commonly as far behind or above the fleeting spoken language as the firmament with its stars is behind the clouds. *There* are the stars, and they who can may read them. The astronomers forever comment on and observe them. They are not exhalations like our daily colloquies and vaporous breath. What is called eloquence in the forum is commonly found to be rhetoric in the study. The orator yields to the inspiration of a transient occasion, and speaks to the mob before him, to those who can *hear* him; but the writer, whose more equable life is his occasion, and who would be distracted by the event and the crowd which inspire the orator, speaks to the intellect and heart of mankind, to all in any age who can *understand* him.

No wonder that Alexander carried the Iliad with him on his expeditions in a precious casket. A written word is the choicest of relics. It is something at once more intimate with us and more universal than any other work of art. It is the work of art nearest to life itself. It may be translated into every language, and not only be read but actually breathed from all human lips; —not be represented on canvas or in marble only, but be carved out of the breath of life itself. The symbol of an ancient man's thought becomes a modern man's speech. Two thousand summers have imparted to the monuments of Grecian literature, as to her marbles, only a maturer golden and autumnal tint, for they have carried their own serene and celestial atmosphere into all lands to protect them against the corrosion of time. Books are the treasured wealth of the world and the fit inheritance of generations and nations. Books, the oldest and the best, stand naturally and rightfully on the shelves of every cottage. They have no cause of their own to plead, but while they enlighten and sustain the reader his common sense will not refuse them. Their authors are a natural and irresistible aristocracy in every society, and, more than kings or emperors, exert an influence on mankind. When the illiterate and perhaps scornful trader has earned by

Similarities between reading the stars and reading books?

how?

enterprise and industry his coveted leisure and independence, and is admitted to the circles of wealth and fashion, he turns inevitably at last to those still higher but yet inaccessible circles of intellect and genius, and is sensible only of the imperfection of his culture and the vanity and insufficiency of all his riches, and further proves his good sense by the pains which he takes to secure for his children that intellectual culture whose want he so keenly feels; and thus it is that he becomes the founder of a family.

Those who have not learned to read the ancient classics in the language in which they were written must have a very imperfect knowledge of the history of the human race; for it is remarkable that no transcript of them has ever been made into any modern tongue, unless our civilization itself may be regarded as such a transcript. Homer has never yet been printed in English, nor Æschylus, nor Virgil even, —works as refined, as solidly done, and as beautiful almost as the morning itself; for later writers, say what we will of their genius, have rarely, if ever, equalled the elaborate beauty and finish and the lifelong and heroic literary labors of the ancients. They only talk of forgetting them who never knew them. It will be soon enough to forget them when we have the learning and the genius which will enable us to attend to and appreciate them. That age will be rich indeed when those relics which we call Classics, and the still older and more than classic but even less known Scriptures of the nations, shall have still further accumulated, when the Vaticans shall be filled with Vedas and Zendavestas and Bibles, with Homers and Dantes and Shakespeares, and all the centuries to come shall have successively deposited their trophies in the forum of the world. By such a pile we may hope to scale heaven at last.

The works of the great poets have never yet been read by mankind, for only great poets can read them. They have only been read as the multitude read the stars, at most astrologically, not astronomically. Most men have learned to read to serve a paltry convenience, as they have learned to cipher in order to keep accounts and not be cheated in trade; but of reading as a noble intellectual exercise they know little or nothing; yet this only is reading, in a high sense, not that which lulls us as a luxury and suffers the nobler faculties to sleep the while, but what we have to stand on tip-toe to read and devote our most alert and wakeful hours to.

I think that having learned our letters we should read the best that is in literature, and not be forever repeating our a b abs, and words of one syllable, in the fourth or fifth classes,

[margin notes: only poets can read poets?]

[margin notes: reading for information vs. reading for insight and pleasure]

[margin notes: active reading]

sitting on the lowest and foremost form all our lives. Most men are satisfied if they read or hear read, and perchance have been convicted by the wisdom of one good book, the Bible, and for the rest of their lives vegetate and dissipate their faculties in what is called easy reading. There is a work in several volumes in our Circulating Library entitled Little Reading, which I thought referred to a town of that name which I had not been to. There are those who, like cormorants and ostriches, can digest all sorts of this, even after the fullest dinner of meats and vegetables, for they suffer nothing to be wasted. If others are the machines to provide this provender, they are the machines to read it. They read the nine thousandth tale about Zebulon and Sephronia, and how they loved as none had ever loved before, and neither did the course of their true love run smooth, —at any rate, how it did run and stumble, and get up again and go on! how some poor unfortunate got up on to a steeple, who had better never have gone up as far as the belfry; and then, having needlessly got him up there, the happy novelist rings the bell for all the world to come together and hear, O dear! how he did get down again! For my part, I think that they had better metamorphose all such aspiring heroes of universal noveldom into man weather-cocks, as they used to put heroes among the constellations, and let them swing round there till they are rusty, and not come down at all to bother honest men with their pranks. The next time the novelist rings the bell I will not stir though the meeting-house burn down. "The Skip of the Tip-Toe-Hop, a Romance of the Middle Ages, by the celebrated author of 'Tittle-Tol-Tan,' to appear in monthly parts; a great rush; don't all come together." All this they read with saucer eyes, and erect and primitive curiosity, and with unwearied gizzard, whose corrugations even yet need no sharpening, just as some little four-year-old bencher his two-cent gilt-covered edition of Cinderella,—without any improvement, that I can see, in the pronunciation, or accent, or emphasis, or any more skill in extracting or inserting the moral. The result is dulness of sight, a stagnation of the vital circulations, and general deliquium and sloughing off of all the intellectual faculties. This sort of gingerbread is baked daily and more sedulously than pure wheat or rye-and-Indian in almost every oven, and finds a surer market.

The best books are not read even by those who are called good readers. What does our Concord culture amount to? There is in this town, with a very few exceptions, no taste for the best or for very good books even in English literature,

differences between lasting art and the merely popular?

WHY NOT?

whose words all can read and spell. Even the college-bred and so-called liberally educated men here and elsewhere have really little or no acquaintance with the English classics; and as for the recorded wisdom of mankind, the ancient classics and Bibles, which are accessible to all who will know of them, there are the feeblest efforts anywhere made to become acquainted with them. I know a woodchopper, of middle age, who takes a French paper, not for news as he says, for he is above that, but to "keep himself in practice," he being a Canadian by birth; and when I ask him what he considers the best thing he can do in this world, he says, beside this, to keep up and add to his English. This is about as much as the college-bred generally do or aspire to do, and they take an English paper for the purpose. One who has just come from reading perhaps one of the best English books will find how many with whom he can converse about it? Or suppose he comes from reading a Greek or Latin classic in the original, whose praises are familiar even to the so-called illiterate; he will find nobody at all to speak to, but must keep silence about it. Indeed, there is hardly the professor in our colleges, who, if he has mastered the difficulties of the language, has proportionally mastered the difficulties of the wit and poetry of a Greek poet, and has any sympathy to impart to the alert and heroic reader; and as for the sacred Scriptures, or Bibles of mankind, who in this town can tell me even their titles? Most men do not know that any nation but the Hebrews have had a scripture. A man, any man, will go considerably out of his way to pick up a silver dollar; but here are golden words, which the wisest men of antiquity have uttered, and whose worth the wise of every succeeding age have assured us of;—and yet we learn to read only as far as Easy Reading, the primers and class-books, and when we leave school, the "Little Reading," and story books, which are for boys and beginners; and our reading, our conversation and thinking, are all on a very low level, worthy only of pygmies and manikins.

lack of attention to "active reading" in schools

I aspire to be acquainted with wiser men than this our Concord soil has produced, whose names are hardly known here. Or shall I hear the name of Plato and never read his book? As if Plato were my townsman and I never saw him,—my next neighbor and I never heard him speak or attended to the wisdom of his words. But how actually is it? His Dialogues, which contain what was immortal in him, lie on the next shelf, and yet I never read them. We are under-bred and low-lived and illiterate; and in this respect I confess I do not make any very broad distinction between the illiterateness

*how does this
compare with
reading
habits now?*

influence

*societal
values
and
education*

of my townsman who cannot read at all and the illiterateness of him who has learned to read only what is for children and feeble intellects. We should be as good as the worthies of antiquity, but partly by first knowing how good they were. We are a race of tit-men, and soar but little higher in our intellectual flights than the columns of the daily paper.

It is not all books that are as dull as their readers. There are probably words addressed to our condition exactly, which, if we could really hear and understand, would be more salutary than the morning or the spring to our lives, and possibly put a new aspect on the face of things for us. How many a man has dated a new era in his life from the reading of a book. The book exists for us perchance which will explain our miracles and reveal new ones. The at present unutterable things we may find somewhere uttered. These same questions that disturb and puzzle and confound us have in their turn occurred to all the wise men; not one has been omitted; and each has answered them, according to his ability, by his words and his life. Moreover, with wisdom we shall learn liberality. The solitary hired man on a farm in the outskirts of Concord, who has had his second birth and peculiar religious experience, and is driven as he believes into silent gravity and exclusiveness by his faith, may think it is not true; but Zoroaster, thousands of years ago, travelled the same road and had the same experience; but he, being wise, knew it to be universal, and treated his neighbors accordingly, and is even said to have invented and established worship among men. Let him humbly commune with Zoroaster then, and through the liberalizing influence of all the worthies, with Jesus Christ himself, and let "our church" go by the board.

We boast that we belong to the nineteenth century and are making the most rapid strides of any nation. But consider how little this village does for its own culture. I do not wish to flatter my townsmen, nor to be flattered by them, for that will not advance either of us. We need to be provoked,—goaded like oxen, as we are, into a trot. We have a comparatively decent system of common schools, schools for infants only; but excepting the half-starved Lyceum in the winter, and latterly the puny beginning of a library suggested by the state, no school for ourselves. We spend more on almost any article of bodily aliment or ailment than on our mental ailment. It is time that we had uncommon schools, that we did not leave off our education when we begin to be men and women. It is time that villages were universities, and their elder inhabitants the fellows of universities, with leisure—if they are indeed so well off—to pursue liberal studies the rest of their lives. Shall the world be confined to one Paris or one Oxford forever? Cannot students be boarded here and get a liberal education under the skies of Concord? Can we not hire some Abelard to lecture to us? Alas! what with foddering the cattle and tending the store, we are kept from school too long, and our education is sadly neglected. In this country, the village should in some respects take the place of the nobleman of Europe. It should be the patron of the fine arts. It is rich enough. It wants only the magnanimity and refinement. It can spend money enough on such things as farmers and traders value, but it is thought Utopian to propose spending money for things which more intelligent men know to be of far more worth. This town has spent seventeen thousand dollars on a town-house, thank fortune or politics, but probably it will not spend so much on living wit, the true meat to put into that shell, in a hundred years. The one hundred and twenty-five dollars annually subscribed for a Lyceum in the winter is better spent than any other equal sum raised in the town. If we live in the nineteenth century, why should we not enjoy the advantages which the nineteenth century offers? Why should our life be in any respect provincial? If we will read newspapers, why not skip the gossip of Boston and take the best newspaper in the world at once?—not be sucking the pap of "neutral family" papers, or browsing "Olive-Branches" here in New England. Let the reports of all the learned societies come to us, and we will see if they know anything. Why should we leave it to Harper & Brothers and Redding & Co. to select our reading? As the nobleman of cultivated taste surrounds himself with whatever conduces to his culture, — genius — learning — wit — books — paintings —statuary—music—philosophical instruments, and the like; so let the village do,—not stop short at a pedagogue, a parson, a sexton, a parish library, and three selectmen, because our pilgrim forefathers got through a cold winter once on a bleak rock with these. To act collectively is according to the spirit of our institutions; and I am confident that, as our circumstances are more flourishing, our means are greater than the nobleman's. New England can hire all the wise men in the world to come and teach her, and board them round the while, and not be provincial at all. That is the *uncommon* school we want. Instead of noblemen, let us have noble villages of men. If it is necessary, omit one bridge over the river, go round a little there, and throw one arch at least over the darker gulf of ignorance which surrounds us.

plea for "modernism"

active reading and "self-reliance".

Jonathan Swift
A Modest Proposal (1729)

For Preventing the Children of Poor People From Being a
Burthen to Their Parents or Country, and for Making Them
Beneficial to the Public.

It is a melancholy object to those who walk through this great
town, or travel in the country, when they see the streets, the
roads, and cabin-doors crowded with beggars of the female
sex, followed by three, four, or six children, *all in rags*, and
importuning every passenger for an alms. These mothers,
instead of being able to work for their honest livelihood, are
forced to employ all their time in strolling, to beg sustenance
for their helpless infants, who, as they grow up, either turn
thieves for want of work, or leave their dear Native Country to
fight for the Pretender in Spain, or sell themselves to the
Barbadoes.

I think it is agreed by all parties that this prodigious
number of children, in the arms, or on the backs, or at the
heels of their mothers, and frequently of their fathers, is in the
present deplorable state of the kingdom a very great additional
grievance; and therefore whoever could find out a fair, cheap,
and easy method of making these children sound useful
members of the commonwealth would deserve so well of the
public as to have his statue set up for a preserver of the nation.

But my intention is very far from being confined to
provide only for the children of professed beggars; it is of a
much greater extent, and shall take in the whole number of
infants at a certain age who are born of parents in effect as little
able to support them as those who demand our charity in the
streets.

As to my own part, having turned my thoughts, for many
years, upon this important subject, and maturely weighed the
several schemes of other projectors, I have always found them
grossly mistaken in their computation. It is true a child, just
dropped from its dam, may be supported by her milk for a
solar year with little other nourishment, at most not above the
value of two shillings, which the mother may certainly get, or

the value in scraps, by her lawful occupation of begging, and it is exactly at one year old that I propose to provide for them, in such a manner as, instead of being a charge upon their parents, or the parish, or wanting food and raiment for the rest of their lives, they shall, on the contrary, contribute to the feeding and partly to the clothing of many thousands.

what was a burden becomes an asset

There is likewise another great advantage in my scheme, that it will prevent those voluntary abortions and that horrid practice of women murdering their bastard children, alas, too frequent among us, sacrificing the poor innocent babes, I doubt, more to avoid the expense than the shame, which would move tears and pity in the most savage and inhuman breast.

The number of souls in this kingdom being usually reckoned one million and a half, of these I calculate there may be about two hundred thousand couple whose wives are breeders from which number I subtract thirty thousand couple who are able to maintain their own children, although I apprehend there cannot be so many under the present distresses of the kingdom, but this being granted, there will remain an hundred and seventy thousand breeders. I again subtract fifty thousand for those women who miscarry, or whose children die by accident or disease within the year. There only remain an hundred and twenty thousand children of poor parents annually born: The question therefore is, how this number shall be reared, and provided for, which, as I have already said, under the present situation of affairs, is utterly impossible by all the methods hitherto proposed, for we can neither employ them in handicraft, or agriculture; we neither build houses (I mean in the country), nor cultivate land: they can very seldom pick up a livelihood by stealing till they arrive at six years old, except where they are of towardly parts, although I confess they learn the rudiments much earlier, during which time they can however be properly looked upon only as *probationers,* as I have been informed by a principal gentleman in the County of Cavan, who protested to me that he never knew above one or two instances under the age of six, even in a part of the kingdom so renowned for the quickest proficiency in that art.

cattle?

cool calculations

question

the art of stealing?

"usefulness" of the children

human merchandise

I am assured by our merchants that a boy or a girl, before twelve years old, is no saleable commodity, and even when they come to this age, they will not yield above three pounds, or three pounds and half-a-crown at most on the Exchange, which cannot turn to account either to the parents or the kingdom, the charge of nutriment and rags having been at least four times that value.

announces the proposal

the proposal in detail

I shall now therefore humbly propose my own thoughts, which I hope will not be liable to the least objection.

I have been assured by a very knowing American of my acquaintance in London, that a young healthy child well nursed is at a year old a <u>most delicious, nourishing, and wholesome food,</u> whether stewed, roasted, baked, or boiled, and I make no doubt that it will equally serve in a fricassee, or a ragout.

I do therefore humbly offer it to public consideration, that of the hundred and twenty thousand children already computed, twenty thousand may be reserved for breed, whereof only one fourth part to be males, which is more than we allow to sheep, black-cattle, or swine, and my reason is that these children are seldom the fruits of marriage, a circumstance not much regarded by our savages, therefore one male will be sufficient to serve four females. That the remaining hundred thousand may at a year old be offered in sale to the persons of quality, and fortune, through the kingdom, always advising the mother to let them suck plentifully in the last month, so as to render them plump, and fat for a good table. A child will make two dishes at an entertainment for friends, and when the family dines alone, the fore or hind quarters will make a reasonable dish, and seasoned with a little pepper or salt will be very good boiled on the fourth day, especially in winter.

I have reckoned upon a medium, that a child just born will weigh 12 pounds, and in a solar year if tolerably nursed increaseth to 28 pounds.

I grant this food will be somewhat dear, and therefore very proper for landlords, who, as they have already devoured most of the parents, seem to have the best title to the children.

Infants' flesh will be in season throughout the year, but more plentiful in March, and a little before and after, for we are told by a grave author, an eminent French physician, that fish being a prolific diet, there are more children born in Roman Catholic countries about nine months after Lent than at any other season; therefore reckoning a year after Lent, the markets will be more glutted than usual, because the number of Popish infants is at least three to one in this kingdom, and therefore it will have one other collateral advantage by lessening the number of Papists among us.

I have already computed the charge of nursing a beggar's child (in which list I reckon all cottagers, labourers, and four-fifths of the farmers) to be about two shillings *per annum*, rags included, and I believe no gentleman would repine to give ten shillings for the carcass of a good fat child, which, as I have

details and outrageous "proposals" increase

said, will make four dishes of excellent nutritive meat, when he hath only some particular friend or his own family to dine with him. Thus the Squire will learn to be a good landlord, and grow popular among his tenants, the mother will have eight shillings net profit, and be fit for work till she produces another child.

Those who are more thrifty (as I must confess the times require) may flay the carcass; the skin of which, artificially dressed, will make admirable gloves for ladies, and summer boots for fine gentlemen.

designates authority

As to our City of Dublin, shambles may be appointed for this purpose, in the most convenient parts of it, and butchers we may be assured will not be wanting, although I rather recommend buying the children alive, and dressing them hot from the knife, as we do roasting pigs.

proposal "refined" by a third party

A very worthy person, a true lover of this country, and whose virtues I highly esteem, was lately pleased, in discoursing on this matter, to offer a refinement upon my scheme. He said that many gentlemen of this kingdom, having of late destroyed their deer, he conceived that the want of venison might be well supplied by the bodies of young lads and maidens, not exceeding fourteen years of age, nor under twelve, so great a number of both sexes in every country being now ready to starve, for want of work and service: and these to be disposed of by their parents if alive, or otherwise by their nearest relations. But with due deference to so excellent a friend, and so deserving a patriot, I cannot be altogether in his sentiments; for as to the males, my American acquaintance assured me from frequent experience that their flesh was generally tough and lean, like that of our schoolboys, by continual exercise, and their taste disagreeable, and to fatten them would not answer the charge. Then as to the females, it would, I think with humble submission, be a loss to the public, because they soon would become breeders themselves: And besides, it is not improbable that some scrupulous people might be apt to censure such a practice (although indeed very unjustly) as a little bordering upon cruelty, which, I confess, hath always been with me the strongest objection against any project, however so well intended.

debate between "friend" and the speaker increases horror

But in order to justify my friend, he confessed that this expedient was put into his head by the famous Psalmanazer, a native of the island Formosa, who came from thence to London, above twenty years ago, and in conversation told my friend that in his country when any young person happened to be put to death, the executioner sold the carcass to persons of quality, as a prime dainty, and that, in his time, the body of a plump girl of fifteen, who was crucified for an attempt to poison the emperor, was sold to his Imperial Majesty's Prime Minister of State, and other great Mandarins of the Court, in joints from the gibbet, at four hundred crowns. Neither indeed can I deny that if the same use were made of several plump young girls in this town, who, without one single groat to their fortunes, cannot stir abroad without a chair, and appear at the playhouse, and assemblies in foreign fineries, which they never will pay for, the kingdom would not be the worse.

*answers
squeamish
critics*

Some persons of a desponding spirit are in great concern about that vast number of poor people, who are aged, diseased, or maimed, and I have been desired to employ my thoughts what course may be taken to ease the nation of so grievous an encumbrance. But I am not in the least pain upon that matter, because it is very well known that they are every day dying, and rotting, by cold, and famine, and filth, and vermin, as fast as can be reasonably expected. And as to the younger labourers they are now in almost as hopeful a condition. They cannot get work, and consequently pine away for want of nourishment, to a degree, that if at any time they are accidentally hired to common labour, they have not strength to perform it; and thus the country and themselves are happily delivered from the evils to come.

*but the
"digression"
is the subject*

*long list of
"advantages"
follows*

I have too long digressed, and therefore shall return to my subject. I think the advantages by the proposal which I have made are obvious and many, as well as of the highest importance.

For first, as I have already observed, it would greatly lessen the number of Papists, with whom we are yearly over-run, being the principal breeders of the nation, as well as our most dangerous enemies, and who stay at home on purpose with a design to deliver the kingdom to the Pretender, hoping to take their advantage by the absence of so many good Protestants, who have chosen rather to leave their country than stay at home, and pay tithes against their conscience to an Episcopal curate.

Secondly, The poorer tenants will have something valuable of their own, which by law be made liable to distress, and help to pay their landlord's rent, their corn and cattle being already seized, and *money a thing unknown.*

Thirdly, Whereas the maintenance of an hundred thousand children, from two years old, and upwards, cannot be computed at less than ten shillings a piece *per annum,* the

everyone
"profits"

nation's stock will be thereby increased fifty thousand pounds *per annum*, besides the profit of a new dish, introduced to the tables of all gentlemen of fortune in the kingdom, who have any refinement in taste, and the money will circulate among ourselves, the goods being entirely of our own growth and manufacture.

Fourthly, The constant breeders, besides the gain of eight shillings sterling *per annum*, by the sale of their children, will be rid of the charge of maintaining them after the first year.

Fifthly, This food would likewise bring great custom to taverns, where the vintners will certainly be so prudent as to procure the best receipts for dressing it up to perfection, and consequently have their houses frequented by all the fine gentlemen, who justly value themselves upon their knowledge in good eating; and a skillful cook, who understands how to oblige his guests, will contrive to make it as expensive as they please.

Sixthly, This would be a great inducement to marriage, which all wise nations have either encouraged by rewards, or enforced by laws and penalties. It would increase the care and tenderness of mothers toward their children, when they were sure of a settlement for life, to the poor babes, provided in some sort by the public to their annual profit instead of expense. We should see an honest emulation among the married women, which of them could bring the fattest child to the market, men would become as fond of their wives, during the time of their pregnancy, as they are now of their mares in foal, their cows in calf, or sows when they are ready to farrow, nor offer to beat or kick them (as it is too frequent a practice) for fear of a miscarriage.

Many other advantages might be enumerated: For instance, the addition of some thousand carcasses in our exportation of barrelled beef; the propagation of swine's flesh, and improvement in the art of making good bacon, so much wanted among us by the great destruction of pigs, too frequent at our tables, which are no way comparable in taste or magnificence to a well-grown, fat yearling child, which roasted whole will make a considerable figure at a Lord Mayor's feast, or any other public entertainment. But this and many others I omit, being studious of brevity.

projected
results

Supposing that one thousand families in this city would be constant customers for infants' flesh, besides others who might have it at merry-meetings, particularly weddings and christenings, I compute that Dublin would take off annually about twenty thousand carcasses, and the rest of the kingdom (where probably they will be sold somewhat cheaper) the remaining eighty thousand.

I can think of no one objection that will possibly be raised against this proposal, unless it should be urged that the number of people will be thereby much lessened in the kingdom. This I freely own, and it was indeed one principal design in offering it to the world. I desire the reader will observe, that I calculate my remedy for this one individual *Kingdom of Ireland, and for no other that ever was, is, or, I think, ever can be upon earth.* Therefore let no man talk to me of other expedients: *Of taxing our absentees at five shillings a pound: Of using neither clothes, nor household furniture, except what is of our own growth and manufacture: Of utterly rejecting the materials and instruments that promote foreign luxury: Of curing the expensiveness of pride, vanity, idleness, and gaming in our women: Of introducing a vein of parsimony, prudence, and temperance: Of learning to love our Country, wherein we differ even from* LAPLANDERS, *and the inhabitants of* TOPINAMBOO: *Of quitting our animosities and factions, nor act any longer like the Jews, who were murdering one another at the very moment their city was taken: Of being a little cautious not to sell our country and consciences for nothing: Of teaching landlords to have at least one degree of mercy toward their tenants. Lastly, of putting a spirit of honesty, industry, and skill into our shopkeepers, who, if a resolution could now be taken to buy only our native goods, would immediately unite to cheat and exact upon us in the price, the measure, and the goodness, nor could ever yet be brought to make one fair proposal of just dealing, though often and earnestly invited to it.*

Therefore I repeat, let no man talk to me of these and the like expedients, till he hath at least some glimpse of hope that there will ever be some hearty and sincere attempt to put them in practice.

But as to myself, having been wearied out for many years with offering vain, idle, visionary thoughts, and at length utterly despairing of success, I fortunately fell upon this proposal, which as it is wholly new, so it hath something solid and real, of no expense and little trouble, full in our own power, and whereby we can incur no danger in *disobliging* ENGLAND. For this kind of commodity will not bear exportation, the flesh being too tender a consistence to admit a long continuance in salt, *although perhaps I could name a country which would be glad to eat up our whole nation without it.*

[margin notes:]

the other "expedients" are good solutions which he wants to dismiss

But he gets them said in this form

Speaker contrasts "vain" thoughts (read "good") with this "proposal" (read "preposterous")

Double irony here— consistently says one thing and means another—

After all I am not so violently bent upon my own opinion as to reject any offer, proposed by wise men, which shall be found equally innocent, cheap, easy, and effectual. But before something of that kind shall be advanced in contradiction to my scheme, and offering a better, I desire the author, or authors, will be pleased maturely to consider two points. First, as things now stand, how they will be able to find food and raiment for an hundred thousand useless mouths and backs. And secondly, there being a round million of creatures in human figure, throughout this kingdom, whose whole subsistence put into a common stock would leave them in debt two millions of pounds sterling; adding those, who are beggars by profession, to the bulk of farmers, cottagers, and labourers with their wives and children, who are beggars in effect. I desire those politicians, who dislike my overture, and may perhaps be so bold to attempt an answer, that they will first ask the parents of these mortals whether they would not at this day think it a great happiness to have been sold for food at a year old, in the manner I prescribe, and thereby have avoided such a perpetual scene of misfortunes as they have since gone through, by the oppression of landlords, the impossibility of paying rent without money or trade, the want of common sustenance, with neither house nor clothes to cover them from the inclemencies of the weather, and the most inevitable prospect of entailing the like, or greater miseries upon their breed for ever.

Summary and humble submission of the "proposal"

I profess in the sincerity of my heart that I have not the least personal interest in endeavoring to promote this necessary work, having no other motive than the *public good of my country, by advancing our trade, providing for infants, relieving the poor, and giving some pleasure to the rich.* I have no children by which I can propose to get a single penny; the youngest being nine years old, and my wife past child-bearing.

Ronald Primeau
Literature Is the "Stuffy" Art *

A student recently confronted me with the maxim that most poets, novelists, and playwrights suffer from a disease he called "universal stuffiness." Trying to be "relevant," I agreed that literature on the whole was perhaps the stuffiest of the stuffy pursuits called the arts. I then assigned him a term project calling for the demonstration of his statement. By the time we talked about his investigations the next week, he had reached some tentative conclusions: the stuffiness of literature is pervasive throughout the whole of English and American literature; it transcends movements, traditions, and mainstreams; Shakespeare was the stuffiest of them all by far; and it really isn't so bad to be stuffy after all, if it's done right. We agreed, then, that the primary business of reading literature is an effort to experience as much of its stuff as possible. Hence, the stuffiness of critical writing, teaching, and so on. Our discussion finally led, surprisingly enough, to a question worthy of Socrates: What, then, is the stuff of stuff?

So it really isn't all that bad to be stuffy. After all, Whitman describes the grass as "the flag of my disposition, out of hopeful green stuff woven." And Whitman himself is "stuffed with the stuff that is coarse and stuffed with the stuff that is fine." He is large and contains multitudes—of stuff. We sat there and discussed all this, starting to throw around quotations. And we didn't think much of it was in any way significant at first. But then we began to see that writers refer to various kinds of stuff quite regularly and that they use the term with deliberation and at crucial times in their works, and that the term often serves a function where no other will do— expressing an almost non-verbal experience bringing the medium of language to perhaps it farthest limits. My student's research thus had me looking for an explanation of why being stuffy on paper isn't so bad after all.

Embarking on a study of this phenomenon, I wanted ultimately to check precisely how people use the word "stuff" in everyday language. The dictionary says it's "(1) material to be

---

*© 1973 by Loyola University, New Orleans. Reprinted by permission of the *New Orleans Review.*

worked up in manufacture or out of which anything is to be or may be formed; raw material; hence, any material regarded indefinitely; as lava is curious *stuff,* (2) the elemental part; essence; as, he was of good *stuff.*" We stuff envelopes and turkeys, in basketball a center stuffs a basket, a pitcher puts stuff on his curve ball, we stuff ourselves with food, we display stuffed dummies and animals, we ask someone if he has the stuff for one thing or another—and such stuff (there I go again). But the word in most of these usages reaches beyond the realm of explainable language and thought, carrying a groping toward essences that cannot be verbalized. Because this sounds very much like the experience literature often seeks to convey, it naturally gets a bit stuffy at times.

Shakespeare is worse than most. A. C. Bradley dealt with his stuffiness long ago actually: "His tragic characters are made of the stuff we find within ourselves and within the persons who surround them." Bradley also saw in *King Lear* Shakespeare's attempt to "free himself from the perilous stuff that weighed upon his heart." And so he "wrought this stuff into the stormy music of his greatest poem." Sounds stuffy, indeed; but let's trace the kind of stuff we find in his plays.

In *Romeo and Juliet,* Capulet describes Paris as "stuffed, as they say, with honorable parts." Simple enough description. Similarly, Portia in *The Merchant of Venice* matter-of-factly declares, "what stuff 'tis made of, whereof it is born, I am to learn." And Don Pedro in *Much Ado*: "The barber's men hath been seen with him; and the old ornament of his cheek hath already stuffed tennis balls." Seemingly frivolous uses multiply: "What stuff wilt have a kirtle of?" and "I'm stuffed, cousin; I cannot smell."

But we look to Shakespeare for an explanation of the stuff of life, and the more famous references provide such eminently quotable philosophy. Prospero's "We are such stuff as dreams are made on" and Sir Toby's "Youth's a stuff will not endure" are among the most remembered. Yet there is also the ironic "Yet do I hold it the very stuff of conscience to do no contrived murder" and the poignant "Horribly stuffed with the epithets of war" of *Othello* as well as Antony's "Ambition should be made of sterner stuff" in *Julius Caesar.* In each case, the stuff is the dynamic energy of life itself, and the creation of being is a structuring of this primal stuff. In his plays on the whole, Shakespeare is attempting to wring meaning out of this human stuff.

The bard thus uses his stuff carefully. In response to Hamlet's apostrophe to man speech, Rosencrantz replies: "There was no such stuff in my thoughts." Speaking to the Queen, Hamlet cries, "And let me wring your heart; for so I shall, if it be made of penetrable stuff." And the King tells Laertes, "you must not think that we are made of stuff so flat and dull that we can let our beard be shook with danger and think it pastime." Plotting against Edgar, Edmund confides, "If I find him comforting the king, it will stuff his suspicion more fully." Finally, *Macbeth* carries in it the heavy stuff that Bradley refers to. Lady Macbeth expresses her approval of her husband's actions: "O proper stuff." And yet Macbeth seeks a remedy for his wife's strange malady as he seeks to "cleanse the stuff'd bosom of that perilous stuff which weighs upon the heart." Characteristically, literature becomes as stuffy as it can at this point and the doctor advises Macbeth as he must: "Therein the patient must minister to himself." All this is reason enough for George III to ask if there was ever "such stuff as great as part of Shakespeare" and to follow with "Is there not sad stuff?"

My investigations led me to the discovery that Shakespeare's use of the stuffy found further expression later in American literature and that perhaps the word itself had become more Americanized than the stuffy English would like to admit. But I also found it in use regularly from Dryden to Auden, from Browning to G. K. Chesterton. While Dryden was to refer to "such woeful stuff as I or Shadwell write," Dr. Johnson voiced his critical opinion of *Ossian*: "Sir, a man might write such stuff forever, if he would *abandon* his mind to it." And like Shakespeare, Browning approaches the elemental in his stuffiness: "I count life just a stuff to try the soul's strength on." Less profound with perhaps the same basic meaning is Chesterton's "Lord Lilac was of slighter stuff. Lord Lilac had had quite enough." Finally, Auden half-whimsically philosophises: "Loose ends and jumble of our common world. And stuff and nonsense of our own free will."

Wandering between categories of English and American literature, I found stuffiness even creeping into the tales of Lewis Carroll, the nonsense verse of Edward Lear, and the revered *Rubáiyyát* of Omar Khayyám. In Fitzgerald's translation we find some stuff among the loaf of bread, the jug of wine, and thou: "one half so precious as the stuff they sell." Significantly also, there is a dimension of the stuffy in Alice's Wonderland: "'I have answered three questions and that is enough,' said his father; 'don't give yourself airs! Do you think I can listen all day to such stuff? Be off or I'll kick you downstairs.'" That is one way to deal with a stuffy monologue, and here the meaning is closer to my student's original assertion. But I'm not so sure Edward Lear's reference lends any further support: "How pleasant to know Mr. Lear! Who has written such volumes of stuff! Some think him ill tempered and queer, but a few think him pleasant enough." Is Lear really so far from Shakespeare or from Josiah Royce who, changing Prospero a little, says that "The world is such stuff as ideas are made of "?

In any case, when the stuffy art crossed the ocean, some things changed, some remained the same. Predictably, the Franklin D. H. Lawrence called "cunning little Benjamin" also knew his Shakespeare: "Dost thou love life? Then do not squander time which is the stuff life is made of." Alongside Whitman's "hopeful green stuff" we can place Melville's "Here's stout stuff for woe to work on," the "coronation stuff" in *Moby Dick*, and Henry James' "the lost stuff of consciousness" in "The Beast of the Jungle" as well as his further references in *Wings of the Dove*: "with such stuff as the strange English girl was made of, such stuff that . . . she had never known." Even Faulkner refers to "that same figment-stuff warped out of all experience." Characteristically, Hemingway has Robert Jordan tell himself to "cut out all that dying stuff." And in *The Sun Also Rises* Bill quips, "Road to hell paved with unbought stuffed dogs."

Beyond these mere cursory mentions, Eliot's concern with a certain kind of stuff is central to "The Hollow Men": "We are the hollow men. We are the stuffed men. Leaning together." And in his commentary on the poem, Donald Heiney uses the same motif: "The hollow men are the citizens of modern Western culture, synthetically stuffed with opinions, ideas, and faiths they cannot feel." Whether dealing with primal stuff or simple stuff, American writers have long recognized their stuffiness. Thus a collection of WPA writings in 1937 was entitled *American Stuff*.

A significant body of Black American poetry reflects a similar probing of elemental stuff. Frank Horne speaks of "The wise guys who tell me that Christmas is Kid Stuff," hoping that "we can get back some of that kid stuff born two thousand years ago." And in "Symphony" Horne builds up through a catalog effect toward the elemental "stuff of the symphony of life." Similarly, Helene Johnson describes "the way your hair shines in the spotlight like it was the real stuff." Commenting on the excesses of emotion, G. C. Oden asks, "Does flight depend upon such feathered things? Or is it air? I do not trust the stuff."

In the American tradition, the drama has been the predominant vehicle for the pursuit of stuff. From O'Neill to Albee, the theatre has strongly upheld the tradition of the stuffy.

Mr. Brown in O'Neill's *The Great God Brown* says, "Billy's got the stuff in him to win, if he'll only work hard enough." And in Sherwood's *The Petrified Forest*, Squier thinks Gabby has "heroic stuff in her." In Odets' *Awake and Sing*, Ralph declares, "I got the stuff to go ahead." Behrman's *End of Summer* displays two distinct kinds of the stuffy. Kenneth is in the pattern we have been observing all along when he says, "I deal scientifically with the human stuff around me." But Will is a little more colloquial in his "when you are stuffed and inert with everything you want, then will be the time for me." Then there's Nick in Saroyan's *The Time of Your Life:* "I stood behind that bar listening to the God-damned stuff and cried like a baby"—and also his "They give everybody stuff they shouldn't have." Finally, Albee's Martha brings it all home as she spits out, "Maybe Georgie-boy didn't have the stuff." In varying degrees, the stuffiest parts of these plays carefully examine the elemental stuff of human existence in an effort to shape it into desirable patterns of reality, wringing a meaning out of that stuff which approaches the undefinable. At the limits of language the strengths and limitations of literature's stuff meet.

Now what does all this stuffiness mean? My student presented his conclusions in a kaleidoscopic impression of the peculiar kinds of stuffiness literature affords its audience. In literary history the project resulted in a developing motif through periods, traditions, genres. And there was a visual dimension to the study in an attempt to deal with the experiences available at the limits of language—where the word "stuff" serves where no other will do. Every study has its stuff—history the stuff of events, philosophy the stuff of truth and being, the sciences the stuff of the physical world and living organisms, anthropology the stuff of man's origins and behavior. Literature's stuff may just be the stuff of stuff.

Summary/Review

Getting started on paper and discovering the organization within your own thoughts help develop a topic which you can follow through to a finished product. Using an outline of the structure of your own thinking, you should be able to limit or focus a topic and then emphasize specific points within a larger context. A study of sample essays written from marginal comments and inductive outlines illustrates the relationships between a writer's earliest recorded responses, developed marginal notations and outlines, and a detailed and smooth finished product.

6/ Building Momentum: Transitions

Readers find meaning in what they read when they perceive pattern, when they discover relationships between statements. Writers communicate with their audiences by establishing clearly observable relationships between words, phrases, sentences, and paragraphs. The methodical use of transitional words and phrases is a primary technique through which the writer builds pattern and momentum into an essay. Attention to marginal comments again helps a reader to understand and to develop personal thinking in the form in which it works best.

Human beings generally respond to external stimuli in some kind of pattern. Although the shape of any response is not always easy to see, the progression from statement to statement determines the organization and ultimate meaning. This pattern that emerges from within is generally known as context. A reader who takes a statement "out of context" is assigning a meaning without regard to the relationship of that statement to others that lead up to or follow from it. To put a remark "in its context" is to look for pattern and to relate each part to an overall whole.

Now all this may sound rather abstract and may seem like a long way around to why effective transitions are crucial in marginal comments. Quite simply, any reaction in the margin makes sense only in relation to other reactions. Initial impressions build up to more developed responses. A reader adds to, qualifies, draws conclusions from, or even changes responses while reading. Marginal comments must reflect the shape of your thinking as a reader if you are to be able to return to your notes for accurate representations of your reading. Similarly, a writer must use every device available to build pattern and momentum in every stage of his or her thinking from marginal comments to finished product.

Transitional words and phrases are an essential part of any attempt to communicate more than one statement at any one time. As a reader, your ability to record your responses and then to communicate them in writing depends, to a significant degree, on your ability to watch carefully the patterns in your reading and to reproduce the patterns for your audience.

When you have recorded your reactions to what you have read in marginal comments and organized your responses from within by creating a unified point of view, you must then build momentum into the form you choose to reach an audience. Transitional words and phrases are the most direct way to make first impressions cohere even in the very first stages of marginal comments. Such structural cohesiveness is especially important because a writer's audience cannot be expected to see the internal workings of the writer's thinking as it developed. It is the writer's job to make that pattern observable.

Even when a workable system of marginal comments gets going, it needs momentum to keep itself going. The most significant, subjectively enriched, and "gutsy" essay isn't much without organization. Often the difference between effective structure and the unintelligible is little more than transitions that tie things together in the organization the writer wants. The writer's job again is to re-create in the finished product—through the use of transitions—the unity and development operating in his or her own developing responses. Once more the organizing principles lie within subjective responses, and the transitional devices are the grammatical counterpart of that inner unity that allows a writer to put together what he or she wants to say effectively.

Marginal comments cohere and form wholes if, as we have seen, the writer builds a pattern inductively rather than imposing a possibly restricting order from outside. The process is similar in an effective use of transitions. Just as tone, point of view, and organization of "argument" arise from a thorough exploration of one's thinking as it develops, so also the momentum of an essay results from making explicit the transitions already implicit in the writer's earliest responses as reader. Again a means is needed to determine not what a rule book says about transitions but what one's own developing responses as recorded in marginal comments dictate about the pace and momentum necessary to make an essay intelligible and convincing. Further self-exploration and use of one's own marginal comments as sources outline a process for re-creating the actual stages in thinking through an issue. Some possible exploratory questions may make this whole process clearer.

Assuming you have tried a method like the one described in this book and are looking for further ways to make what you have done hold together, the following questions should help (remember you're not using transitions so much to make your thoughts "better" as you are to make it clearer exactly what your thoughts are and how you want your audience to see them as a whole):

1. What is the relationship between my first statement and the one I choose to follow it? Why does one follow the other? Could I reverse the order?

2. Does the second statement add something to the first? qualify something about the first statement? make a concession to someone about the first? conflict with the first?

3. Does the information in the second statement follow from the first? Is there causality working either way?

4. Does the second statement contain an example of a principle stated in the first?

You can, of course, make up endless varieties of such questions exploring all the possible relationships between two statements that happen to follow each other. The point is that establishing such relationships ahead of time makes an essay intelligible and establishes the momentum for an argument. Distinguishing carefully for your readers between a statement of causality and the granting of a concession steers them more easily to how your thinking is taking shape. When your readers can understand your premises and presuppositions as they develop from sentence to sentence, then you're letting them in on your responses at a level in which your thinking was more intelligible to you in the first place.

Take two of the simplest assertions for illustration:

1. It was cold.
2. I started the car.

To combine these assertions in one sentence and show the relationship of each to the other, one might try any of the following:

(1)		(2)
It was cold.		I started the car.

A— moreover
   furthermore
   and

B— yet
   however
   but
   nevertheless

C— because
   since
   for

D— therefore
   thus

In A, (2) is merely an addition to (1).

Coldness and car starting merely happened together with no specific assertion about their relationship.

In B, (1) is a concession preceding the assertion in (2).

Car starting in spite of coldness, coldness that might affect car starting but didn't.

In C, (2) causes (1).

Coldness caused by car starting—which is ludicrous

without some very special conditions.

In *D*, (1) causes (2).

Car starting caused by coldness. Typically destructive coldness causes the "I" to start and run the car to warm it up. . . . Even this statement can be examined for logic because the coldness caused the attempt, not the starting itself.

Taking this simple statement one step farther:

(1)	(2)
It was cold.	I started the car.

E— While
    Although

F— Because
    Since
    Inasmuch as

G— As if
    As though

E is very like *B* with sentence variation now possible.

In *E*, (1) is a concession preceding assertion (2). In spite of the fact that (this phrase is itself a transition) it was cold, the car started.

F is again a ludicrous (1) causing (2), unless we have an engine that starts only in cold weather.

G expresses some doubt followed by an inference about (1) and an assertion in (2). From the way the car started, we can infer coldness, or some such thing.

Obviously what is being said changes in all these examples. But a more important and less obvious point is that one relationship can be inferred in the absence of the one you want. "It was cold and I started the car" does not convey causality. In fact it infers a lack of causality. Stated in this way, the two assertions suggest that none of the other relationships is intended by the writer. The result at the worst is total confusion; at the least the writer misses an opportunity to re-create most effectively for an audience the gut reactions as they happened. Again, if you say it explicitly as it made most sense to you, you are building momentum into what you say and your reader can better experience it with you.

Granted, lengthy repetition about starting a car in cold weather is boring. But a close look at one of the most famous statements in philosophy to depend on a transitional word can perhaps better illustrate the significance of perceived pattern and momentum. In attempting to prove his own existence, the seventeenth-century French philosopher René Descartes concluded "*Je pense donc je suis.*" The statement is equally famous in Latin, "*Cogito ergo sum,*" and in English, "I think, therefore I am." Notice that if a reader knew no other French or Latin and yet knew *donc* and *ergo* meant "therefore," he or she would understand that B followed from A or that A caused B. Without the explicit transitional structure, however, the relationship between the two statements is obscure and the meaning is lost.

Descartes meant that he knew he existed ("I am") because he was aware of being in the process of thinking ("I think"). His consciousness of being a thinking being brought into existence his awareness of consciousness itself. Descartes' views led ultimately to a split between thought and existence. What came to be known as a Cartesian dualism between "I think" and "I am" developed in the history of the philosophy of the past three hundred years. The point here is simply that the transitional word actually carries the main burden of meaning in his classic statement. To illustrate the primacy of the transitional relationship, one need only substitute freely for Descartes' "therefore."

<u>(1)</u>
I think

A— moreover
  furthermore
  and

B— yet
  however
  but
  nevertheless

C— because
  since
  for

D— therefore
  thus

<u>(2)</u>
I am

E— While
  Although

F— Because
  Since
  Inasmuch as

G— As if
  As though

D communicates Descartes' meaning. In A, (2) merely occurs in addition to (1). The sense of B is opposed to Descartes in asserting that existence can be felt despite the coincidence of rationality. C reverses Descartes by arguing that consciousness of thinking follows from existence. Or, in other words, existence causes thought. In *E*, existence is documented in spite of thinking. *F* is very close to Descartes' meaning, but not quite the same. "I think" therefore "I am" does not necessarily mean "I am" because "I think." Again, *G* is obscure and its sense is bizarre if there is any at all in this example. These examples are intended not as pseudo philosophy but only to illustrate the startling shifts in meaning caused by the slightest variation in transitional pattern.

Transitional words, then, map out the direction of a reader's marginal comments as they structure from within the written communication of his or her responses as reader. But in addition to the words alone, carefully selected repetition of one's most important terms and phrases allows the reader continually to look ahead and back while reading the record of thoughts in progress. Repetition of crucial terms is an essential part of the development of inductive outlines and is crucial in paragraph building—especially in the writing of effective topic and ending sentences. Momentum in an essay arises, in part, from the writer's picking up strands of the previous paragraph and looking forward to the next paragraph in one unified movement.

In addition to transitional words and the repetition of most important terms and phrases, careful use of references such as 'this" and "these" can link one sentence or paragraph to another sentence or paragraph and achieve momentum.

Exercises

1. Make a list of all the possible transitional words like the following:
   furthermore
   in order that
   because
   therefore
   although
   nevertheless
   however

Include in your list any word that ordinarily establishes relationships between what has gone before and what is to come after. Explain the relationship each normally expresses. Does changing the positioning of any of these terms ordinarily change its function in a sentence?

2. Use five or six of these transitional words in your marginal comments on any essay. Discuss the effects of each.

3. Make an inductive outline of (2) using the transitional words as organizing factors.

4. Write a paragraph of 100 words using at least 8 transitional words. Then delete the transitional words in a second version. Compare the two versions in terms of the effects of the "transitionless" and "transition-ful" on an audience.

5. Rewrite the paragraph in (4) with no transitional words while repeating key words and phases and using "this" judiciously to create momentum.

6. Write a poem expressing only "gut" reactions linked with transitional words.

7. Create a collage illustrating a development requiring transitions. How do you create transitions through pictures alone? Find an audience and ask them to evaluate your effectiveness in creating momentum.

8. Compare two writers' styles according to their use of transitions.

9. "Read" a page in any foreign language with the vocabulary for transitional words only in front of you. What can we infer about the structure of argument or the momentum of the assertions on that page?

10. Discuss similarities between film techniques used for momentum and transition and transitional devices in writing.

11. Write a five-minute speech using the suggestions put forth in the first five chapters of this book. Pay special attention to transitional words and phrases. Present the speech before an audience and ask for feedback particularly on your ability to create momentum. Can your audience follow the shape or pattern in your speech? Then write an essay on the same topic and compare your essay with your speech. Which form, essay or speech, requires the most careful attention to transitions? Discuss your findings.

12. Observe carefully a speaker delivering a speech, a television ad, and a movie. Notice especially the gestures, intonations, or contrasts used to create effective transitions. What kind of transitions do you find most/least effective and why? Point out examples of especially good or especially bad transitions and discuss the specific effects on you as audience.

Summary/Review

What an audience takes to be your meaning will depend on observable *relationships between* all the statements you make. It is not enough to merely record your responses as they emerge in marginal comments and outlines. Because human beings generally respond best to pattern, you must make the structure of your thought clearly observable to an audience. Effective transitions can be the difference between what reaches an audience and what merely records your thoughts. Transitions provide the momentum that not only keeps an essay going but also attaches the reader to the direction of that movement. When marginal comments preserve the momentum within your thinking, later outlines and drafts should better be able to reflect relationships which will otherwise be taken as disjointed parts of a whole. Four principal transitional devices build pattern into sentences, paragraphs, and larger structural blocks. These include transitional words, careful pronoun and adjective references, repetition of crucial concepts and terms, and the orchestration of major thoughts through restatement in different contexts.

7 / Paragraph as Structure of Response

In a writer there must always be two people—the writer and the critic. And, if one works at night, with a cigarette in one's mouth, although the work of creation goes on briskly, the critic is for the most part in abeyance, and this is very dangerous.

—Leo Tolstoi, *Talks with Tolstoi*

Tolstoi wrote in the morning, when his head was "fresh." Dostoyevski wrote at night. For many busy people today, evening is the best time for uninterrupted marginal notation, morning the best time to find the structures that make intense personal responses effective as communication. This book stresses the need for finding ways of recording for future use one's initial personal reactions. Inductive outlines suggest that form and structure arise from within rather than as impositions from outside. The morning and evening metaphor is worth considering. If paragraphing is a critical activity of "the morning" which Tolstoi refers to, it is an activity accomplished only if the work of the creative "evening" is done and preserved effectively. A paragraph is no more than an idea finding its own internal structure, a thought completing itself in a form of sufficient complexity and intensity to reach an audience. An idea "forms" itself by taking structure. And structure helps ideas develop.

Almost anything can be said in a paragraph. If one has no more and no less space, any subject can be summarized, digested, explored in a paragraph. A business person preparing an advertising brief, a reporter outlining a story, a writer writing a book—all probably do or could write their whole effort (in abstracted form) in a single paragraph. In digest form a writer can "cover" any subject by developing one central idea in a paragraph. When the range of material to cover and the complexity of the subject require increased length, the writer can expand the original summary paragraph into parts which are then once more explored in paragraph structures similar to that of the original. In this sense, writing an essay is like growth from an original single cell into thousand-cell complexity. Of course none of this is new. The similarities of organization between the single paragraphs making up an essay and the structure of the whole essay are the basis of the technique of outlining. "I, A, 1, a" outlines illustrate the process of subordination and structural development reflected in paragraphing.

We have heard all this before. But how to decide where one paragraph ends and another begins or what is or is not a complete and effective paragraph is another matter. Much stream-of-consciousness fiction will run twenty or thirty pages with seemingly no paragraphing. But given the nature of the expression as free association of ideas, all thirty pages probably belong in one paragraph. In such a case, decisions about where one thought is fully developed and another begins are almost meaningless. Such might be the situation also in marginal comments consisting of intense personal reactions. If the purpose of your paper were to re-create the state of your mind as you experience what you read, stream-of-consciousness exploration of your gut reactions would be most appropriate. If, however, your purpose is to describe accurately, to present information, or to construct an argument, then your particular purpose should dictate the kind of decisions you'll have to make about structure and organization. Given clusters of gut-level reactions, how can they be put together for effective communication?

Let's assume, in this chapter, that the earlier work of marginal comments, listing and grouping, and developing inductive outlines is complete. You thus have much of the often ignored crucial earlier stages of writing to build on. All you really need at this stage is a brief check list to use in assessing the effectiveness of paragraphs built from inductive outlines. If sufficiently intense and complete, recorded gut reactions are the kind of thoughts moving toward completeness that paragraphs depend on. In these terms, again a paragraph is simply a basic unit of complete thought; the thought is stated in a topic sentence, outlined and more fully expressed in the body, held together through the use of transitions between the several parts, and "concluded" in an ending sentence that sums up, points ahead, or suggests the implications of what's been said. The topic sentence usually emerges from one of the crucial marginal comments recorded earlier; it also assumes a place of importance on initial lists and later inductive outlines. Similarly, the ending sentence of a paragraph—often overlooked—can be traced to earlier marginal comments.

Faced with problems in "paragraphing" a rough draft, then, it is logical to look back to earlier stages of marginal comments, lists, and outlines to see where if anywhere the process of developing gut reactions into complete thoughts could have been short-circuited. The process of working from paragraphs back to the materials the paragraphs grew out of reverses, of course, the growth from within of the inductive outline. And this reversal can often be put to use as a very good check on paragraphing. If there are many things to be said and the structures holding all the content seem shaky, it is often very effective simply to back away from the complicated structures and prepare a brief and simple list of the basic points you wish to make. Looking squarely at your subject and audience, simply list on a separate sheet off to the side exactly what you want to communicate. In essence, you'll be once again re-creating some personal responses you stated earlier in the marginal-comments stage of prewriting. Freeing yourself from paragraphs that now look settled, you can rethink the paragraphing needed to best represent your thoughts.

You may find, for example, that one paragraph is an expression of four or five complete thoughts while another lacks even one. Or your brief list may reflect a relationship between two or three ideas that your paragraphing obscures. Perhaps the three ideas belong in one paragraph with one overriding idea unifying all three. Brief lists can also point to the exact spots in paragraphs where transitions are needed. Because carefully prepared lists tend to point toward conclusions, such rethinking can isolate paragraphs that really have no—or perhaps at best an ineffective—ending sentence.

Building paragraphs according to set patterns such as causality or parallel structure may not work. Such attempts can become replacements for the personal responses needed to bring writing to life. But again, as a check list in determining what makes a paragraph work, such means of development are useful. Patterns of movement from the general to the particular or particular to general, simple time sequence, cause and effect, and comparison-contrast are convenient and effective ways to gather together otherwise disconnected statements. Similarly, the use of examples or analogies for illustration or the building up of details or withholding crucial evidence for suspense—all these techniques can help structure a complete idea as it is expressed.

Relating the paragraphs of an essay to one another and to the whole essay is also a matter of discovering structure from within. Again based on a procedure like that of inductive outlining, the chief task is to determine the logical progression within your own views. Marginal comments can once more be of help, as can effective transitional links between shifts in thought. One or two practical suggestions might serve as final checks on paragraphing. It might help, for example, simply to number each paragraph in a rough draft—assigning a number to a paragraph only when you're satisfied that it says as much as you want it to and no more. Consecutive numbering can then be checked once more to determine if any two paragraphs could or should be reversed in order. If they should be switched, switch them; if you can't really tell, chances are the order and transitional devices are not as effective as they could be. Basic changes can often be made in rough copy by mere cut-and-paste rearranging. But in addition to wholesale reversal, often such a numbering technique reveals total change of subject, lack of development, or excessive repetition. Because such gaps and repetition are inevitable, they should be seen as the necessary stages in the whole process rather than failures. It is often necessary, in fact, to rewrite a whole idea two or three times in two or three repetitious paragraphs before you can get it just the way you want to say it. In fact, such may be an important method of paragraph development: repetition of the same idea three different times giving way to a single-paragraph mosaic of the best of the three versions.

Exercises

1. Beginning from the stage of marginal comments and inductive outlines, write a one-paragraph response to something you have read recently.

2. Write the paragraph of #1 at least two other ways—not worrying about repetition. Then combine the best of all three versions and check that single paragraph for topic sentence, transitions, and effective ending sentence.

3. Choose any paper you have written in the past few weeks. Concentrate on especially complex and confusing passages, making a list of essential points on the side. Then use the list to improve paragraphing in the essay.

4. Number the paragraphs in the essay you are working on for #3—and determine whether the order can be changed at all. Then on a separate sheet alongside each number identify the principal means of development used in that paragraph: cause-effect, time sequence, deductive or inductive, comparison-contrast, and so forth. Compare this final version to the inductive outline prepared from marginal comments.

5. Describe a striking scene in one paragraph. Then develop each sentence in that description into a full paragraph by adding sufficient detail. Compare the final version to your initial paragraph.

6. Read three or four articles on one topic in magazines or professional journals. Then write a single-paragraph summary or abstract of each article in which you state the main thesis and follow the steps of the argument. Compare your one-paragraph digest to the article itself.

7. Examine the differences between paragraphing techniques in news stories and in feature articles in newspapers.

8. Can the "scene" in film as consisting of a series of frames and shots be compared to the paragraph in writing? Use several examples and point out the difficulties in making such a comparison.

Summary/Review

As the central element in written structure or pattern, the paragraph is an expanded statement or idea finding its own form. A paragraph is a thought completing itself and, as such, may vary significantly in length and complexity. From a single developed thesis or topic statement to an abstract of an essay, a brief of an advertising promotion, or the digest of an entire book, a paragraph can be expansive or compressed. Your purpose, control of focus, and the logical structure within a developing thought should determine paragraph organization. Again systematic marginal comments and inductive outlines provide the responses upon which paragraphs are built. As a useful check on the organization of your material, you should make a brief list of your major points and determine whether your paragraph breaks reflect the logical patterns in your own thinking.

8/ Focus and Forming Conclusions: Generalizing from Detail

Everyone has heard the brainbuster, "All generalizations are false, including this one." The same witty fellow who made that proclamation may also have warned, "My mind is made up; don't confuse me with the facts."

Every writer has to be able to balance generalization and detail if the writing is to be clear, thorough, convincing, or make sense at all. The most forceful generalization is suspect without supporting details; the most vivid details are pointless unless the writer selects them and builds a pattern that shapes generalizations. Unstructured detail and unspecified generality are equally ineffective in any stage of composition from marginal comments to finished product.

One further technique for building marginal comments into a finished product is the writer's careful blending of generalization and detail. Marginal comments that are all large generalizations restrict a reader's ability to see beneath the surface of what is being read. If, on the other hand, the comments are specific but unrelated, a reader blocks his or her ability to see pattern.

As first graders, we all knew how to perceive. Ask small children to describe anything, and they'll give you long lists of what they experience through their senses. But as they learn to abstract from such details to draw conclusions, they come to deemphasize the senses in favor of the conceptualizing intellect. Where both develop simultaneously, the potential from within is limitless. Unfortunately, oftener than not the development of the abstracting intellect has been at the expense of the perceiving mind, and students forget that even the most perplexing concepts come to them through specifics. In fact, they may—if the tendency toward abstraction is reinforced

148

to excess—forget *how* to perceive through the senses. And so a writer might easily walk in the world blind and deaf, unaware of touch and smell all around, piling abstraction on top of abstraction and wondering why an audience doesn't understand what is written.

This book argues repeatedly that too much insistence on abstraction, impersonality, and "objectivity" can inhibit you as a reader when you read or as a writer when you write about what you have read. We have all heard much about the progressive dulling of our senses, the narcotizing of our awareness of anything short of extremes, and our need for "remedial experience" ranging from sensitivity sessions to merely opening our eyes. Looking for "objective" and "impersonal" insights, we often fail to recognize our most real responses. But for the writer trying to communicate personal reactions, the problems caused by unspecific abstractions are acute. No one likes an overly opinionated loudmouth—someone who always takes a strong position on an issue, whether or not he knows anything about it. But what is usually wrong with the know-it-all's comments is not that they are opinions. Rather, what is most objectionable are unexplored generalizations and simple-minded obviousness. To *unexplained* as well as unsupported generalization, an audience is likely to say, "So what?" or, "What's so special about that way of seeing things?" or simply, "Tell me more and then I'll decide if it's worth listening." In a sense, all these objections would apply to marginal reactions that abstract from specifics and then don't include any of the specifics that the abstractions were abstracted from. "Beautiful" or "good," "I agree" or "that's not right" mean little without specifics. Generalizations without the concrete details that formed them produce "objectivity" in a vacuum without the specific and often subjective responses to concrete particulars that make up pattern.

It's not necessary to give up all abstractions or lament the abuses of our educational system to restore a balance between generalization and detail. In any system of marginal comments, to re-create valuable personal responses for your audience, you as a writer must be able to communicate immediacy through concrete description. You must be able to trace for your audience *how you came to* the conclusions you now hold. In order to work back to the specifics of your thinking you must preserve your *specific* reactions for what they were when you had them rather than for what any imposed order from outside says they should be. If you can get no farther than unsupported generalization, your problem lies either in your perception or in your choice of a topic.

Everyone who has ever studied seriously "how to write" has tried exercises on description and the use of concrete detail. Most people have had enough examples of the "happiness is a warm puppy" variety. Tirelessly, writers try to describe "love," "cold," "sharp." Instructors and editors constantly advise that writers clarify the vague or obscure and enrich the obvious. More red ink has been blotched over "be specific," "make this concrete," "offer an example" than for perhaps any other single writing problem. Attempts to describe odors, smooth surfaces, emotions, bodily contact, tastes, movements are difficult and yet rewarding exercises for senses that are too readily lazy and too easily swayed by the well-worn phrase or the comfortable current jargon. If marginal comments are to represent a reader's responses in any kind of complete way, they require language at least specific enough to re-create the details and images that typically flash before a complex and thinking mind. No matter how much you as a reader might initially respond in generalities, *what you think* follows from the specifics in *what you read* and in your own experience. If you think in specifics and respond only in generalities you may simply need to bring your responses more in contact with the complexity of your own thinking. As difficult as this process is, it is something you as a writer can teach yourself.

No matter how good a writer becomes, he or she must forever remember to be more specific. A writer who runs dry or gets stale must often reach back and examine his or her own thinking more closely. Of course the kind of description necessary to communicate complex thoughts presupposes that the writer has complex thoughts. In accord with the overall premise of this book, it is assumed that writers have difficulties precisely because they *have* more to say than they know *how* to say. Put another way, problems multiply when writers' techniques for recording their thoughts lag behind their intuited sense that they have something to say. In the best writing, one perceiving mind reaches another—through *specifics*.

If you've ever been told that your writing has "too much fact" in it, you may have experienced difficulty in making details "add up." This chapter so far has been about the need for focus and the importance of creating detailed description before a writer's perceptions are abstracted away. But it is entirely possible that a writer might have all the necessary details and still not be able to communicate them.

Once again, balancing concrete details and abstract generalizations is necessary simply to perceive realities around us. According to the philosopher Hegel, perception of reality actually *is* an interaction of the particular and the general in the development of the human personality. Particularity (concrete, detailed description in writing) actualizes the potential of objectivity (abstract generalizations in writing). Each without the other is unfulfilled and hence ineffective. Just as unparticularized abstraction has no vitality, so ungeneralized particularity can exist only as unactualized potential.

A common criticism of reliance on one's own personal reactions in writing is that intensity rather than complexity is the identifying factor of such response. In its initial stages, one's personal reaction is primarily intense rather than complex. In drawing upon the intensity of his or her own "gut" reactions the writer can breathe vitality and force into what might otherwise be lifeless prose. But as is often the case, a chief strength can often be a downfall, and such is true if personal responses are allowed to grow in quantity and intensity without a corresponding development in quality and complexity.

In a sense the selection, arrangement, and presentation of concrete details is itself a series of choices that generalizes from the details. Carefully chosen, purposefully arranged, and effectively presented, details *are* in themselves an embodiment of the generalizations they are intended to support. The old adage is true here that a person who presents evidence well enough doesn't really need to spend much time explaining conclusions that an audience can figure out for themselves. If you have been accused of using "too much fact" in your writing, the problem most likely lies in (1) lack of careful selection of details, (2) ineffective arrangement of details, or (3) ineffective presentation of facts you have. Any or all of these in combination will usually produce details that "don't add up," details that lead nowhere, or "gut-level" response that might be intense but lacks all complexity. You most likely have been warned against *not* "too much fact" but rather a tendency not to do anything with the facts you have. And as a result you may have left your reader with no answer to his query of "so what?"

To enrich the complexity of their personal reactions, readers must relate their responses to something outside their own immediate associations. They must explain their implications, and in general, answer their audience's quite justifiable, "So what?" In generalizing from details, writers not only state their point but also communicate at least implicitly *the significance* of the point. Writers make their case as they assemble the evidence; they balance particulars and generalizations, which reinforce each other. Structure from within results in part, then, from a clustering of particulars like those found in an inductive outline of marginal comments. Each bunching of particulars (just as in an outline each major heading) represents a generalization that is supported as it is stated. A whole spectrum of writing difficulties—"lack of unity," "no evidence," "too opinionated," "doesn't go anywhere"—are thus caused by a lack of balance between the particulars and generalizations as they develop from within recorded personal responses.

The need for limiting the subject and creating sharper focus becomes clearer when a writer develops a system of effective marginal notation. Initial "gut" reactions tend to be either very general or very specific; undifferentiated almost vague intensity seems to alternate with a kaleidoscopic bombardment of seemingly unrelated individual impressions. But as generalizations form from clusters of particulars, the selection and arrangement of details should be further influenced by the generalizations that come to mind. Thus further marginal comments tend to focus more sharply on details relevant to the generalizations taking shape. In responding to what he or she is reading, a writer also focuses personal response on details that fit into the pattern of his or her *general* responses and impressions. General impressions are, of course, shaped by the details you focus on. The work of reacting in a margin is a reciprocal process in which a writer (a) states a point and cites details to support the point, and at the same time (b) develops the point based on the details cited. When this kind of sensitive response is carried over into an essay, the writer's credibility with an audience is strengthened. It becomes clear that he neither makes up his mind ahead of time (unsupported generalizations) nor merely responds to everything without ever making up his mind about anything (concrete details that "don't add up").

Credibility with an audience raises further questions about distinctions between assertion and demonstration in drawing upon "gut" reactions. Mere assertion often draws upon an intense response but fails to develop the complexity necessary for demonstration. While it is good to study logic and the danger of logical fallacies, quite simply a point is stated *and* proved only when one can combine forceful generalizations with a corresponding effective selection, arrangement, and presentation of details. No matter how intense, "gut" reactions are not effective communication if they are mere assertion. Somehow the forcefulness of assertion always collapses when concrete support is lacking.

Details and generalizations must recur throughout an essay and reinforce each other. But the question of the order and prominence given to one over the other deserves careful consideration. You have no doubt often been advised to get to the point immediately, to state your position emphatically at the outset and then proceed to the proof. On the other hand, it is also effective to demonstrate a point chiefly through the accumulation of specific details and statement of the argument such details demonstrate as a finishing clincher or even a form of résumé or restatement at the end of an essay. One or the other (or a combination of the two) is suggested for a variety of audiences, subjects, and purposes. For a relatively direct and simple argument or when facing a sympathetic audience, the former is most effective; when presenting a very complex argument, when addressing a hostile audience, or when you wish to create suspense, the latter approach works best.

Again looking for organization within is the best means for developing the balance between general and specific. When an argument will progress more smoothly or is easier to follow as the pieces fit together, then a details-first followed by generalization pattern would represent an argument at its best. Then, too, if an intense "gut" response rests on a conclusion that is best explored when details are withheld until after the initial assertion, it is best to state a position and then put together for a reader the steps that led to your conclusions. It's a matter of your audience approaching your responses in one of two ways: they might want to know first what and how you're thinking as you respond to a subject and then see how you put things together in reaching conclusions. Or they may wish to hear a statement of position first and then raise questions about what led you to think the way you do. In either case, they will be there with the "So what?" that requires a balance of general and particular in whichever order you choose to present them.

One final warning: to urge a balance of particulars and generalizations is not to rule out contradictory responses leading to conclusions that are not entirely clear or conclusive. In order to reach effective generalization, a writer must not force clear conclusions where there are none. Effective

generalization means adherence to the details that support it—contradictory
or unresolved though they might be.

Exercises

1. Begin with your marginal comments on some controversy you have
read about. Write a descriptive passage of about 500 words in which you take
a stand on that controversial issue. Argue a point and construct your evidence
(without statements) through the selection and arrangement of detail. Include
no generalizations. Your concrete description must "state" and support your
point.

2. Write a thesis statement on the same topic you chose for #1 and build
an essay around your marginal comments, as you did in earlier chapters. Then
blend the statementless details from your descriptive passage into your
revised essay. Check for a persuasive balance of generalization and detail.

3. Describe the most intense experience you can either recall having or
can imagine being possible. Then write an essay *about* that experience.
Review your finished product for generalization and detail.

4. Create a collage which "describes" any abstraction through visual
images only.

5. Write a scenario for a five-minute film on any subject. Work out
carefully the directions to the camera man on camera movement, exact
scenery, costumes, lighting, color, exact actions and timing for the actors;
exact editing for the final product. Your instructions should be self-contained
and sufficiently detailed so your film can be "experienced" by your audience.
Notice that abstractions and generalizations can occur *only* when your
concrete details create pattern.

6. Study your film scenario closely. Look at it as a film essay and
compare the camera and the persona of an essay. Notice that the movie can
mean only what the accumulation and arrangement of perceptual images can
make you see.

7. Record your initial "gut" reactions to the following controversial
subjects:

interracial marriage
reformed abortion legislation
pollution control and big business
premarital sex
individual rights and governmental surveillance

Develop the complexity as well as the intensity of your personal reactions by generalizing from concrete details as they form clusters. As you did earlier, develop inductive outlines, but concentrate here on an effective balance of generalizations and concrete details.

8. Proceed as in #7 in response to your reading on a chosen subject. Develop a system of marginal comments to record your reactions and then identify the most significant generalizations and details present in your marginalia. Again develop an inductive outline using generalizations as major headings and concrete details to fill in the record of your total impression.

9. Looking back to your responses in #7 and #8, distinguish between initial assertion and a more developed demonstration of facts. Bring mere assertion closer to demonstration by making the details and generalizations reinforce each other. Trace your methods of limiting your subject and sharpening your focus based on the funneling effect of early generalizations. To what extent are you able to focus details more sharply after you have formulated at least some preliminary tentative generalizations? How does this process influence your selection, arrangement, and presentation of details? Be specific in your answers.

10. On a graph that might be called an "intensity thermometer," place your "gut" reactions to a current debate along a continuum from "most intense" to "bland."

> most intense
> intense
> neutral
> weak
> bland

Then, using a similar graph—a "complexity thermometer"—rank the same reactions to their simplicity or complexity.

> most complex
> complex
> moderately involved
> simple
> overly obvious

To what extent do you find the two graphs overlapping? Is there an inverse relationship between intensity and complexity in the earliest stages of gut reactions? Can the two be brought together as you develop an effective balance between particulars and generalizations in your later responses?

11. As you move toward a finished product, experiment with the two basic approaches to alternating generalizations and specific details in an essay. In your first essay state your conclusions at the outset and follow with supporting details; develop your argument deductively. In the second version, withhold your generalizations until after you have selected, arranged,

and presented the essential details that support your position; develop your argument inductively. Compare your two versions of essentially the same essay in terms of their effectiveness in dealing with your specific subject and in reaching your specific audience.

12. Find in your reading an example of the effective use of abstract words.

Summary/Review

To communicate any personal reactions or opinion, it is crucial to balance generalizations and details. To reach an audience, you must state not only what you think but also how and why you came to such conclusions. Unsupported generalization leaves an audience uninvolved. Merely saying something doesn't make it so. Too much emphasis on abstraction dulls our ability to see or hear what is in front of us. Often the selection and arrangement of concrete details makes for better statement of a point than what it is possible to convey in a concept. At the same time, details that don't add up only confuse and frustrate an audience. Lengthy lists or catalogs are burdensome when no pattern is discernible. Because human reactions often occur in abstractions and unpatterned specifics, marginal comments can often reflect an imbalance of generalization and detail. In an essay based on personal responses, you must take care to examine the complexity as well as the intensity of your own views. Techniques for presenting generalization and detail vary according to purpose and audience. Inductively, specifics build to conclusions; deductively, concrete details follow from stated generalizations. The interaction is crucial in either format.

9 / Film Editing and Revision as Process*

The historic debate on whether a writer succeeds through genius or craft seriously affects our attitudes toward revision. If you assume that a writer either has "talent" or doesn't, you might opt for the view that the successful writer is most often a genius who communicates through inspiration. In such a view, even the "tortured genius" experiences torture in a wrenching creative act that is assumed to be distinct from the boredom of revision. Of course there is some truth in this position, but its implications can be fatal to all of us who are not geniuses. In these terms, revision becomes remedial work (at best as interesting as an autopsy) rather than a part of the continuity of the writing process itself.

The classic argument pitting genius against craft has never been more sharply delineated than in Ben Jonson's criticism of Shakespeare. To counteract the growing assumption in his time that Shakespeare was a wild, unregulated genius who never "blotted out a line" once he had written it, Jonson retorted, "Would he had blotted a thousand."[1] We find this harsh comment surprising, and to call it a compliment would surely be stretching a point. After all, Jonson contends (in rather harsh terms) that Shakespeare's *"Phantsie"* flowed with facility "that sometime it was necessary he should be stop'd." And again: "His wit was in his owne power; would the rule of it had beene so too." But while wishing that Shakespeare had revised more than he did, Jonson further proclaims that he "redeemed his vices, with his vertues.

---

*Portions of this chapter appeared in somewhat different form in "Film Editing and the Revision Process: Student as Self-Editor," *College Composition and Communication* 25 (December, 1974), 405–10. Reprinted by permission of the National Council of Teachers of English.

1. Ben Jonson, "Timber: or, Discoveries" (probably written during the years 1620–35, and posthumously published in 1641), in *Criticism: The Major Texts*, ed. Walter Jackson Bate (New York: Harcourt Brace Jovanovich, 1970), p. 112.

There was ever more in him to be praysed, then to be pardoned." It is, of course, risky to tamper with reputations of such renown, and such was not Jonson's purpose. Rather, in arguing that even a genius like Shakespeare would have profited from further revision, Jonson calls attention to the importance of the writer's craft at every level of expertise. Further, he picks up something about Shakespeare that the German Romantics and Coleridge after them later described in greater detail, namely, that the creative artist creates through an interaction between craft *and* "genial" inspiration. In letters, journals, essays, interviews, and in their memoirs, writers consistently describe revision not as something they impose medicinally upon their expression but rather as an integral part of the creative act itself. Tolstoi, to name only one, is reported to have wished he could go on revising novels years after their publication.

It seems obvious, then, that apprentice writers should also see revision as an integral part of the compositional process. To isolate it as something that merely cures the ills of earlier drafts—as if it were an imposition of structures and rules from outside rather than growth and development from within—makes it more difficult to develop individual techniques and style. The remedial theory of revision appeals to almost no one beyond would-be editors.

If one can "hold off" long enough, the process of revision can be a most satisfying climax to the writing experience. A writer who attempts to revise too soon, however, most likely will stifle his or her productivity and enjoyment with standards of "excellence" that are too rigid to seem valuable. Revision is not patchwork applied to earlier processes; it is an advanced stage of more of the same, but better. Handbooks or guides to usage provide invaluable checks on the effectiveness of one's final product; but before such agreed-upon conventions of usage can do their job, the writer must be able to rethink original thoughts, to re-create full subjective responses to the subject, and—through self-discipline and self-exploration—to force his or her views into larger and at the same time more sharply focused contexts.

Emphasis on revision will most likely modify several conventional assumptions about the quantity of work required in a writing course. You will most likely be asked to do fewer *new* writing assignments so that you will have the time and energy to devote to the various stages of drafting and redrafting but a few *major* pieces of writing. The revision process that goes beyond mere "correction" is the kind of revision that authors of books, dissertations, and articles go through over a period of weeks, months, or years. If you expect to "churn out" ten or fifteen themes during a term, you will be unable to sustain the reworking of each assignment. Emphasis on creative revision assumes further that you will learn a great deal (and much that will last beyond any one writing course) if during a term you bring one major essay to as high a level of polish as your abilities and the limitations of time will allow. One danger is, of course, the boredom that might ensue in redoing the same work several times. But an expanded understanding of revision as the process that enriches and expands one's insights through successive drafts will itself sooner or later convince each writer that in revising he or she is creating something new each time rather than merely sifting the remains of the old.

Links between revising on paper and similar processes in other media and art forms dramatize that you cannot successfully "revise" before you are ready. The key to successful "revision" or "editing" in photography or filmmaking lies in the production of sufficient shots or footage to make the selection and arrangement of materials meaningful. Just as film editing requires several shots from various (or even from the same) angles, so also the writer must try out various ways of saying and developing a point. Similarly, the dancer who rehearses or the painter who revises on a canvas does not consider the earliest movements, shapes, or colors to be useless if either content or technique is modified or replaced in the process of artistic creation. Early drafts in any medium or art form are looked upon as warmups or stimulants serving to engage the artists themselves in a process. If the earliest activity is looked upon as what must often be done in order to get where one is going, then initially revision is an actual part of the shaping and reshaping—the flexing of expression, the exercising, the warmups—which form the bulk of early drafting. Revision in this sense of trying out various forms of expression (rather than "correcting" in accord with a norm) is part of a continuous creative process that unfolds along a continuum rather than in halting stages. Revision as an invaluable force in the generating of written creativity suggests, therefore, nothing of the purgative remediation or the images generally associated with editor-as-vulture.

Film editing provides a useful analog between print and nonprint media. Obviously, filmmakers experiment with every possible way to "say" what they want to express with a camera. Repetition is for them at first a technique to achieve shades of variation rather than a problem requiring remediation. Filmmakers use variations on camera angle, duration of shots, juxtaposed sound pattern—in short, everything from the manipulation of single frames to the building of an overall unity and rhythm—in order to expand their range of cinematic expression. In filmmaking it is easy to see the continuity between "drafting" and editing. The initial process generates material that is qualitatively and quantitatively ready for editing which is an almost indistinguishable extension of the filming process itself. From Eisenstein to Pudovkin to the present, film editing has been an integral part of cinematic art. Ernest Lindgren's appraisal clarifies the central position of the editing process in the creation of the final product: "The fundamental psychological justification of editing as a method of representing the physical world around us lies in the fact that it reproduces this mental process in which one visual image follows another as our attention is drawn to this point and to that in our surroundings. Insofar as the film is photographic and reproduces movement, it can give us a lifelike semblance of what we see; insofar as it employs editing, it can reproduce the manner in which we usually see it. This explains why the modern film is so much more vivid and interesting and lifelike than the primitive film, which was limited to the artificial, unreal manner of the theater."[2] Through editing, filmmakers discovered that they could change the meaning of the whole by rearranging, without necessarily altering the content of, an existing sequence. Throughout the history of the cinema, whether filmmakers espoused realism or, like the Russian experimenters, emphasized a nonrepresentational "building" of scenes, the editing process emerged as a central part of the creative act itself.

Dziga Vertov's "kino-eye" technique underlines the importance of assembling and rearranging materials as the filmmaker perceives with the camera and then relies for his effects "solely on the choice of the material and the way in which it was ultimately assembled at the editing table."[3] Briefly stated, "kino-eye" assumes that the camera is a tool for research in "the endless process of taking creative notes on film."[4] After "the endless process of observation with camera in hand," the filmmaker must "establish the order of exposition of what has been shot" by assessing the "thousand possible combinations" and then actually creating in the editing process: "The school of Kino-Eye requires that the cine-thing be built upon 'intervals,' that is, upon a movement between the pieces, the frames; upon the proportions of these pieces between themselves, upon the transitions from one visual impulse to the one following it." Vertov was also aware of the striking similarity between his "kino-eye" and the writer's use of editing in the development of his craft: "I am a film writer. A cinepoet. I do not write on paper but on film. As with every writer, I have to make work notes. Observations. Not on paper, however, but on film. Together with longer poems I write short novels, sketches, verse. . . . All this will be possible only with the organization of the endless research, filming, and editing work." Vertov actually suggests parallels between filmmaking and the compositional process at every stage of the creativity necessary to each. Though his view is often considered an extreme assertion of the significance of editing, writers—as editors of their own material—must look at their own drafts with the understanding that their own creativity lies in experimenting with, rearranging, expanding, compressing, and polishing the shape of their own perceptions. John Harrington has noted the chief contribution of Pudovkin, Eisenstein, Griffith, and others in recognizing the "artificiality" of the film medium: "By seeing that film was not recorded reality but artistic material capable of manipulation, they advanced the art of the film."[5] Similarly, writers must understand that the goal of creative editing is the artifice of verbal discourse. As their own editors, they will be helped significantly if they are able to understand parallels between

---

2. *The Art of the Film* (New York: Collier Books, 1963), p. 67.
3. Ibid., p. 97.
4. Dziga Vertov, "Kinoks—Revolution" (Selections), in *Film Makers on Film Making*, ed. Harry M. Geduld (Bloomington and London: Indiana University Press, 1967), pp. 79–105. Geduld collects several excerpts from Vertov's Manifestoes, most of which he wrote between 1922 and 1934.
5. *The Rhetoric of Film* (New York: Holt, Rinehart & Winston, 1973), p. 128.

the job of the film editor and the process of composing and building patterns on paper.

It is not necessary to go far into the film editor's tasks to see similarities with the way writers work. It is of course the editor's job to fix the sequence of film shots which are rarely taken in the order the finished film reflects. Similarly, when writing an essay, you need not draft pages in the order you expect to achieve in final copy. Understanding this flexibility in initial drafts will enable you to invest less psychic energy in "getting things right" the first time and thereby free you from a sometimes crippling reluctance to make productive revisions later. The film editor and the student as editor share the jobs of selecting and arranging details, structuring and pacing materials for emphasis, blending sequences together through effective cuts and transitions, and establishing unity and continuity by fixing sequence and pattern and rearranging the parts to enhance the effects of the whole. Thus the earliest stages of the writing process or camera shots as well as the third or fourth revision or splicing are all part of the continuous creative activity common to print and film.

What Ernest Lindgren calls the filmmaker's reproducing the *manner* in which one perceives provides further clues to the essential purpose of a writer's revisions. Writers who attempt to communicate what they see *and* how they see it must also be able—at an even earlier and therefore more crucial stage—to re-create *for themselves* what they see and how they see it. They must, in short, develop techniques for representing accurately and in great detail all the stages necessary before revision is profitable. Like filmmakers, writers explore thoroughly what they see. Through words, they approach their subject from different angles, and with varying intensity, achieving appropriate tone, rhythm, and overall unity. And writers—once again like the film editor—develop techniques for determining how to simultaneously expand and compress in order to create through the building of patterns. In order to maintain this continuous process, writers also keep a record of their own thinking in a form that captures the shape of that thinking as it developed.

When you are ready to revise an essay, an immediate conflict between writing (perhaps assumed to be creative) and revising (almost always assumed to be merely remedial) is often arresting. Further, an artificial gap between your initial reactions (thoughts, feelings, ideas about what has been assigned and what you have written about what was assigned) and the actual writing and rewriting of these responses may restrict your ability to reexamine your thinking in ways that could make revision profitable. In earlier chapters, I have suggested some techniques that might enable you to supply the missing link between two phases of your education: the full range of experiences in your reading and thinking (which often remain private) and public discussion of your experiences in the classroom and in papers.

Developing a system of marginal notation and linking that record of personal response to the revision process will help soften one time-honored piece of advice that is sound and yet often seems intimidating. Perhaps you have at some time been told that you are too close to your material and that in revising you must achieve the objectivity associated with distance. Of course this is true, and almost everyone with any objectivity about himself can see that it is valuable advice. But too often the advice implies that someone else is always needed to provide the objectivity suggested. Assuming, however, that most writers must ultimately provide their own "distance," you need more than the self-evident maxim that you should let a paper "cool off" by putting it aside for a while and then returning to it with a fresh point of view. In order to shape the mass of their personal responses successfully into a structured whole (in other words, in order to either compose in the first place or edit), writers must be able to accomplish the dual task of (1) reliving their "gut" responses with intensity and complexity, and (2) maintaining some perspective on their own responses to enable themselves to rethink their thinking and thereby to move closer to "objectifying" it in a form understandable to their audience.

Revision is, then, a paradoxical process of getting more involved in personal responses while one achieves, at the same time, a distance that is often mistakenly associated with noninvolvement. This combination is understandably not easy to achieve. But it is often made even more unreachable by our own assumptions about the alleged connections between "correctness," impersonal criticism, and "objectivity." Just as the impersonality of third person and passive voice ("it is to be assumed" rather than "I assume") is often mistaken for an "objective" stance, so also the function of the uninvolved editor can be overemphasized in discussions of the activities necessary for revision. Perhaps too the confusion over "objective" and "subjective" masks a larger issue about what actually constitutes the *improvement* arrived at through editing. Because some noticeable results can be obtained through impersonal or "noninvolved" distancing, it does not necessarily follow that the writer's own talents are being improved in the process. Writers sometimes complain that editors, who are working from a "distance," are learning more than the writers, who have not yet been "let in on" the editing process. Before writers can consistently revise their own material with anything approaching the "unbiased critical eye" called for in an appeal to "distancing," they must first learn how to get more rather than less involved with, closer to, rather than farther away from, their own developing responses.

We sometimes forget that revised thinking and expression must generally become broader and deeper as well as more clear. Obviously, a writer's audience looks for insight as well as clarity or correctness. Revision therefore involves an enriching of what may still be (no matter how correct it is) merely intense though undeveloped personal responses. Quite simply, a piece of writing may not be ready for revision of mechanics, grammar, and conventions of usage as early as we think it is. Difficulty in revising may be caused by the fact that there is still a considerable gap between what you are struggling to communicate and the actual communication you have achieved. No amount of distanced revision can make what might be rather bland responses any more than that. A futile result of overlooking the kinds of revision one needs is the flawless yet uninspiring paper which "gets the hook."

In the initial stages of revision it is probably best not to "dwell on" what you have already written. Instead, you should go back to the marginal comments in which you earlier had recorded your responses to the readings assigned in class. You can then more effectively rethink your own reactions and reformulate the issues you are writing about. Only after such re-visioning of your thinking should you write out again your personal reactions—this time in response to both the assigned reading and your own earlier record of your reactions. In this process, you will be revising your own responses not in order to bring them into accord with what someone else thinks (though all writers naturally consider such things). Rather, you will be shaping and reshaping your writing according to your own developing standards and in line with what your own presumably more involved and developed response calls for.

We have all experienced the horror looking back some years later to something our earlier and less enlightened self had composed and then cut loose. After recovering from the shock, we hopefully come to see our earlier responses as valuable stages on the way to where we are now. Had we not been what we were then, we could not be what we are now; the various starts and stops were all activities necessary to "get through." So too, with revision. While we are not, in a work-in-progress, chronologically as far away from our earliest responses, living through and then *preserving in verbal form* the earliest responses may have deepened, modified, and even changed significantly our thinking, degree of perception, and sensitivity to language. Careful attention to such changes as they occur will often result in a re-*vision* worth editing in the conventional sense of the term. There is simply a lot of pure psychology in revising—as there is in every stage of the compositional process. How successfully you will be able to revise early drafts often depends as much on the atmosphere you are able to create for yourself as it does on how well you know the rules of usage. Motivation and ease of operation become as important in sustaining meaningful work in revision as any information about language that you can and should have as a part of your tools.

On sound psychological principles again, it makes sense for each writer to develop individual effective and easily repeatable ways to keep preliminary materials together and in an order he or she can understand. Drawing upon your own *and* your instructor's marginal comments, you should collect far more than you can ever use each time you set out to rewrite a paper. You will then find yourself in the position of the filmmaker or the photographer who is about to edit shots. You must be ready at that point to admit something's usefulness in serving its function and then throw it away when its use has "peaked out." While you surely don't save every paper you have written over

many years in school, if you look seriously at your own development it would
be difficult to reject the value of any one paper for what it was worth in the
whole process of learning to develop your potential with language. What is
needed is less investment of psychic energy in early drafts and a greater
ability to let go of what you know deep down should go. You might then be
less apt to say, "I've spent two hours getting that first paragraph just right,
and I'm not going to change it—far less throw it out completely—for
anything."

It's crucial to understand that discarded writing is not useless effort. To
repeat, countless discards generally bring writers closer to where they want to
be. As their own sensitivity increases and their perceptions sharpen, writers
shape for themselves new and more productive directions through their own
sharpened sense for selecting, rearranging, and discarding if necessary. As
you learn what doesn't work, you are also learning to judge better, and so to
create, what does work. Many writers even insist that for them—without the
agonizing work of countless discards—nothing approaching what they want
can ever result. In this view of creativity, what makes subjective responses
most effective is one's ability to see one's own responses as they develop and
to *let them develop effectively in various stages*. Writers must ultimately look
upon their material as a mass of prized possessions ready to be packed for
moving. If, when packing, they conclude that it is more expensive to move
something than it is really worth, they shouldn't move it anyway because it's
theirs and they won't let loose. If the price for moving first drafts into final
copy is the forfeiture of later complexity that goes undeveloped, the earlier
material must be acknowledged for what it was worth and sent on its way.

One might say that this rhapsody on revision is all well and good but that
many successful writers do, in fact, write well without revising at all. Students
often shrewdly suggest that professional writers must meet deadlines and
therefore generally have little time for extensive revisions. They simply must
get their writing done on first copy. A very shrewd student once even cited as
his authoritative example Samuel Johnson, who allegedly fed copy for his
Rambler essays page by page to the printer's boy waiting at the door. You stop
my "this is all true, but . . . " with a simple request: "Why don't we learn how
to write first-copy prose and pass by all the extra time required by this
revision business?" Perhaps I could show you manuscripts depicting the
successive revisions of a great work and we could study its evolution from
marginal comments to finished product. In any case I would simply have to
admit that writing polished first-copy prose with no need for revision *is an
ideal goal* of learning how to revise. As your writing becomes increasingly
proficient in various stages of creative revision, you will progressively have
less and less need for more and more of the activities you have mastered. You
will then be able to accomplish much revising in your head or in the initial act
of thinking on paper. If exercises in revision seek primarily to program
themselves out of existence, revision is, then—like all stages of the writing
process—a means to an end rather than an end in itself. Once stated, this

conclusion seems obvious and we could agree that revision is part of a continuous creative act.

As one more means for seeing that continuity, it helps to develop flexibility in the earliest stages of drafting and redrafting. Too often the most exploratory stages of thinking on paper are most easily stifled by worries about, for example, repetition. Because a writer doesn't always know at first whether any given views are going to be major or minor points, whether they're going at the beginning or the end of an essay, or even whether they're leading somewhere or nowhere, he or she has to try out different ways of saying things. Because of indecision (or even lack of discovery as yet) about content or structure, the writer must always engage in a form of repetition that may even serve as an indispensable tool for the generation of ideas. Sometimes the only way to get something said (or to get to the point where one finally has something *to* say) is to phrase and rephrase the same idea. When exact repetition gives way to alternative ways of perceiving and verbalizing, then revision and early drafting merge in ways that the standards of correctness cannot approach. Rather than cutting off repetition in early drafting, you should recognize it for what it is, keep it as long as it is productive, and then discard later what becomes a hindrance rather than a help. Often this means gathering what you have said many times into one place—synthesizing a hodgepodge into one thrust while carefully selecting the best structures formed out of the composite. While the conglomerate of repetitions may look like the assembling of a collage, the final product should aim toward the unity of impression achieved by the dominant points you want to emphasize.

Likening revision to the making of a collage is far from stretching comparison. If reordering the parts of early drafts means endless rewriting and recopying, you probably won't do it—no matter how sound you might feel it is to do so. Any means that can lessen the physical busywork of revision should become automatic to the writer. Such well-known devices include writing on every other line so that revisions can be made between the lines rather than in a whole new copy; writing on one side of a page only so a writer can cut out materials or tape new passages onto a page without sacrificing copy on a second side; cutting and pasting for patchwork rather than recopying at any point possible; using photocopy machines to copy quotations from sources. Any technique that helps you to see writing as an ongoing process, as an art ("artifice"), as the putting together of materials in various stages to achieve meaningful wholes, will help you to see that the editor is a creative artist rather than a mere "corrector."

The physical makeup of early drafts—the way they look on a page—also helps establish the sense of editing as a continuous process. A daily journal or notebook of ideas will not only provide a repository of sources but also will help fix a continuity between note taking, successive drafts, and creative revision. Composing on a roll of paper that approximates the continuity of the movie reel may actually highlight larger patterns. Looking at the relationships between the parts of a draft in the perspective provided by a movielike manuscript may enable you to see more clearly the similarities between editing prose and splicing film as two related means of building structure inductively. Though writing on a roll of paper rather than on separate sheets smacks of gimmickry, as a reinforcer of continuity it may break down the often rigid barriers imposed by assignments measured in page length or word counts. Whatever devices a writer uses (and this should often depend on learning to shape personal idiosyncrasies to advantage), the point is that there's too much substantive work in revising to waste time on busywork that advances the final product no more than what could be accomplished by shortcuts or even gimmicks.

Such shortcuts might also, of course, cause problems. The same psychological principles that make these shortcuts sound practice can, when carried to extremes, bring about the writer's undoing. If you use "patchwork" editing solely to save old readily available material that should be discarded or fill a page with quotations produced by a hyperactive copy machine, you will find yourself aborting the process of revision in favor of a return to the inadequate or a substitute of the unoriginal. (Yellow, green, or pink felt-tipped pens marking out long passages seem to be a current rage. One difficulty is that if one marks out three-fourths of a page and provides no verbal notations at all, then one has, for all practical purposes, marked nothing at all. Of course, any sort of unconscious notation can become counterproductive by serving merely to soothe one's subconscious guilt over one's uninvolved reading. Needless to say, filling the margins with unintelligible or unrelated "commentary" in order to convince oneself that "reading" is going on is a danger students should be reminded of.) Marginal commentary and its attendant difficulties will never be easy, but on sound psychological principles alone you should record more, think more (and think more about what you are thinking), and hopefully synthesize more about what you read for the class regardless of what you at first record or how you record it. Once the process is set in motion and the writer is in control of his or her own responses, revising a first or second draft may be seen as an extension of the earliest systematized records.

One final note on how marginal quotations can contribute to a process of revision. It often happens that in the midst of several drafts and increasingly complex themes and structures, the central points a writer is trying to make can get lost. In the midst of complexity, often a simple device for sorting can be best. To avoid reproducing a maze of interrelated ideas, you might simply stop and ask yourself what one, two, or three points you are trying to make at any given time and then list them off to the side of your copy in plain English and in simple sentences. When trapped in disorganized complexity, you can simplify the structures and then form simple statements again with the help of your marginal notations. The goal is, of course, to reestablish a degree of complexity while communicating in a straightforward way. Ultimately, the chief aim of revision is to achieve complexity in a way that looks simple.

The following brief excerpts from longer essays illustrate a few of the ways in which revision can work in every stage of the writing process. The object of most revision goes way beyond "correction" and involves a rethinking of one's reading, marginal comments, and first drafts. The annotator of Thoreau's "Reading" (the chapter from *Walden* and marginal comments are reprinted in chapter 5) wrote the following in her first draft. (Sentences are numbered to make discussion easier.)

(1) Thoreau wrote that "in dealing with truth we are immortal, and need fear no change or accident." (2) Reading was Thoreau's link with that truth of the past. (3) When a reader is in contact with the past he becomes as much a part of that past as it is of him. (4) The glory that an ancient philosopher finds in the truth is that same glory that a reader experiences today. (5) Reading takes training. (6) Reading books is like reading the stars and requires as much concentration and active interest and attention. (7) Thoreau feels that the printed word is "the work of art nearest to life itself." (8) But he also felt that the people of his times read little that was good, and they read poorly. (9) He also claims that if more money was spent on education instead of "conveniences" people might learn "to pursue liberal studies the rest of their lives." Thoreau wants people to wake up and live in the present. (10) His warnings could apply now.

Beyond minor stylistic and grammatical problems that are a part of any early draft, this excerpt can be revised by expanding from within. The short piece raises more questions than it answers and therefore is excellent material upon which to build an essay. The writer has at least three sources available for such an expansion. First, her copy of Thoreau's "Reading" and her own annotations can take her through closer study of the material *and* her own reactions to the material. Second, the first draft she has written from the annotations explores questions she can come back to for further discussion. And finally, her own careful reading and *annotations on* the first draft itself will give her thinking a nudge in more expansive directions.

Again, the writer can discover more about what she wants to say by studying carefully what she has already said. Examples of annotations on her own paper would include the following (in the margins alongside the sentences indicated by number): (1) Expand on the quotation. (3) Explain relationship between past and present. Sounds like Beatles' song "I am you and you are me. . . ." (4) Quote Thoreau. (5) Break paragraph and expand this idea. (7) Paragraph break. Show how print contrasts with other forms. Or maybe drop this idea because it belongs in another paper. (8–9) Two sentences go together and call for a section on society's lack of commitment to education. (10) Include examples of what applies today and how.

The writer of this essay on "Reading" reacted to her own first draft in these and other marginal comments. Following her own suggestions in the margin she then greatly expanded her next draft. Excerpts follow:

Thoreau wrote that "in dealing with truth we are immortal, and need fear no change or accident." In the midst of the changing fortunes of wealth and fame and acknowledging even the passing of human relationships, he detected an eternal state of timelessness in man's perception of truth. Reading was his link with the past as well as the past's link with his future. Through reading Thoreau saw "as fresh a glory" as did the ancient philosopher. Though the learning and insight of reading happen in time, they are also beyond time: "That time which we really improve, or which is improvable, is neither past, present, nor future."

When a reader is in contact . . .

(EXPLANATION AND REFERENCE TO BEATLES FOLLOW. SENTENCE FOUR IS INCORPORATED ABOVE.)

Reading to come into this full contact with the past takes training.

(TRANSITION FROM LAST PARAGRAPH IS FOLLOWED BY EXAMPLES OF TRAINING AND QUOTATIONS FROM THOREAU. INCLUDES SENTENCE SIX AND DEVELOPS REFERENCES TO ASTRONOMY AS READING.)
(AFTER DELETING SENTENCE SEVEN, LACK OF READING IS EXPLAINED IN THE FOLLOWING:)

Despite his own sensitivity to the values of reading, Thoreau finds the conversation and reading of his society to be "on a very low level, worthy only of pygmies and manikins." Reading as "a paltry convenience" or "to keep accounts" overlooks the challenge and pleasure of its "nobel intellectual exercise." Thoreau describes how the masses of Concord were raised on "easy reading." He describes at length what he calls a "sloughing off of all the intellectual faculties" among people who are too lazy or ignorant to read responsively.

(MORE FOLLOWS ON THE MISEDUCATION OF THE MASSES.)

But Thoreau's concern goes beyond the "dulness" or "stagnation" of the uneducated or miseducated. He attacks especially the misguided reading of even the so-called "literate." Since "the best books are not read even by those who are called good readers," many ignore "golden words, which the wisest men of antiquity have uttered." Past and present fail to meet and Emerson's "self-reliant man" lets others make his decisions and dictate his values. Thoreau concludes in a scathing indictment of the educational process of his own times: "We are under-bred and low-lived and illiterate; and in this respect I confess I do not make any very broad distinction between the illiterateness of my townsman who cannot read at all and the illiterateness of him who has learned to read only what is for children and feeble intellects."

Thoreau blames society's neglect of education on an even larger mix-up in values.

(TRANSITION FROM EIGHT TO NINE. A LENGTHY DISCUSSION OF "LIBERAL EDUCATION THE REST OF THEIR LIVES"–WITH EXAMPLES–FOLLOWS. THE LAST SENTENCE OF THIS EXPANDED PARAGRAPH IS A TRANSITION BETWEEN THIS TOPIC AND THE APPLICATION OF HIS IDEAS TO TODAY.)

This necessary continuing of true education throughout one's lifetime requires that men "soar higher" in their "intellectual flights" than "the columns of the daily paper."

Such warnings apply perhaps even more in our age of mass culture and the electronic media. Do we still allow "Harper and Brothers and Redding and Co. to select our reading?" Do best-seller lists and ratings determine our tastes?

(MANY EXAMPLES FOLLOW–INCLUDING PARALLELS BETWEEN EVENTS NOW AND THOREAU'S CRITICISM OF HIS SOCIETY.)

Thoreau's emphasis finally is on values. He argues that since men can afford what they want, "expense" is always a poor excuse for neglecting education: "If it is necessary, omit one bridge over the river, go round a little there, and throw one arch at least over the darker gulf of ignorance which surrounds us." It is time we begin to consider the number and kind of bridges we are building over the gulfs in our society. . . .

This essay is by no means complete, and the revisions here are not final. The writer is still rethinking and expanding her thoughts on the subject. She is thinking on paper by studying her own responses to Thoreau and to her own first draft. Further marginal comments in this draft may enable her to clarify and be more specific and thorough as she goes along. Eventually she will select from an overproduction of drafted material and refine the style and grammar of the final draft. The point is that until the writer develops fully what she wants to say, mere "correction" can only stifle the growth of ideas. Again, discovering what she wants to say is primarily a matter of responding fully and then studying her own responses. In all these revisions the writer can save time and see her own thinking in a new perspective by rearranging sections and building a new organization through the cut-and-paste method. By using devices similar to film editing, the writer can delete or add material easily, and she can rearrange various sections for emphasis or logical order. Consider the effects of various schemes of rearrangement, and add details that would change the meaning or emphasis in this essay on Thoreau's "Reading."

Another way of drafting from marginal comments and then developing a series of revisions can be seen in the following section from a paper on Mark Twain's *Pudd'nhead Wilson*. The student was assigned to observe the structure of the novel and to describe its effects on her reading. The first step was to annotate her copy by recording her reactions and identifying structural blocks. From these annotations, she wrote the following:

> The structural plot development of the novel moves along four lines, each centered respectively in the events associated with Pudd'nhead Wilson, Tom Driscoll, Roxy, and the others, chiefly Judge Driscoll and the twins. Each group has a story to tell. Wilson solves a mystery and emancipates himself. Roxy attempts to order the chaos and savor the joy which result from her switching the babies. Tom is an heir, a "nigger," a murderer. The twins create sensation in the town, and the Judge both wins an election and fights a duel.
>
> Although everything happens together, a certain emphasis determines four main structural divisions in the action. In chapters 1–6, two developments are in the center of our attention. Wilson is socially ostracized, and Roxy switches Tom and Chambers.
>
> In the transition of chapter 7, there is a hint of the coming crime—Wilson sees the "girl" in Tom's room.
>
> In chapters 8–10, the emphasis is on Tom and his relationship to Roxy's blackmail and the Judge's will. At this time chapter 11 knits the novel tightly together in the meeting at Wilson's house of the protagonists of the various developments of action—Tom, the twins, the Judge, and, of course, Wilson.

The action in chapters 12–20 centers on Tom's attempts to please the Judge, triumph over the Pudd'nhead, incriminate the twins, and maintain a working relationship with Roxy. Tom's conflicts lead to murder and the "framing" of Luigi— leading to the final division of the novel.

The final chapter, 21, is the denouement, where Wilson triumphs in court. Here, and in the Conclusion, the action of all four lines of development is resolved.

These structural divisions are not rigid and are based on an emphasis, a focusing of the reader's attention on the part of the novelist. The reader is aware that the events in the novel occur simultaneously. The novelist, though, realizing everything cannot be said at once, creates structural divisions in which emphasis is the isolating factor. Each division is identified by a certain focus on different characters. In the four divisions stated above, the emphasis is respectively on the people in the town, Roxy and Tom, Tom alone, and finally Wilson.

To expand this early draft, the writer need only follow her own thinking and answer several questions that arose when she reread what she had written. Although the first paragraph is a good overview of the subject, each of the "four lines" calls for further examples and explanation. How does the author present each person or group with a story to tell? Do their stories overlap, or is there a sharp four-part structure? How does the organization affect the reader's knowledge about events and her feelings toward the characters? The writer answers some of these questions. But the discussion is still sketchy in this example. Drawing upon your own responses as a reader, annotate these seven paragraphs on *Pudd'nhead Wilson*. Include suggestions for clarifying and expanding the subject. Write a letter to the author of this selection stating your recommendations for her later drafts. In this letter you will of course be a different audience depending on whether you read the novel or not.

In many ways this chapter describes revision as an endless process. Writers can always write "more of the same, but better." They can always expand, overdraft, then cut back to their best for emphasis and effect. "Warmups," "rehearsal," experimentation with structures, juxtaposition to create new patterns—all are processes for discovering ideas in the process of writing itself. Chapter 10 examines questions about the relationship between the discovery, expression, and arrangement of messages. Revision is a central part of these three stages of communication. To keep the process going and to minimize confusion about "correcting" and "editing," a writer should as a matter of course annotate, write, and then reannotate what he or she has written.

Exercises

1. Authors often revise a manuscript by first annotating it with their re-thinking or re-visions and then incorporating additions and changes into the new and expanded version. In her revised edition of Harold Innis' *Empire and Communications* (Toronto and Buffalo: University of Toronto Press, 1972), Mary Q. Innis explains that the author had written "in the margins of his copy new ideas, suggestions, quotations, references" (p.xiv)—all of which could be used in a new edition of the work. The revisions re-create the author's later thinking on his subject.

Using a similar technique, annotate one of your own completed essays and then follow your notes and write a revised and expanded version. Pay careful attention to the techniques you find effective and explain why and how such techniques work for you. This will no doubt take several weeks to complete.

2. Look into the history and theory of film editing and study in greater detail the similarities between manuscript editing and the views of Eisenstein and Vertov.

3. Explain the statement "Revision is more of the same, but better." How similar are "invention" and "revision"? Examine similarities in your own techniques for "drafting" and "revising" essays.

4. Following the method described in this chapter, edit one of your finished essays by cutting it apart and rebuilding it. Think of the process as the discovery of new patterns and an opening up to new ideas, examples, and questions that will expand your own thinking. Use whatever cut-and-paste technique you find most productive.

5. Illustrate the essay you have revised (in #4) by making a pictorial collage. Then compare the way you structure the essay and the collage. Show how you are composing, developing, and revising in each example.

6. Explain the difference between marginal comments that involve a reader in an activity and unconscious underlining that substitutes for, rather than records, thinking on paper. Give examples from your own reading of textbooks.

7. Observe closely, in the next movie you see, how the filmmaker uses editing as a creative device for building structure and meaning. List specific examples of edited "cuts," "transitions," shifts in the camera's "point of view," and the special effects created in the "collision" or "juxtaposition" of apparent opposites. Explain the effects of such techniques. Compare the filmmaker's original "shooting" or "drafting" and his later creation by editing.

8. Explain the psychological advantages of the particular kind of cut-and-paste editing technique which you find most effective. Distinguish

between advantages that are primarily time-saving and others that help you discover ideas and develop a topic.

9. Why are writers reluctant to "throw out" copy that doesn't "fit" what they are doing? Why the hesitancy to delete what is quite obviously not working?

10. Cite examples of one essay that leads to another. Suggest ways to "salvage" deleted material that might itself develop into another essay. Outline a method for best using such "discarded" material and support your method with specific illustrations from your own work.

Summary/Review

Genius in writing is more hard work than inspiration. The work of revision is not "correction" but an indispensable part of the creative process. Learning to write most probably means writing few "new" pieces and instead expanding and reworking one selection to fully develop its potential. Revising an essay is like editing a film. Early drafts or warmups develop into a pattern that emerges through the writer's or filmmaker's manipulation of possible form. "Drafting" and "editing" are therefore one continuous process. Effective revision once again demands a workable system of marginal comments to which you can return in rethinking your responses. Moreover, you may provide further marginal comments on your own first drafts as a record of your later and presumably more developed responses in a topic. Again the systematic record of such responses is crucial. Similarly, the physical disposition of successive drafts—the way words actually get on paper—can make revision creative rather than corrective. As you become better at revision, you have less and less need for more and more of the activities you have mastered.

10/ Writing Beginnings at the End, or How Do I Know What I Am Going to Say Until I've Said It?

How *do* you know what you want to say until you say it? How can a writer begin an essay without knowing what he or she will say in the essay? And then hasn't the essay already begun? Maybe this seems to be only meaningless double-talk; but consider the problem of actually beginning an essay even after marginal comments and outlines are working for you. Even with much to say, "how to begin" is a crucial make-or-break decision that will affect everything that follows.

The trouble with writing beginnings is that writers almost always write them too early. Contrary to a sacred old adage, it is not always the best policy to begin at the beginning. A closer look at revision (chapter 9) shows that essays, to paraphrase Vertov on cinema, are not written but *built*. A writer builds an essay in progressive stages by pushing off from a beginning that does more than get things started. Anything that is built depends on structure. To be able to respond to the structure of an essay, an audience must be ready for what is coming.

To prepare the reader for what is coming, you as a writer must write a beginning *after* you know not only what you are going to say but also the pattern in which you will present what you will say. When you are in close contact with your own thinking, when you have carefully thought out your reactions, recorded them in marginal comments, discovered outlines from within, built momentum and pattern through transitions and paragraphing, developed the complexity of your thoughts in sufficient detail and generalization, and engaged yourself in the complex stages of the revision process—then and only then are you ready to write a beginning that makes legitimate promises about what is to come. You cannot "set up" a reader for what is to follow until you know how you got to where you are. To write the beginning at the end is to make the map when one is most qualified to describe the territory.

Rhetoricians 2500 years ago and communications experts today are saying many of the same things in different terms. Classical orators and media specialists alike insist on a "game plan" for an audience. Through a careful plan, the writer strengthens his or her essay by predisposing the reader to respond in predictable patterns. The introduction or beginning of an essay should therefore do the job of what classical rhetoricians called the *dispositio*. It should gain attention, present facts, define terms, outline procedures, and set up a progression that will help shape the audience's responses as they develop. This early "contract" between writer and audience takes the form at once of a promise and a controlling outline. This sort of beginning helps create solid exposition and argumentation. And it is also sound psychology.

The classical rhetorician's model for beginnings applies even in our media age. *Narratio* presents the facts the orator will work with; *expositio* tells the audience what the orator is going to do and defines the terms that the audience must know in order to comprehend; *divisio* illustrates for the audience concretely *how* the orator is going to accomplish goals by previewing the outline and steps of the argument. All these steps set the stage for the *confirmatio,* or the actual proof; the *confutatio,* or the anticipation and discussion of possible objections; and the *peroration,* the summing up and plea for action.

The beginning of an essay is not, then, a representation of where a writer began, but rather a reflective preview of coming attactions. It is an announcement of what is to come from the point of view of one who has been there. In addition to generating interest in one's subject, the writer prepares the reader to respond in certain patterns. Because people generally get someplace more easily when they know where they are going, the writer sets the stages for the readers' responses. In the beginning of an essay, the writer sets up the rules for his game, tells the reader what to expect, and outlines briefly the exact route by which the essay will proceed.

This emphasis on beginnings assumes that writers exercise choices in their efforts to reach an audience, that they discover what to say often in the process of thinking on paper, that they reshape and structure their materials in order to create the best possible interaction between form and content, and that they take special care in writing and rewriting beginnings to ensure that all such good things will happen for their audience upon reading what has been written.

But this logic of structure, maps, game plans, and *dispositio* is not always so easy to see in an age conditioned by the media. Although it is not always clear why, emphasis on methodical schematic pattern doesn't seem consistent with the way people actually communicate today. Assuming even the best of motives and the largest reservoir of energy, the student of media might verbalize frustration by saying, "If I do everything in the introduction, what's left to do in the essay?"

But classical rhetoric updated appears everywhere in the media. Marshall

McLuhan on the viewer's role in the creation of the TV image perceived, Dos Passos and Joyce opening up to the cinematic and journalistic structure of modern fiction (read *rhetoric*), Eisenstein or Vertov on film editing and the origins of the creative process—all reflect a meshing of classical premises and the workings of contemporary print and nonprint mass media. Classical *dispositio* can be seen in advertising techniques, in film, in collage/montage effects of all sorts, and in the complex structure of nonverbal communication in the nonprint media. To map the old onto the new in these instances is to sneak in the back door the timelessness of the classical. With eyes and ears tuned by nonprint media, we can observe techniques in classical rhetoric that less oral sensibilities wouldn't even know how to look for.

Basic examples will suggest directions for writers who are influenced by the media every day. In television advertising, for example, surprisingly the typical one-minute spot is becoming more rather than less like the classical rhetorical model. What is presented as the facts opens most commercial pitches *(narratio)*. What follows is usually the speaker's "Tell you what I'm going to do" or "I will show you" *(expositio)* and "I'll do this right before your very eyes by looking at X, Y, Z." *(divisio)*. In fact most advertising overwhelms with *dispositio* and then has neither the time nor the inclination for the *confirmatio*, or proof proper. And curiously, *confutatio* (in the increasing deprecation of other name products specifically or at least by implication) and *peroration* ("See, ours is the best; go out and be the first to have it") are becoming more frequent.

All this is obvious; it is, after all, the typical rhetoric that one would expect in verbal advertising. But as all advertisers know, suggestion, allusion, and inference build up more from the nonverbal and can therefore be more subtly persuasive than direct appeal. This same rhetorical model stressing the *dispositio* can be found in the visual and symbolic representations and in the musical backgrounds or counterparts for the one-minute commercial. If we were accustomed to seeing rhetorical patterns in written prose, we would more readily understand the unique nonverbal extensions of such devices as classical *dispositio*. The visual representation that opens many commercials lets the audience see pictured for them "the facts" as they infer ("Look, we are so much happier now that we have ———") this *narratio* is a "given." Letting the viewer in to observe a "real life" enactment (taking bleach away from some "poor sucker") or to watch a careful arrangement of structural blocks on a screen (pain pills racing to a stomach) performs the task of the *expositio* and, if it is elaborated, the *divisio* as well (the visual image beckons that we "come along and look at all these people all over the country who are right now discovering the joy of ———"). The viewer is brought to the brink of the *confirmatio* and then generally urged to provide that for himself (the picture and joyous music cry out that "you must try our product, in order to be ———" or even less verbally, "you too can do/just what you see/hear right now"). The rhetorical patterns of subliminal, nonverbal communication are closer to the techniques of the media than we might ordinarily think.

Classical *dispositio* is perhaps most readily observable on film in documentaries and cinema vérité, especially in the conscious manipulation of materials so as to persuade through seeming artlessness. Vertov's "kino-eye" is again instructive in its assumption that the camera is a tool for research in the "endless process of taking creative notes on film." The actual creative process takes place in the highly rhetorical work of editing: "The school of kino-eye requires that the cine-thing be built upon 'intervals,' that is, upon a movement between the pieces, the frames; upon the proportions of these pieces between themselves, upon the transitions from one visual impulse to the one following it." Again this process appears to be so contrived (especially when it is verbalized) that it is easy to overlook the subtle nonverbal rhetorical structures in cinematic montage. Even there, collage and montage rely on observable pattern which by definition must be fixed (so as to be able to vary later) at the outset.

Perhaps more difficult to see are the parallels between the highly verbal *dispositio* of traditional discourse and similar rhetorical structures in nonverbal communication. But again we must first look on silent languages, adumbrations, symbolic gestures, the movements of infants—all complex interactions involving initial signal networks very like the groundwork of classical *dispositio*. As Haig A. Bosmajian has shown in *The Rhetoric of Non-Verbal Communication* (Glenview, Ill.: Scott, Foresman, 1971), law journals abound with studies of the communicative force of the nonverbal. What all such studies point to is exploratory and problematic. Yet such legal precedent may further point the way to the responsibility of readers and writers to watch rhetoric updating itself and to educate ourselves in the process.

Exercises

1. Select two or three essays that you have already developed from marginal comments through outlines and revisions to a finished product. Rewrite the beginnings of each essay to set up what follows in the manner of classical *dispositio*.

2. Describe fully (a) a one-minute television advertisement, (b) the opening scenes of a recent film, and (c) the first two or three minutes of a lecture you have attended. Analyze the rhetorical structure of each with special reference to the *dispositio, exordium, narratio, expositio, divisio, confirmatio, confutatio,* and *peroration*. When are these rhetorical techniques explicit and when are they present through subtle implication?

3. Describe any entirely nonverbal communication that you have experienced or witnessed. How far into the experience did you realize what

was happening? When did you begin to see the shape of the message being sent? How much did an effective beginning contribute to your perceiving the overall pattern?

4. In what specific contexts would a "map" or "set-up" beginning be less effective than holding back information from the reader? Find examples and explain why some type of beginning other than classical *dispositio* would be more effective.

5. Find examples of ineffective or less than fully effective beginnings in magazine articles and feature stories in newspapers, as well as in your own work. Suggest changes in these beginnings and then rewrite at least one of them according to your suggestions.

6. Compare classical *dispositio* in the beginning of an essay with a preliminary lab report for a science experiment, a briefing on a legal case, and a prospectus for a business report. Show how the intent and format are similar in each procedure.

7. Write a fully developed beginning (following classical *dispositio*) for a speech on the problems caused by boredom in our society.

8. Write five beginnings for essays that you would like to write (if you had time) or that you would like to read if someone else would write them. Include at least one beginning for an essay that "needs to be written, but for a variety of reasons probably never will be."

9. Reread one of your own completed essays. Pay special attention to the ending. Try rewriting the ending as a beginning that fully previews what is to come.

10. Study your own marginal comments from which you have written an essay. What kind of marginal comments are most likely to find their way into the beginning of an essay? into the conclusion? What kind of marginal comment makes the best opening sentence? transition? thesis sentence? closing remark? title?

11. Review the discussion throughout this book of organizing and developing your ideas. Look back at the essays you have built and revised and compare your thinking on structure in an essay and structure in nonverbal communication. Compare the pattern of movement in mime and the organization of a speech or an essay. Make a list of similarities and differences in the ways film, mime, speech, and the essay structure what they communicate.

12. Study the advertisement on page 179 which explains techniques for creating a slide show. Note especially

    (a) the emphasis on knowing your audience

(b) the importance of meaningful order in presentation

(c) the building of ideas through the rearrangement, addition, and deletion of slides

(d) the attitude toward revision as "creation" rather than just "correction"

(e) the notion of rehearsal as a rethinking or revisioning of ideas

(f) the development of ideas forward *and* backward and deciding on a beginning only after it's clear what the purpose and direction of the slide show will be

Follow the suggestions in the ad and make a short slide presentation. Again, compare your techniques to composing and editing written copy.

How to Give a Better-than-offhand Talk Without Being a Showman[*]

1. Think about:
   What does my audience have in common?
   Why are they coming?
   How much do they know already?
   How much more do they want to know?
   What attitudes will they bring with them?
   What do I want to change or accomplish with my
   message?

2. "Multimedia" presentations can be written and produced for you by professionals. There are occasions where more modest efforts of your own might be more appropriate. Make sure this is one such.

3. Get a pack of 4″ × 6″ index cards.

4. Draw a large box in the upper left-hand corner of a card. In that box draw a crude sketch of what comes into your mind when you concentrate on one of the principal points you want to make. It may be a chart, clipping, symbol, diagram, or a photo of a person, place, or thing. Underneath state the point in as few words as needed to cue yourself to the thought.

5. Do a similar card about the thought that leads into the thought you have just expressed. Now do one about the thought that follows the first one. Keep going like that.

6. When you run out of ideas to tack on ahead or behind, think of the important points that haven't fallen into sequence yet. Make cards for them. Always work up the sketch before the words. (If lively words flow out of you too easily to work that way, probably anything you'd say on any subject would fascinate any audience. In that case you hardly need any of this advice.)

7. Arrange the cards on a table in an order that makes sense.

8. Now get critical. Is the development of the ideas too plodding? Would some other scheme of arranging the cards liven up the beginning and the end? Which cards should be

---

[*]Reprinted courtesy of Eastman Kodak Company.

tossed out? Where are you skipping too fast? Where are you trying to pack too much into a single card? Make out the additional cards you need.

9. Now get critical about your stack of cards from the standpoint of practicality. Some of your sketches would take too much time and art talent to turn into presentable slides. Substitute images easier to obtain from internal sources or the public domain. If you (and perhaps your secretary) are on your own for this, the KODAK EKTAGRAPHIC Visualmaker kit can much simplify your slide-making problems, both in copying extant material and in snapping originals.

10. Run through the talk. Make believe your sketches are already slides on the screen. Speak from the cues you've written under the sketches. (When you give the actual talk, the slides themselves may suffice as cues. Then you wouldn't be reading at all. Why assemble an audience just to hear you read?)

11. Decide whether you have too much or too little material. Discard or add cards accordingly.

12. Now you are ready to prepare your slides. Worst of the pitfalls is type or other detail that the important but shy people in the back row can't quite make out on the screen. To avoid this and other mistakes, send for the free Kodak publication "Slides with a Purpose." Address request to Dept. 55X, Kodak, Rochester, N.Y. 14650. We'll throw in literature about the KODAK Visualmaker and other handy products.

13. You're on!

14. You're great!

Summary/Review

You can write an effective beginning only after you know where you are going. The primary job of a good beginning is to predispose the audience to respond to what is to follow in the rest of the essay. In classical rhetoric this map or preview was called the *dispositio*. Classical orators first gained attention, presented facts, defined terms, outlined procedures, and set up a pattern the audience could then expect to follow. On the surface, the *dispositio* doesn't seem to apply to sensibilities conditioned by electronic media. But examples from advertising, film, and nonverbal communication point to similarities in the structures of classical oration and contemporary media. Certain identifiable "summary" marginal comments will most likely provide the best material for beginnings.

11 / Keeping Track of What You Think: Library Notes, Research Papers, Essay Examinations, Speeches, Letters, and Other Marginal Comments Not in the Margin

In Plain Speaking: An Oral Biography of Harry S. Truman (New York: Putnam, 1974) Merle Miller refers to Mr. Truman as "a great underliner, a great writer of marginal comments, usually about things with which he disagreed" (p. 26). His comments were more often than not "Bunk!" "He doesn't know what he's talking about!" "That's not True!" "Where did he ever get a damn fool notion like that?" Similarly, next to a passage he found especially good, he would write "True! True! True!" Mr. Truman's habits of making notes in margins are fairly typical of the busiest people who nonetheless find time to read actively. It is fairly safe to assume that a President of the United States spends a good portion of the day reading, listening to briefings, seeking and giving advice, giving speeches, and in general thinking on paper, out loud, and in formal presentations. Systematic notes and marginal comments would seem to help busy people to keep track of their own thinking and make it available in its best form when they need it. In this example, marginal comments provide the starting point for a variety of finished products from position papers to responses in a press conference.

What Miller underscores in President Truman's active reading is important for at least two reasons. First, the technique has many uses beyond simply writing about what one has read. It serves primarily to record what otherwise might be lost; moreover, it provides a source of material for any form of communication. Second, a system of marginal notations seems most useful to the exceptionally busy person who must keep records of his or her own thinking on a variety of subjects and for a variety of uses. Even though marginal comments impress almost everyone as a good idea, the strongest resistance to responding in the margin generally comes from those who claim to have no time to slow down their reading. "Good idea but too slow" overlooks the fact that reading effectively means thinking through something well rather than merely skimming the surface of a great bulk that remains a puzzle. True, a reader must select carefully passages worth careful thinking and annotation. But truly busy persons can ill afford *not* to record their reactions as they move quickly through large amounts of material. It is often said that "if you want something done right away, give it to a busy rather than an idle person." The systematic discipline evidenced in the reading habits of busy people may be one of the chief reasons that they are generally effective communicators.

Discovering and expressing ideas by annotating *one's own books* has been the subject of much of the first ten chapters. But marginal comments have a much broader use also in the writing of speeches, letters, examinations, and term papers. Often readers cannot preserve their thinking in the margin because the books they are reading are not theirs. This is especially true in any kind of research where most of the sources are library copies of books and periodicals. Everyone learns how to take notes of some sort for future reference. But the purposes and format for taking notes are often overlooked or misunderstood. Too many readers merely copy passages and fail to include their own thinking on those passages. Or else they may summarize a large amount of material or jot down key words and phrases so they can recall at least the high points of what they have read. But unless such notes record their own responses to what they are reading, they will be no further along in understanding or developing their own thinking. In short, taking notes in a library requires the same kind of systematic self-exploration that is essential in marginal comments.

A brief look at one workable system for note taking will illustrate some ways in which readers can record their thinking in marginal comments without writing in the margin. Suppose you have just read a chapter in a library book. After recording all the necessary information such as author, title, place and year of publication (so you can get back to the book when you want to), you might first write a concise one-paragraph summary of the chapter. Special attention to the author's thesis will force you to get to the point faster. And *brief* quotations will enable you to reread the author in his or her exact words later when the book isn't immediately available. It is, of course, easy to waste time copying long passages that you may never use. Very lengthy passages that are essential can be photocopied and marked in the margin of the copy. The procedure so far is fairly standard. It is most important, however, to follow all this summarizing and quoting with your own reactions and questions about what you have read. Whatever system of marginal comments you generally use in marking your own books should also become a part of any note taking in the library.

Drawing from active reading and annotating in the library, research papers are dialogues between writers and their sources. Methods presented throughout this book for recording your responses are useful techniques for writing reports, term papers, or longer studies requiring extended library work. Alternating quotations from a source with the writer's own interpretations will provide at least first-draft material for a research study. A writer often begins writing an essay when he or she records initial reactions in marginal comments. So too a "research paper" often begins in the notes that summarize not only the material in books but also the reader's responses to what is read in the books. An entire essay may develop from one or two comments on note cards. Or one set of responses may lead to further questions that will, in turn, alert a reader to look for certain things in further research. And a reader should record further responses in marginal comments when looking back at notes later.

The procedures for responding in the margin can be useful even in taking essay examinations where there are usually no books to annotate. Or course notes made while studying can make reading and preparing for the exam simpler and more meaningful. But during the writing of the essay answers as well, a brief initial period of "annotation" can build forcefulness and direction into otherwise "sprawling" responses. Simple and direct lists of points to cover, brief jottings of "topic sentences," and decisions about what to emphasize will organize material in its most informative and persuasive format. "Thinking in the margin" before answering the question directly not only helps structure a response but also is itself a process for discovering ideas and translating them from head to paper. All in all, systematic note taking can always be a process that is developmental. One thing leads to another. Note taking is not merely copying information. It is a recording of one's thinking in order to explore, develop, and then communicate that thinking.

The most effective system for taking notes depends on how one will use the notes later. A reader will record different kinds of responses in preparing a speech and writing an essay. For a speech one will focus on information that can be retained in a single hearing rather than what requires several readings or extensive study. Similarly, more quotations and more methodical detail in notes are needed for a research paper than when reading for pleasure and information. Whether taking notes for a speech, essay, research paper, or pleasure, a reader will most likely record far more information and responses than will actually be used. But keeping the detailed record is a first essential step before any selection and arrangement of materials can be meaningful.

The busiest people often keep the best notes because they have learned not only to use time effectively but also to record their own thinking so they can build on it when time does become available. For example, if you are to respond to a speaker when you have no prepared text ahead of time, you must take concise and responsive notes and prepare your remarks as you listen to the speech. Or in a debate tournament the participants respond to one another with the aid of notes taken on the spot. Many dinner speakers, especially when called upon unexpectedly for "a few remarks," are known to jot down key words and phrases or punch lines on paper napkins or the backs of matchbook covers. Essays and research papers may just as likely begin in marginal comments, systematic note taking in a library, or scribbling on a paper napkin. Again, recorded responsiveness preserved for later development is an essential starting point for creative thinking and effective writing.

One final suggestion seems in order on the purposes and extent of systematic note taking. Notes, like marginal comments, must strike a balance between thoroughness and conciseness depending again on what use the reader plans for them. Thoroughly detailed responses for use in writing must nonetheless remain focused if the reader is to avoid wasting time. And for certain kinds of oral presentations, concise cues are better than lengthy passages which necessarily create the impression that the speaker is reading remarks word for word. In conducting an interview, for example, the questioner will generally refer to notes that are detailed enough to be helpful yet brief enough to maintain flexibility and spontaneity.

Marginal comments in one's own books, notes on reading in the library, note cards used to deliver a speech or conduct an interview, and even the briefest scribblings on paper tablecloths in order to reply to a speaker—all are devices used by busy and often famous people simply to keep their thoughts together or express themselves in writing or public appearances. But for nonprofessional writers and for students who have completed their formal education, the most important form of written communication is the letter. In business and professional communication, notes written in margins or spoken into dictaphones are generally the "annotations" from which formal correspondence is derived. Quite simply, the content of a letter often begins as anything from marginal annotations of another letter, reactions to written proposals submitted for consideration, or notes taken in a meeting.

Letters are marginal comments with an audience. A letter writer is keenly aware of the letter reader's presence while writing. In perhaps no other written form is the writer's purpose easier to see. Writer, audience, and subject are well defined, and the purpose is always either obvious in itself or stated explicitly.

Because a letter writer's range of styles is as wide as the intended audiences, the letter is an appropriate form in which to express the broadest scope of thoughts and feelings. Systematic notes based on extensive research go into the preparation of letters written in formal job applications. Casual correspondence or love letters, on the other hand, might read like expanded annotations on one's experiences and beliefs. Letters to the Editor express—formally or informally—reactions to the writer's reading or to current events. In biblical writings, "Epistles" often take the place of speeches or essays in teaching theology.

Because the audience in a letter is clearly determined in the heading ("Dear ———"), the writer can develop and control the persona (see chapters 2 and 3). Marginal comments can therefore grow in one central direction and speak directly to the announced audience. If a reader writes a letter to the author of a book that he or she has read, that letter can be at once a review of the book and an essay on the issues the book raises. And if that letter were intended for publication, three focal points (reader, the book's author as direct audience, and what might be called "audience intended to overhear") would shape its form and purpose. If you write a letter to Michelangelo about the Sistine Chapel, you obviously do not intend what you say for Michaelangelo's eyes. Choosing the specific direct audience may help you to organize your thoughts and reach with greater impact the real audience who is intended to "overhear" what you have written.

Examples throughout literature readily illustrate the potential of the letter as a form. A section of James Baldwin's *The Fire Next Time* is subtitled "Letter from a Region of My Mind." Eldridge Cleaver's *Soul on Ice* is written as a series of letters from prison. Martin Luther King's "Letter from a Birmingham Jail" was an influential social document in the civil rights movement. Poems written as letters by Alexander Pope and John Keats used the form to organize many themes and techniques. Entire novels have been written as a series of letters—as in Tobias Smollett's *Humphry Clinker* (1771).

Thinking in the margin is an important part of all written communication. At first, the audience for the reader's marginal comments is most often the reader. In fact, a memo to oneself (a reminder to keep an appointment, pay bills, or buy tickets to a concert) may be the purest form of annotation. Initial marginal notations and finished product, writer and audience, are all rolled into one. And more sophisticated recording devices are making it easier for a reader to "talk out" his or her reactions to what is read. The "annotator" can then listen to an "instant replay" of personal reactions while rereading the original selection. Locating specific comments on a tape and rearranging various sections are still difficult, however. Until complex retrieval devices catch up with advances in actual recording mechanisms, a pencil or pen is likely to remain the best equipment for "thinking on paper."

Exercises

1. Develop an extensive set of "marginal comments" on cards or notepads without marking the book you are reading.

2. Check your notes in #1 for an effective balance of quotations and your own reactions to those quotations.

3. Write an essay using your notes and the processes described in earlier chapters on marginal comments.

4. Listen to a speech as if you were to respond to the speaker's remarks as soon as she finishes. Take notes for your reply. Deliver your reply orally and then write a more formal response in an essay.

5. Answer a letter you have received recently by first preparing detailed notes from which to conduct a formal response.

6. Enter into a formal debate with a group of interested parties on a topic mutually agreed to. Keep careful notes of your responses to each other and then write a series of essays arguing both sides of the question under discussion.

7. Prepare a series of notes for use in interviewing a famous person. Then study your notes and use them to conduct research and write an essay on that person.

8. Look back over any set of notes you have prepared after reading this chapter. Respond to your own notes in marginal comments, expand the notes further, and write an essay based on the more developed record of your thinking.

9. Look into the techniques of famous people who habitually record their thinking "in the margin." (Look back to the Exercises of chapter 3 for suggestions.) If the well-known annotators discuss their reading or work habits, explain how they save time in the process. Describe the habits you have developed as an annotator through the exercises in this book.

10. Write a very brief research paper in first-draft form by creating a dialogue between yourself and your major sources. Alternate direct quotation and your own interpretation of the source.

11. Compose two or three "essay questions" and write the "set ups" for answers in brief "marginal" annotations. Then answer one in detail following the direction and structure suggested by your "jottings." Compare your techniques to the processes of "inductive" structure discussed in chapters 4 and 5.

12. In "Epistle from My Heart" (reprinted on p. 187), Herbert Woodward Martin brings together autobiography, poetry, and argumentation in the form of a letter. Martin creates a sense of "urgency" not only from what he says but also because his is a direct plea to a specific reader, at a clearly defined time, and in the highly personal form of a conversational letter written on a first-name basis. "Epistle" expresses ideas that its sender had been "thinking about for some time now" and which he hopes to "fit together" in the letter itself. The expression of this range of ideas and experiences might be thought of as marginal comments with an audience. Several passages convey strong feelings that might often take root at many different times and places in some form of thinking "in the margin." Annotate these passages and reply to them in an "Epistle" of your own.

Herbert Woodward Martin
Epistle From My Heart*

February 16, 1972

Dear Roy:

This is a rather long letter. I have been thinking about it for some time now. I am not sure all of the parts are here, nor am I sure what is here will fit together by the end. But, because we are committed to enduring, I suspect, I have the same hope for this epistle that I have for the world and the predominant presence of Mankind.

There are any number of impulses that I could point to as causes for the poem I will soon quote in its entirety, and they are equally the growing militant resolution (black and white), frustration, dissatisfaction, and apathy (students, middle and lower class America) and ultimately the realization that however far the black man has come, *He has not come far enough!* It is not his fault. The forces which disfranchised him, robbed the Indian, and have systematically made niggers out of: women (black and white), and every minority beyond the blacks: prisoners, homosexuals and, indeed, every reactionary voice that has cried out, along with every liberal voice of warning. We have killed them all, allowed them to be killed or we await their execution. It is part of our nature as men to ignore prophets; it is also part of our nature to rid ourselves of these men. There we do not lack the conviction Yeats warned 20th century Man about. Poor Poets! The dark is always around them!

Let me quote to you that poem which seems to be the initial impetus.

> *God is a prisoner behind the blackman's teeth,*
> *Where the tongue has forgotten the taste of Human things.*

---

*Reprinted from *Rap* (March 1972), pp. 27–30. © copyright 1972 by Herbert Woodward Martin. Reprinted by permission of the author.

Herbert Woodward Martin, Associate Professor of English at the University of Dayton, is the author of *New York the Nine Million and Other Poems* and *The Shit-Storm Poems* as well as many poems, articles, and plays appearing widely in journals and collected works.

Death, my brother,
My distinguisher,
Count my fingers,
Count my bones,
We need each other to see.

My intention in the first two lines here attempts imagistically to deal with traditional white stereotype beliefs. They are: All Negroes have white teeth, God is white. There are other more important things which seem to me equally necessary and they are that the teeth represent bars; they are weapons that protect that paradoxical instrument of good and evil: the tongue. When the tongue forgets what it is, essentially, to be human, then it is time that we give up, and turn everything over to the computers. Perhaps, as I am given to saying to my student writers, "All of what you were aiming at did not come through," and so the poem had better be done over. What I think is really wrong with these lines, and so many others like them is that liberals and conservatives would like for them to vanish, and with that process, perhaps, the problem itself would also disappear. No such thing is ever likely to take place! James Baldwin warned us of our inconsiderateness in *The Fire Next Time*, and we have foolishly and unwisely ignored not only him but everyone else pre-Baldwin or post-Baldwin. I think we are likely to go on repeating our errors until the last man passes away. We are inexorably committed to that: both blacks and whites, Americans and Russians, East and West. This is the fate of the world as we know it, sad as it may seem, it is the truth. And that my dear friend is the one thing we are not often given to telling ourselves.

Confess, as I must, that there are innumerable freedoms open to the black man in America these days, I am still bothered by the fact that things have never had to open up for anyone else, who came to this country, in quite the same way. The old adage is still applicable.

If you're white, all right.
If you're brown, stick around.
If you're black, get back.

And if it is not applicable in the same terms we may say then it is only because the new black has simply reversed the axiom. If the Constitution had truly meant *all men*, and that word implies and includes women as well, then there might have been less of a problem, and maybe none at all. But, it truly did not, and *that has been the essential problem!*

Do not mistake me, I am a firm believer in the fact that you cannot legislate the minds of the people, but the fact that whites have all along known The Constitution was for them, has made them slow in recognizing anyone or thing except those in their own interest. One can be certain that this is why we are distrusted so much abroad. It is the combination of facade democracy, and self-entrapping interest, as opposed to, say, the Russians who really do not pretend when they buy an interest in a country. We have witnessed time and time again how they have put down those who owed them allegiance. I hastily add that I do not suggest we adopt the Russian posture, or even so close a thing as the Kent State affair. Alas, this is why every group in America we can think of is crying out "Liberation!"

Again, if the truth is told they shall be crying for a long time to come, mainly because *we have stopped caring about each other*. Secondly, we have killed off every ray of hope that we might have possibly had to make things better, or possibly show us the way. It is no wonder we are withdrawn; the sixties were so violent. If the peace and order which is to come is tyrannical in any way then we can look to the eighties for a replay of the sixties.

I am this hopeless and this despairing because I have had a chance to reflect on how the world regards blacks. They are less liked than any other group I know. We are still that exotic, that rare unknown commodity. We favor, look alike and, I dare say to paraphrase Shylock, are subject to the same joys, ills and hand of fate that others are subject to. But that has not elevated blacks in any sense to a level of freedom. Let me relate to you several personal incidents.

When I was in Italy last summer I happened to be walking alone down a street, when suddenly I was confronted with a young Italian boy's laughter. I suspect he was twelve or thirteen. It dawned on me quickly he was laughing at me. Surely in this age of modern technology he must know that there are black people in the world. Or, take for instance when I was again walking (this time with a friend) on a street in Germany, a small child of some five years asked why I was so dark? His interest was more tolerable. At least somewhere in his memory is locked the fact that he has seen someone darker than he is and an explanation as to why it is so. The first incident is unforgiveable; the second is. There is a third example. I was sitting quietly in a restaurant in Switzerland, and a little boy who was with his mother left her and came over to my table and sat down. He was genuinely friendly. He was even younger than the second child. He, too, perhaps, even knew I was different in terms of color, but I was a man, and that seemed grounds enough upon which to be friendly. We broke bread together, and I strained my French to make sense to him. When I left he offered me his hand to shake. I was surprised, indeed pleased. I hope against all the odds that the last child, and even the second will not mature into an individual like the first boy. For I confess were I not committed to doing something worthwhile in this world I might very easily have jumped into one of those Venetian canals and ended it all. And I know the same kinds of depression that hounds every black from Watts to the South of Chicago to Harlem, and truthfully, it hounds every other minority from the poorest white to the poorest Mexican and Puerto Rican. There is no true or real progress until we are willing to take the peripheral fringes of society with us. This world moves more and more toward the extremes of Haves and Have-nots, and the middle class is caught exactly in the middle. It is no place to be! It is no man's land! It is the Gaza Strip! It is that indistinguishable line between black and white. It is that place where the old are committed and the young never visit. It is true, what we do to ourselves, we do to others, and so if we do not hold ourselves in high regard we are not likely to hold anyone else in high regard either. I am aware of those individuals who believe prejudicially that they are better ——— (fill in the blank) but it is another fact that they do not enjoy themselves either, less perhaps. Our values, morale and self-appreciation have fallen into a hole from which we are unlikely to ever retrieve them again. We may attribute most of our problems to arrogance, vanity and assumption.

It is to this latter problem that I should like to turn my specific attention. The basic assumption that if one is born White, Anglo-Saxon, Protestant, all is O.K. Even with the poorest of whites the assumption is still there, but it is not there for men of darker humanity. And that is a major crime, No, *sin*! It is so because as Americans (whites, that is) one still hears, "Wait," "Be patient!" And I hear my brothers and sisters replying "What the hell for?" I know essentially they are right! If one is not moved by metaphors, then we had better get back to listening to the heart, and be moved by emotion, or ultimately there will be such an unleashing of frustration and anger that no one on earth will be able to turn the tide, and it will be squarely the fault of those who cried, "Wait." There is simply no more time! We must get to work!

I said I was to speak for a moment on assumption. Let me put it this way. In 1972 it is still a miracle if a black man escapes from the ghetto into which he is born. It is no wonder, black men have come to hate so vocally. They have been bought and used by everyone including themselves that they no longer trust anyone. It is because there are those who have been shrewd enough to get all of the power (real, as opposed to illusory) and more important most of the money. Indeed, that is where most of the power in the world is: in money. Money is influence and vice-versa. There is no way around it. The most astute Black, Negro, Afro-American (choose one) has always realized this as a matter of course on his way to middle class existence. This process has necessarily separated him from less fortunate blacks, and is the basis for much of the problems that exist among blacks.

It may well be true that the Uncle Toms and the Aunt Jemimas sold out, but I maintain they bought us something even more precious: *Time*. And it would be to our benefit to use that time well through an investment in intelligence, politics and economics. These are the necessary factors which serve as impulse and thrust to this world and specifically to the American Society as we know it. There should be no apologies for those individuals who bought time for their survivors, only praise. We are their heirs, and I know of no better way of spending an inheritance than by passing along as much of my own particular heritage to younger generations. I aim at giving each one a sense of his own individual self. It is out of the pride for the individual self that the appreciation of the group is solidified. It can happen no other way. The facade of all of the Afro-American trend matters very little unless the individual is happy with himself. What I am saying, and this is vital, is that there must be something internal for both black and white to work from or it is all for naught. Before the voices of righteous indignation are raised against me, let me say I am for the Afro (except in theatres where they keep me from seeing) and I am for all the costume clothing. I am for the sincere student of those cultural influences which have their roots in African and/or Afro-American blackness, *but when these things are studied to the exclusion of everything else a distortion occurs. That, also, has been the single problem all along with white education.* Black contributions have been ignored (except when it was outright stealing to make money), and one need only look at the scientific and artistic influences to realize the wealth of contributions blacks have made under the worst possible conditions.

The more I teach, the more I learn one implicit fact and that is that we are a divided nation, people, race, and what is even worse is that we are divided against ourselves. We are not individually together. Mainly, this is true because blacks have finally been convinced by the past that they are not a desirable part of the American condition, and so they have turned even more inward. The retreat seems final! I regret it. I am even at some loss to convince these young people that their thinking is false, especially when I continue to find people who are prejudiced, and who subtly discriminate. I realize how foolish I must sound by saying that one has to trust. Such an attitude clearly asks for further deception.

Let me truthfully say that blacks and whites, young ones especially, realize that for this society to succeed the problem still is building a substantial two-way street which will support the activities of common goals. If this is not done, of course the society will go on being frustrated and divisive. It is, quite frankly, this very factor which has allowed those less liberal Americans to maintain the slavery that some hundred years ago, in costly blood, was declared illegal.

The assumptive naivete that individuals can absolve themselves of the problem is no longer valid! We are all heirs to the crimes committed in the past. If we, then, reap the wealth of those crimes, we must answer, in turn, for the faults of those crimes. That is to say, we are at that juncture where we can no longer say the problem is solvable only by a certian group of people or that they must find responsible answers for themselves. Good God, this buck passing is mainly why we have so many dissatisfied factions in America—young and old, rich and poor, black and white, men and women, militant and gay, hip and conservative, Catholic, Protestant and Jew, and in the center of all of this frustration stands the most isolated minority of all, the middle class. They are, alas, the buffer zone to good and bad, and when there is controversy they are the ones who suffer the most. It is the middle class who stands between anger and peace, so it is no wonder that they seem to be the most distraught of all the wanderers rushing to the outskirts of suburbia as fast and as soon as they can afford to. Soon there shall be no place to run, for rich, middle or lower class. The world as we know it shrinks by the minute every day. We had better get together; we have no choice! *A first imperative step is regarding every individual as a man,* and I hasten to add this has nothing to do with like or love. Think about it. I say again the assumptive naivete that individuals can absolve themselves of the problems of this world, white or black, rich or poor, East or West is no longer tenable!

Summary/Review

Marginal comments are of course useful for more than writing essays. They are a way of systematically keeping track of thinking that might otherwise be obscured in a maze of distractions. Contrary to the objection that marginal notations take more time than they merit, the busiest people seem to make best use of techniques that save the most time. Beyond their use for writing essays, marginal comments are essential in all forms of note taking, in preparing for speeches or debates, in writing letters or while reading library books that cannot be annotated. Taking notes is not just a useful tool; it is an art cultivated by the busiest and most effective writers and speakers. Note taking is actually the beginning of communication. Writing marginal comments in the form of a letter is often an effective way to choose an audience and to structure one's communication for that audience. While recording his reactions in notes, a reader begins to clarify and develop thinking that might otherwise remain an undifferentiated mass.

12/How to Annotate
Your Television Set

The statistics no longer surprise anyone. Television has become the principal source of news and entertainment for most Americans. It is also a chief medium through which advertisers reach consumers, and it continues to show limitless potential as a modern art form. Almost everyone has some opinion on the effects of television on education, politics, and the psyches of the viewing audience. Even the most dedicated disciples of the anti-TV movements cannot escape its influence. Audiences are affected just as readers are moved by what they read. Viewer reactions—sought by pollsters, networks, and advertisers—determine to a considerable degree the format and content of programming.

But are television audiences really responsive? Do they watch critically and then pay close attention to the meaning of their own reactions? In a famous book Nicholas Johnson has demonstrated *How to Talk Back to Your Television Set* (Boston: Little Brown, 1970). Just as readers' marginal comments capture their reactions to what they read, viewers' annotations help them to respond actively and self-critically to what they watch.

Of course a viewer doesn't watch TV in exactly the same way or under the same circumstances in which a reader reads. TV viewing is generally recreation; whereas reading, at least for students, is often merely "an assignment." Television is leisure time or an evening-filler, by choice; books are school time or an evening's work, by compulsion. The environment surrounding TV viewing and reading helps shape the ways in which audiences and readers engage in an activity. As Marshall McLuhan has documented at considerable length, television invites—in fact, demands—participation from the viewer. One who "watches" a TV screen participates in the creation of a mosaic "picture" from a series of dotted configurations. And the viewer is further engaged in the audience-participation structure of many talk shows,

194

quiz programs, and even situation comedies (complete with laugh tracks). Finally, the fragmented structure of program formats and the collage effect of advertising by suggestion call for the involvement of the viewer in what is perceived. In sharp contrast, reading calls for the less active involvement of a reader. McLuhan's analysis of the invention of movable type (see chapter 1) points to the uniformity and repeatability of books that allow the reader to remain passive. The necessity to overcome that passivity through the reader's conscious responsiveness has been the chief argument of this book. The same process of actively annotating one's reactions is crucial also for TV audiences. While television viewers participate more in what they perceive, viewers' participation is satisfying only when they are aware of what they are doing. An audience's need to understand and analyze its own reactions is as much a problem in TV viewing as it is in reading.

The proponents and opponents of television are equally convinced of its positive and negative effects on our society. We hear that the video art is a unique medium of communication that has shaped its own visual and tactile "language"; that the "boob tube" has warped language and helped further to rob young people of the riches of their native tongue; that the "window on the world" has opened up the range of viewers' experiences and thereby expanded the public consciousness; that narrow and formula programming has confined viewers' imaginations and stifled their curiosity about the world not contained in the electric box. These diametrically opposite conclusions are easily repeated and endlessly argued. The truth is generally somewhere in between or in a combination of the seemingly contradictory extremes. TV constricts *and* liberates. It dulls *and* creates—depending as often as not on the awareness of its viewers not only about what they are watching but also about what is happening to them as they interact with an electronic medium.

The effects of television are everywhere. It is ever conveniently available and hence a deterrent to exploration and creative curiosity. And yet as a form, television itself demands involvement and responsive viewing. At once it mesmerizes and stimulates. It numbs and at the same time wraps itself around the viewer. Television does popularize the serious arts and thus risks trivializing artistic values and standards of taste. Yet it also makes art available to mass audiences previously thought incapable of enjoying what had been saved for the privileged.

Television *is* educational. Even in popular network shows, it is a source of knowledge about history and geography and a medium for reaching millions with new discoveries in any field of study. But it can also pervert or distort history through the projection of myths and fabricated images. It can give back to us only a mirroring of ourselves in the hero worship of entertainers and athletes. TV stimulates the economy through advertising, and it warps sensitivities and values by insisting on the now hackneyed cliché that the viewer must "keep up with the Joneses" in order to like himself. The television set helps Americans to regulate time, to relieve boredom, to make the day manageable. It also can merely pass the time; create boredom, and carve out a day of monotony.

The psychological effects of TV are also inexhaustible. Images on the screen create models—sources of identity. They also merely embody the pseudo heroes produced by ratings mongers and Madison Avenue packagers. For the lonely person, the turned-on television set creates a sense of presence. For "small people" in a mass society, it provides a point of contact with the world "out there." At best it involves the individual in world events; at worst it creates an easily collapsible sense of "Security." Network coverage has at once strengthened the national identity and blurred valuable regional differences. Its strongest advocates argue that TV is opening up new modes of perception and stimulating new ways of thinking. Critics insist that it distorts perception and dulls thinking by forcing all into what can be safely (and with profit) programmed. Arguments about hypothetical effects are tireless. Television affects movie viewing; it creates and ever reshapes a "mass audience"; it displaces family and replaces personal expression and initiative. TV arrests action. "Events" come into the living room, so there's no need to go to them. Its effects are pervasive on our legal system, politics, education, the rights of minorities, and the development of violence in our society.

Debates on all such questions are not solvable in these pages. But a system for "annotating" TV will help clarify what happens to viewers as they respond. A system is needed much like the marginal comments used by active readers. And similarly, TV viewers can expand their marginalia into effective communication about their television viewing. In order to illustrate this method of "talking back" to the television set, it will be useful to take news programs as a specific example and then sketch some approaches and methods.

Television news schedules the day with as much regularity as clocks or the sun itself. The three major networks wake up America with news and interviews. The "news at noon" fits into lunchtime formats on most local scenes. Mid-morning and mid-afternoon recaps dot daytime programming. Of course the major newscast of the day is the networks' evening news, featuring the three major national anchormen. In most cities, this network coverage is supplemented by from thirty minutes to two hours of additional news, features, and interviews. Finally the late news becomes a bedtime ritual that plugs the gap between prime time and the late movie or talk show. In larger cities a late-late "summary of headlines" supplies one more report before the cycle returns to another "Today" in the "A.M." and the "Morning News." Variations on this schedule are many, and this summary errs in the direction of omission. Television news can be found on at least one channel at almost any time of the day. When people debate "the effects of television" on today's society, they must always confront the issues of the selection, presentation, and consumption of TV news. Annotating news coverage and programs will help viewers understand the way they respond to the television they watch.

Picture the typical half-hour news show. A sole or principal anchorperson previews the major headlines and sections the program slot into segments of alternating narrative accounts and film "highlights." The format is generally ritualized so that the audience knows exactly when to expect "news," "weather," "sports," entertainment "reviews," and editorial "commentary." Longer shows feature interviews, "in-depth analyses," "film essays," or heavily researched and lengthy follow-up stories. The tone projected in these shows depends on the commentators and station policy. Most news shows are sober "just the facts" narratives of what is happening, though there has been a recent trend toward witty interaction between reporters. Reporting of the news—if not the news itself—has become more and more entertainment. All of this is punctuated, of course, by an increasing number of commercial "messages."

How viewers react to the news depends upon their habits and "qualifications" as television-news consumers. The formula structure calls for predictable responses, and viewers are comfortable in their expectations. But this ritual sameness of format *and* news camouflages the significant effects of television news as a communication medium. Consider the following questions: (1) How does a viewer evaluate the completeness of a news story? (2) Do reporters and writers have access to all relevant information? (3) If anchorpersons present "just the facts," how does a viewer interpret data and reach his or her own conclusions?

Just as readers must evaluate the research that backs up what they read, the television audience must determine the credibility of news "sources." Unique problems in the communication of news arise precisely because the facts to be communicated must be actively sought by the communicator. To what extent, then, do news departments or wire services report and to what extent to they create the news? The questions are too complex to examine with any thoroughness here. What matters is that in order to "annotate the TV," viewers must find ways of answering these questions for themselves as they carefully study their own reactions. Judgments about the accuracy and thoroughness of sources and questions relating to the censorship or overall effects of news telecasts—all depend on viewers' understanding their own responses to what is programmed for their consumption.

The way "news" is presented obviously shapes how it is perceived. Sensationalism confers status on what might in fact be trivial; everyday repetition of "routine" occurrences might cast a veneer of boredom over truly significant but dull events. Effective public relations agents know that strategically positioned publicity can make anything into "news." Audiences seem to demand the bizarre and in the process greatly influence what is presented to them. Several clichés illustrate what becomes news. Not "dog bites man" but "man bites dog" is news. "No news is good news." "Controversy makes news." Controversy also seems to encase newscasting in unending complexity.

Viewers of the evening news are becoming aware of their own decoding of what is presented to them. This awareness follows scathing attacks against the press and subsequent study of issues often taken for granted in television news. Former Vice-President Agnew accused television news commentators of distorting the news by engaging in unacknowledged editorializing, ill-conceived "instant analysis," and "querulous criticism." Others suggested that "visual effects" might dominate over the intrinsic importance of the news in decisions about programming—much as "when the tail wags the dog." Still others have argued that news telecasting protects the vested interest of big government, big business, and worldwide corporate enterprise at the expense of the powerless. Watergate and its aftermath have dramatized the issues on both sides of this debate. In order to observe your own responses to TV viewing more systematically, select several topics from the following Exercises. Each suggests a range of patterns that your reactions might take and calls for annotating and interpreting your own responses as they develop.

Exercises

1. Watch two or three competitive news programs aired during the same hours and compare their coverage of events. Any of the networks' major early morning or evening programs will do. Make a list of stories covered or overlooked, and compare air time, newsreel footage, interviews, or follow-ups to determine relative emphasis. Compare also the ordering of stories and the overall structure of segments in relation to each other and commercial breaks. Include your reactions to the items you list, and then interpret the significance of your findings. Do you detect differences in coverage on issues, selected public figures, political orientation, or attitudes toward what is presented? Do you notice a pattern from network to network or when moving to different formats, anchorpersons, or time of day?

2. Keep notes on the differences between news coverage and editorializing in the same program. For example, how does Walter Cronkite's reporting differ from Eric Sevareid's "analysis" of the news? Or, compare John Chancellor and David Brinkley or Harry Reasoner and Howard K. Smith as reporters as opposed to interpreters in their "comment." If you notice any overlap, explain the effects of mixing editorials with objective reporting. Do you think television audiences are aware of the differences between the two approaches to the same "news"? Based on your marginal notations, write an essay in which you explain to a TV news audience the subtle influences of reporting vs. editorializing on them as news consumers.

3. Select examples from television news programs of (a) major news events which you consider to be significant and (b) "non-events" that make the news because of sensationalism or effective public relations campaigns. Explain in detail the differences between the examples you cite and then show how television coverage helped shape their attraction as news.

4. Observe carefully many different examples of violence in television news coverage. Describe, for example, commentary and films on war, terrorist attacks or kidnapings, or street crime. Keep notes of your reactions to the violence and then examine the effects of language, visual representation, and programming on your reactions. Contrast news coverage of violence with that depicted on police and detective shows. What is the difference between "real" and "staged" murder? From your notes, write an essay on violence in the media—news vs. prime-time adventure programs.

5. Keep notes on your reactions to several television news editorials. Select one or a series on one subject and write a counter-editorial of your own. You may use the form of a letter to the station or commentator to whom you are offering a rebuttal.

6. Follow closely for a week the activities and statements of one major figure in the news. Take careful notes on the person's own statements, comments from his "spokesmen," and reactions of others to your subject's actions and statements. Notice the differences between the image the person projects and the opinions created by others. Study also the contrasts in various networks' and news shows' selection and presentation about the person you choose. Build an essay from your observations, and explain how television news coverage presents or creates the image of your "person in the news."

7. Again choose a major figure in the news, and keep detailed notes on your reactions to that person's public image as it unfolds on the TV news. Study your responses to his or her opinions and accomplishments, and analyze carefully any controversies. Then write a letter to that person expressing your opinions or counter-proposals.

8. Write an essay on the use of "sources" in television news. In addition to careful annotations on your reactions to the news you watch, it will be necessary to do some research on the "Fairness Doctrine" and the debates on "disclosure." When should "equal time" be provided by networks on controversial news issues? And should news reporters be required to divulge the sources of their "leads"? How much trust can be given to "official spokesmen" or "undisclosed sources"?

9. Watch closely news coverage of political campaigns and debates. Compare a candidate's "position" with the image he or she projects. Analyze the differences between direct statements and attempts to "sell" the candidate. Compare footage of the figure in news programs with the image created in thirty-second or one-minute "paid for political announcements." To what extent does the packaged-up advertising slot distort your understanding of what should happen in political campaigns? Keep notes on examples of candidates who attempt to "buy" their way into office through "effective" but often misleading publicity.

10. How useful do you think ratings are as a device for determining the content and scheduling of programs? What is measured by ratings? How do current ratings compare with your viewing habits? If television news depends on successful ratings, to what extent will networks, advertisers, or viewers influence the content and format of news telecasts? Include specific examples.

11. Study several consecutive newscasts for about a week, paying special attention to the advertisements. Based on your notes, do you notice a pattern in the selection or arrangement of ads in relation to different kinds of news segments? How does the presence of advertising influence the overall impact of the show on your responses as a viewer?

12. Keep detailed notes on your reactions to television news images of public officials, women, members of minorities, or any other recognizable group of individuals. Study the contrasts between what you feel are stereotypes or realistic portrayals.

13. Compare your responses to television news with detailed notes on your viewing of other kinds of programs. How do you react to situation comedies, serious drama, soap operas, or sports shows? Do you find yourself reacting in predictable patterns depending on the kinds of programming you are watching? Write an essay on the effects of one kind of program format on you. Then compare your reactions to the two or three different kinds of programs.

14. Do your reactions to TV differ when you are watching it alone or with a group of friends or with your family? Compare your notations as a solitary viewer or as a member of a larger audience? Does the variation depend on the kind of program you are watching? Would a figure-skating competition or Monday night football call for group response and a talk show individual viewing? Where would news telecasts fit in this scheme? Choose several examples and then analyze the causes for the different effects you find.

15. How do your habits as a television viewer affect your responsiveness as an audience of radio, movies, or books? Again, would the differences depend on the various kinds of formats followed in each medium? Keep detailed notes on your reactions to several news programs on television, radio, newsreel documentaries, and newspaper and news magazine stories. Contrast the different effects on your viewing. Do some research on the question and reach some conclusions on the influences of various media on one another. In what unique ways does a TV generation view movies or "read." How do enthusiastic regular filmgoers respond uniquely to books or television?

Summary / Review

Viewers watch television in ways different from the way readers read. The unique characteristics of the electronic media and print demand different kinds of responses. But an audience's need to understand and analyze its own reactions is as much a problem in TV viewing as it is in reading. Because television is so influential in our society, it is particularly important to study its effects on viewers. Endless debates about the values and dangers of TV demand that viewers develop a system for "annotating" programs in order to clarify what happens to them as they respond. News shows are a special source of controversy. Questions about content, format, the use of sources, editorializing, and the nature of "news" itself underline the subtle effects of television programming on media consumers. Notes "in the margin" are a way to "talk back" to your television set and in the process to understand your reactions and develop them into your own thinking on the world that comes into your living room. Similar notes on serious drama, sporting events, soap operas, or situation comedies will reveal the effects of such programs on television's mass audience. Understanding these effects is the first step in becoming a more responsive viewer and more forceful and successful communicator.

DATE DUE

APR 10 '78			
APR 3 1978			
AP 12 '82			
AC 16 '82			
DE 12 '83			
NO 30 '85			
NO 3 '86			
NO 09 '86			

PN
81
P67